FOR KING, CONSTITUTION, AND COUNTRY

The English Loyalists and the French Revolution

ROBERT R. DOZIER

THE UNIVERSITY PRESS OF KENTUCKY

Library of Congress Cataloging in Publication Data
Dozier, Robert R., 1932–
    For king, constitution, and country.
    Bibliography: p.
    1. Great Britain—History—1789-1820.   2. France—
History—Revolution—1789-1793—Influence.   I. Title.
II. Title: English Loyalists and the French Revolution.
DA520.D69   1983   941.07′3   83-1221
ISBN 0-8131-1490-X

CONTENTS

PREFACE

The publication of Albert Goodwin's *Friends of Liberty: The English Democratic Movement in the Age of the French Revolution* (1979) has revealed a noticeable gap in our knowledge of late eighteenth-century history. We know practically nothing about the activities of tens, perhaps hundreds of thousands of Englishmen who rallied to the defense of English institutions and values during the early years of the French Revolution. These people, who called themselves loyalists, formed a movement which had profound effects upon domestic developments as well as upon the workings of the constitution, strengthening its flexible, evolutionary tendencies. Until Goodwin finally classified the nature of the radical movement, however, the nature of the radicals' enemies, the loyalists, was little understood. Because of the size of the loyalist movement, some aspects of it could not be overlooked by historians. Yet its nature, goals, and activities, its continuity and transformations, could never be understood or placed in context until the reasons for its existence, the radical responses to the French Revolution, had been thoroughly explored.

Historians have had difficulty in interpreting the importance of the radicals and loyalists since the turn of the century. In the pre-World War I era, three historians, G.S. Veitch, P.A. Brown, and Elie Halevy, examined the democratic and loyal association movements and concluded that the former was relatively innocent, whereas the latter was part of the Pitt government's policy of repression. Indeed, Halevy insisted that the possibility of England's participating in a revolution at the time had nothing to do with either movement but stemmed from a different emphasis among the possible leaders of the English people. Pointing to the growing evangelical movement, Halevy concluded that the leaders of the working classes were involved in a crusade which offered no threat to the constituted authorities. From this perspective, the loyal association movement was an overreaction, a near panic that had little to do with reality.

This point of view was maintained during the interwar years. G.M. Trevelyan, H.W.C. Davis, D.G. Barnes, and Keith Feiling wrote variations on the theme established by the earlier historians. To Trevelyan, the Pitt ministry, by mobilizing the militia (the spark which generated or increased the activities of loyalists), was attempting only to aid the delusion Englishmen held about the possibility of revolution. Davis, believing that the revolutionary threat was never great, castigated Pitt and his ministers for overreacting and charged that they ruined a good cause by overestimating the importance of the English radicals. Barnes thought Pitt was merely attempting to play upon the fears which divided the Whigs, hoping to make a split in their ranks permanent. Feiling's analysis, on the other hand, lauded the competency of the Pitt ministry in dealing with possible dangers in the domestic situation, although he too believed those possibilities overblown. The loyal movement, he believed, was prompted more by anti-French than by anti-Jacobin sentiment.

While little was added to our knowledge about either the democratic or the loyal movement by these historians, the connection between the radicals and the French was more than once touched upon. That there was a burst of patriotism, all conceded, yet this patriotism, when coupled with governmental influence, was condemned. The loyalists, it appeared, were opposing some of the cherished

ideals of the English, such as free speech, the right of association, and the right of all to have some influence on
government. The radicals, on the other hand, were applauded as the forerunners of later reformers, although
their intentions and numbers made their influence upon
events relatively slight. Although challenged in 1949 by Herbert Butterfield,
this view persisted until Robert Palmer published *The
Democratic Revolution of the West: The Struggle* in 1964.
While still insisting that there was no danger of revolution
in England, Palmer noted new works appearing which opposed his views. Even as he published, four important
works appeared which changed the direction of scholarship
about this period of history. The most important of these
was E.P. Thompson's *The Making of the English Working
Class*. Thompson not only demonstrated the revolutionary
nature and activities of the English radicals, but also
viewed the loyal movement as a semiofficial reactionary
aberration, ruining whatever chances the English might
have had for democratic reforms. While Thompson's goal
was to discover the awakening class consciousness of the
English workingman, he dealt more deeply with the English workingman's response to the French Revolution
than had any previous scholar, and opened avenues for
future research that are still unexplored.

Appearing at the same time were the first attempts to
explore the loyal association movement in itself by Austin
Mitchell, E.C. Black, and Donald Ginter. Mitchell's work
was the best attempt to explain why so many Englishmen
opposed the intrusion of French principles into England,
yet, by examining but a small part of the loyal movement,
he cast it in an ideological framework which allowed an
immediate challenge from Ginter. To oppose Mitchell's
conclusion that practically all of England was turning conservative, Ginter attempted to demonstrate that, because
so many ex-reformers joined the ranks of the loyalists,
they captured a sizable proportion of it. Black's condem-
nation of the loyalists further confused the picture of the

nature of the loyal movement. A step forward had been taken, however, for the increased information published about the radicals and loyalists could not help but connect the two movements and imply that understanding either depended upon understanding the other.

While two works dealing with the English radicals appeared after Thompson's, those of Gwyn Williams and Carl Cone, the basic interpretations remained the same. Goodwin's work, the most complete yet written, is not only a synthesis of works written about the radicals, but also the result of much original investigation of his own. He has made our picture of the radicals more complete than ever before. Intent on understanding the radicals, Goodwin notes not only the ideals but also the blunders and inconsistencies of the movement. His work finally examines the radicals for what they were and creates the context in which the loyalists can be understood.

With the radical stimulus explained, the loyal response can now be understood. For the loyalists were not just the privileged classes in England, but hundreds of thousands of Englishmen in all ranks of life, who not only outnumbered the radicals but also were impressed with a new view of the relationship between the individual and his society which had implications as revolutionary as any doctrines synthesized by the radicals. Now that Goodwin has explained in detail what the radicals were attempting, we can see that their greatest immediate impact was the creation of the loyalists, people who voluntarily joined the system, sometimes led by but at other times leading the government.

To discover the extent and nature of the loyal movement, I have had to consult documents which reveal not only the actions of individuals and groups but also some intimations of the spirit of the times: the prevailing preoccupations which explain somewhat the context in which actions were taken. These were found as much in the counties as in the metropolis. Government records were invaluable, but so were provincial newspapers. In short, I have taken a broad sampling of those sources which reveal

the way Englishmen were thinking. In doing so I have discovered a movement which dwarfed that of the radicals
and which continued, varying in intensity, from the early
months of 1792 until the latter months of 1794. The
effects of this movement upon the radicals, government,
and English public opinion form the substance of my
work.

I wish to thank the University of Montana Foundation
for providing the wherewithal for research in England, and
the faculty of the Department of History, especially
Robert Lindsay and Linda Frey, for pointing out errors in
this work. I am grateful for the support given me by the
University of Montana. I also wish to thank the officers
and clerks in the various local record offices in England for
their help, kindness, and encouragement in my travels
through the countryside. Last, I wish to express my gratitude to my family and friends, who kept me to the task
until it was finished.

Dedicated to my best friend,
who happens to be my wife,
JOYCE

CHAPTER I

THE AWAKENING
OF THE LOYALISTS

On May 21, 1792, George III signed a proclamation warning his subjects that "divers wicked and seditious writings" had been circulated throughout the kingdom which might excite tumult and disorder." He urged his subjects "to avoid and discourage all proceedings, tending to produce riots and tumults." Included in this proclamation was an injunction to all magistrates to do their duty by forwarding all information about seditious activities to the central government. The public response to the proclamation was overwhelmingly favorable. By September, 386 loyal addresses from cities, towns, and counties were presented to the king. To be sure, 10 counties and 80 cities and towns did not respond,[1] but on the whole this was a gratifying answer to the hidden question in the proclamation. Four out of every five Englishmen in the political community agreed with the ministry that the inflammatory literature in circulation, chiefly Tom Paine's *Rights of Man,* posed a danger to the body politic, and they were quite willing to support the government should any ill effects ensue.

The significance of these events was that they revealed a frame of mind in a portion of the English public that would later serve as an identifying mark for group actions. Superficially this large response was rather surprising. The proclamation merely warned Englishmen that certain types of literature were in circulation and asked them not to lose their heads about it. Moreover, the use of addresses to the king or Parliament was an old device, normally utilized by politicians to illustrate the support they held out of doors for measures they wished to defend or oppose in the legislative houses.[2] In the days before public opinion polls, addresses were cumbersome devices to poll the sense of the nation. In this instance, however, the politicians had tapped a new emotional source of support in sections of the body politic that would sustain a movement lasting four years, disappearing only after diffusing its primary impetus into the public generally. The May Proclamation and the subsequent loyal address movement revealed for the first time the emergence of English loyalists, men and women who would in various ways support and sustain the constitution against all proceedings tending to undermine, discredit, or in any way weaken its effectiveness. Because these loyalists were not created overnight, a brief examination of the political and ideological situation in England during their gestation period is warranted.

Although Edmund Burke is often credited as the originator of the "conservative" response in England to the French Revolution, he can be viewed as the first outspoken English loyalist. His *Reflections on the Revolution in France,* published in 1790, was and is an excellent defense of English political and social activities and organizations in the eighteenth century. Burke examined and defended a view of the proper relationships between men in society and between governors and the governed under the English constitution. This evaluation, couched in the form of an examination of the probable effects of French revolutionary reforms, was written in response to the possible approval, and perhaps adoption, of French methods of change in England by some sections of English society. In his work, the English system was held to be the norm and the degrees of absurdity or wrong-headedness of French activities and theories were determined by their departures from the English model. To be sure, Burke did more than that. Viewing Englishmen and Frenchmen, he posed possibilities of human political and social behavior which could be applied to mankind. Yet the basis of his argument was a comparison of the French system and the English, his loyalty to the English pushing him to defend all aspects of it. Ironically the publication of his pamphlet precipitated an intellectual controversy that produced clearer views of the French system, which in turn intensified the very conflict Burke had attempted to quell.

Of the hundred-odd pamphlets published in this controversy,[3] Paine's *Rights of Man*, Part I, stated most simply and clearly the French case, and later became the chief argument of a new class of reformers who wished to modify Burke's constitution more extremely than any had proposed previously. This ironic development can be emphasized too strongly, however. Neither Burke nor Paine wrote about the revolution which stimulated the loyal response. Indeed, events transpired with such rapidity across the Channel that they resembled a process more than events. The revolution Paine defended was not the revolution Burke attacked. Too many changes had occurred in the interval between the publications of their works.

The French Revolution was more than an event or a series of events. It was a complicated process of interrelated phenomena forever changing emphases and directions, in which the actions of its supporters occurred in a medium of values applicable only to themselves. Outside observers might grasp temporary insights and believe they understood developments; could take stands approving or disapproving the actions of the chief actors; but the Revolution continued at varying speeds, so that their conclusions when reached were out of date when published. Burke and Paine disagreed in interpreting some aspects of the process and its origins. By the time their views were published, the French Revolution bore little resemblance to the interpretations of either. Englishmen, however, committed their views to print; therefore notice should be taken of the general tenor of this response.

There can be no doubt that the English intellectual response to the initial efforts of the French was overwhelmingly favorable. With the exception of Burke, practically every English writer of note was stimulated into paeans of praise to the modernity and rationality of French attempts to reform the basic structure of their constitution. In these early years, if there were Englishmen other than Burke who thought differently, their thoughts did not gain notoriety.[4]

The reasons for this overwhelmingly favorable interpretation are fairly obvious. The principles revealed by French actions were part of the English tradition. The Real Whigs could easily appreciate the goals of the French and were to some extent encouraged to push for the realization of similar goals in England.[5] The devolution of power in the French state from the monarch to representative assemblies was similar enough to that of the English historical experience to lead to several congratulatory speeches in the House of Commons. Even Horace Walpole could celebrate the fall of the Bastille as an event agreeable to the best interests of mankind. France seemed to be following the path blazed by the English. Patriotic Englishmen could not help but feel flattered, reformers encouraged, and romantics thrilled by the event.

The greatest pragmatic inducement to the English to felicitate the revolutionaries arose from the implications that the upheaval had upon the prospects for peace in Europe. William Grenville, later foreign secretary, wrote as early as September 14, 1789, that "the main point appears quite secure, that they [the French] will not for many years be in a situation to molest the invaluable peace which we now enjoy." Charles James Fox, leader of the opposition in the House of Commons, when pressing for a reduction in armaments the following year, agreed.[6] The French Assembly's renunciation of the rights of conquest on May 22, 1790, bore out the predictions of these politicians. Whether or not one agreed with the justifications used by the French in remodeling their constitution, the important consequence was that they would not be an international bother until their domestic situation was settled.

These combined views of the activities of the French in the early years partially explain why most Englishmen took little alarm over the activities of those at home favoring the Revolution. To be sure, the sermon preached by Dr. Richard Price at a meeting of the Society to Commemorate the Revolution of 1688 stimulated Burke to write his *Reflections,* but Burke's attack on the good doctor was censured by those who answered him. Throughout most of the eighteenth century the Real Whigs, or Commonwealthsmen, had put forth the same or more extreme views without arousing alarm. The "Church and King" riots at Birmingham in 1791, directed at Dissenters and others favoring the French Revolution, had been deplored by those concerned with stability and order.[7] In these early years, views of the Revolution were not the politically divisive factors they were to become later.

There was another reason for this disinterested tolerance toward clubs or societies which celebrated French activities. These groups—constitution societies, Friends of Liberty, and so forth—were composed of members of the middle and upper classes. The Revolution Society in London, with Dr. Price and Lord Stanhope as members, was a typical club of this caliber. William Pitt had worked in concert with similar organizations earlier during the County Association Movement.[8] These associations, composed of members of the political community exercising their right to organize to gain political or social ends, were a familiar feature of the political system.

One last point should illustrate the dominance of the favorable pragmatic view of the Revolution. Paine published Part I of his *Rights of Man* in 1791, when Englishmen still viewed the Revolution disinterestedly. Lord Mornington's letter, gently chiding Foreign Secretary Grenville, points out the aloof yet generally concerned attitude held by those in the governing classes that similar behavior was being urged on Englishmen. "I wonder that you did not hang the scoundrel Paine for his blackguard libel on King, Lords and commons. I suppose the extreme scurrility of the pamphlet, or the villany of those who wish to disperse it among the common people, has carried it through so many editions. For it appears to me to have no merit whatever; but it may do mischief in ale-houses in England. . . . I think it by far the most treasonable book that ever went unpunished within my knowledge; so, pray, hang the fellow, if you catch him."[9] While the Home Office kept Paine under observation, it made no move to prosecute him, for until revolutionary circumstances in France changed, Paine was merely a disgruntled individual whose pamphlet would only be magnified in importance by official action. The ideas he expressed were not new, although his ability to express them simply and understandably pointed to a wider dispersal of them than ever before. Government thought the wise course of action was to allow the pamphlet to die by neglect.[10]

National and international circumstances changed drastically by 1792. In the early part of the year, tradesmen, shopkeepers, mechanics, and other members of the skilled laboring class formed a society in London and another in Sheffield. Six months later the two societies claimed over 2,000 members. Similar societies appeared in other cities. Their members were reformers, individuals whose stated goals were universal suffrage, annual Parliaments, and the other long-sought ambitions of the Commonwealthsmen through much of the eighteenth century. Although individuals of their social background had participated in debating societies after the American War, their numbers and energetic activities now quickly caught the attention of members of the political community. Their spiritual and ideological backgrounds, traced sensitively and approvingly by E.P. Thompson, leave no doubt that theirs was an English origin, firmly rooted in the English past.[11]

Spiritual and ideological backgrounds, however, do not explain entirely the novel features of such societies, nor the change they worked in the political circumstances of the day, for the class composition of these new clubs was mostly that of skilled artisans, individuals accustomed to making decisions which affected their livelihood. Their economic success or failure depended to a large degree on the wise use of their talents. It is not surprising that the spectacle of a revolution in France abolishing all restrictions on men of talent inspired them to join together to seek political equality at this time. Moreover, as representatives of their class in old England, they may have been naggingly aware that their status was being challenged by the factory wage-earners of the new England, an awareness which would lend some urgency to their cause. They adopted Paine's *Rights of Man* as their chief article of propaganda, and when Part II was published in February 1792, it was added to the bible of their faith. Why they chose Paine's works rather than others equally available and supporting their cause more exactly deserves some attention.

Paine published the *Rights of Man,* Part I, in February 1791 in the pamphlet controversy generated by Burke's *Reflections.* Scholars have had no difficulty tracing the origins of his ideas, in spite of his claims to originality. What made his works so attractive to the artisans was that he spoke to an element of human nature that had had little encouragement before. The *Rights of Man,* both parts, is pure impudence. Paine treated all deferential aspects of English society sarcastically and impiously, laughing at the seriousness with which those in authority viewed themselves. The Crown, for instance, was a "metaphor," titles of nobility were "nick-names," and all pretensions were ridiculed in a like manner. Nor did Paine hide his goals. "There was a time when the lowest class of what we call nobility, was more thought of than the highest is now, and when a man in armour riding through Christendom in search of adventure was more stared at than a modern duke. The world has seen this folly fall, and it has fallen by being laughed at, and the farce of titles will follow its fate."[12] Paine grasped the essential art of the propagandist—that the feelings of the reader, more than his considered judgment, had to be changed before any action was possible. Paine realized that an institution's viability depended upon the respect paid it by men in society. To make change possible, institutions supporting stability had to be held up to ridicule, which, if successful, would diminish the respect supporting them, thus paving the way for social and political modifications.

This was the type of propaganda needed by the artisans. They were undoubtedly aware that their greatest enemy was inertia and ingrained respect among members of the lower classes. What they needed was works which were easily understood, to be sure, but works which attacked the deference of the governed to those in society who ruled. Paine spoke a language they could understand. In their respective fields the artisans were as competent as others in any section of society. Their exclusion from political rights was a result of tradition and custom, based upon nothing more than unspoken agreements which could be viewed as unjust and unfair. Paine provided the mental attitude necessary to take steps to right the political order. By adopting his works as propaganda to rouse others to action, however, the artisans, if they really only desired reform, changed and confused the goals of their movement. For Paine did more than import the cockiness of Yankee Doodle. After rousing his readers, he pointed to the way they should act. "When we survey the wretched conditions of man under the monarchical and hereditary systems of government, dragged from his home by one power, or driven by another; and impoverished by taxes more than by enemies, it becomes evident that these systems are bad, and that a general revolution in the principle and construction of government is necessary." The system demanded to be changed, not only in construction, or structure, but in principle, deviating from custom and tradition and refounded upon the rights of man. Piously, Paine hoped that this general revolution might be produced by "reason and accommodation," but, because this was the "age of revolution," everything was in the reach of those who acted.[13] Paine's works were indeed masterpieces of propaganda, but they were also blatant calls for revolution.

It is highly probable that the artisans' clubs, notwithstanding these calls to revolution in their propaganda, might have been absorbed into the flexible English political system had the timing of their appearance not coincided with two major developments in the revolutionary process in France. The pathetic attempt of Louis XVI to escape his position as constitutional monarch of the new France belied the reform-orientation of the Revolution and placed the moderate French politicians in an intolerable position. A new party, led by a faction from the Gironde, openly advocated warfare as a means of protecting the Revolution. In less than a year, and coincident with the founding of the new clubs in England, two of the practical reasons for the English approval of the Revolution had vanished. It was obviously no reform; Louis XVI now appeared more as a captive symbol than as the representative of the hereditary aspect of the government. And with war fever rising, the pacifism of the Revolution, so much a factor in the earlier evaluations by the English, was now reversed. Should the French go to war, they could not help but threaten the English. These events in France provided the context in which domestic English activities were viewed. From the latter part of 1791 until the end of the revolutionary process in France, Englishmen in the governing classes would almost automatically assume that English democratic agitation was either a reflection of or a part of French plans. As such, the artisans' clubs were seen as posing a danger to domestic peace.

This danger lay in the possibility of discontented Englishmen imitating French methods of reform. Indeed, from the perspective of the twentieth century, it would appear that the French were captured by the spirit that animated Paine's works. Bankrupt, struggling to maintain a facade of legitimacy, yet desirous of continuing a Revolution that promised everything, they defied reality and worked toward dimly seen goals in spite of their seeming impossibilities. This is the very core of the revolution introduced into the Western world by France, and its total revelation would redefine the concept itself. Moreover, the forces at work in France seemed exportable. If one judged the onset of the disease by the creation of ideas and the appearance of groups of men dedicated to the spread of those ideas, the rapid circulation of Paine's works and the growth and energetic activities of the artisans' clubs pointed to the conclusion that England was infected, and that if health was to be restored, steps had to be taken.

The realization of this potential danger to domestic tranquillity occurred very rapidly. Paine published Part II of the *Rights of Man* in February 1792 and the Girondists captured control of the French government in March. Pitt and Grenville, the chief spokesmen for the government in the Commons and Lords, spoke confidently in February of the possibilities of peace in Europe. In March internal struggles began in the Whig opposition over French and English events which were to lead to the disintegration of the first modern political party. The outcome of these struggles was a major influence upon the government's decision to ask the loyalists in England to speak out in support of the constitution.

The Whig opposition, nominally headed by the Duke of Portland, was at this time confronted by the dangers of ideological rupture. The Burke-Fox disagreement over the evaluation of the French Revolution in 1791 had indicated that the old justifications for political alignments were vulnerable to new ideological forces. Burke ended his friendship and political connections with Fox, not on the simple matter of defining what the French were doing, but on the precedent they were establishing for others. In effect, the Revolution cast English political activities in an entirely new light. As J.H. Rose has put it: "It served among other things to confuse the lines of domestic political contro-

versy established in the 1780's. One advocate of reform
was now seen . . . as a diehard of the old order; while
another, respectable enough yesterday, was suddenly
found to be the agent of diabolical subversion."[14] The
issue was no longer whether Parliamentarians approved or
disapproved of the Revolution, if that was ever an issue at
all, but whether they supported or opposed Englishmen
out of doors who did. It was not whether Parliamentarians
wished to imitate French methods of reform or innovation, something no Parliamentarian ever intimated, but
whether they supported individuals out of doors who proposed just that.

The divisiveness of this issue in the early months of
1792 and the difficult position in which it placed individuals within the Whig Party are clearly illustrated in a letter
from Fox to Lord Fitzwilliam, one of the leaders of the
Whig opposition. "Our apprehensions are raised by different objects; you seem to dread the prevalence of Paine's
opinions (which in fact I detest as much as you do) while I
am much more afraid of the total annihilation of all principles of liberty and resistance, an event which I am sure you
will be as sorry to see as I." Fox clearly spelled out the
dilemma facing all politicians in England. Their decisions
had to be made upon possibilities. Fitzwilliam apprehended the possible dangers of the spread of opinions
hostile to the constitution, an apprehension which at this
time may have been exaggerated. Fox, on the other hand,
dreaded the possible destruction of the liberties of Englishmen which might occur if freedom of speech should be
attacked to end the spread of subversive literature, a much
greater exaggeration. Fitzwilliam chose the lesser of the
evils; on April 6 he wrote Henry Dundas, the home secretary, that he and other members of the Whigs were willing
to support measures by the government to silence the
growing wave of sedition.[15]

Others within the Whig party, stimulated to action by
the same considerations, chose a different method of calm-
ing the domestic scene. On April 11 twenty-eight members

of Commons and upwards of seventy other individuals formed the "Friends of the People, associated for the purpose of obtaining a Parliamentary Reform." On April 26 they published a declaration which stated in part that, in order to preserve the constitution in its "true principles," they would promote a reform through Parliament for two goals: "To restore the freedom of election and a more equal representation of the people in parliament. Secondly,—to secure to the people a more frequent exercise of their right of electing their representatives."[16] While Charles Grey, Richard Sheridan, and Thomas Erskine, the Friends' chief spokesmen in Parliament, did not intend to ask for universal suffrage and annual Parliaments—the stated goals of the artisans' clubs—their proposals did touch upon the exact areas of the latter's discontents. The Friends were attempting to implement a "preventive remedy," to remove abuses before they accumulated to the point where only an "eruption" could clear them away.

To be sure, the Friends did not stress the discontents in the nation as an impetus for reform. In fact, their chief argument was that a reform was feasible at that time because of the general tranquillity with "some [mixture] of discontent"[17] which existed in the country. This was obviously a tactical move, an attempt to avoid the clash of reasoned reform and threatened patriotism. In the rest of their address the Friends did note the lessons men had learned through the example of France about the danger of doing nothing while grievances accumulated. Preventive remedies were effective before, not during, the event.

When Grey gave notice on April 30 of his intention to move for a reform of Parliament, the Whigs had already divided over the issues of the Revolution, the threat posed by the spread of Paine's principles, and the steps which should be taken as a consequence. Their disarray offered Pitt the opportunity of making permanent this split in the ranks of his political opponents. Later, in the debates on the May Proclamation, the Whigs supporting Grey and Fox charged Pitt with political opportunism.[18] To a degree they were probably right. Pitt was too astute a politician not to have taken advantage of this opportunity. Had they had the opportunity, the Whigs would have done the same. Pitt's stand against constitutional reform, however, illustrated a pragmatic political philosophy entirely in accordance with his past and future activities which makes it difficult to see any major aberration on his part merely to encourage divisions among the Whigs. Indeed, his response on this occasion indicated for the first time his interpretations of the nature of the Revolution in France, and of the implications of the activities of those in England who wished to modify the constitution.

The foundations of Pitt's "hold fast" philosophy can be seen in his statement of principles when answering Grey's appeal on April 30. The lesson he had learned by studying the French experience was that "reform was the preliminary" to more extreme modifications of the constitution, something eagerly desired by a small number of individuals in England. To reform the constitution at that time would be "to follow a madness which has been called liberty in another country—a condition at war with freedom and good order—a state to which despotism itself was preferable—a state in which liberty could not exist for a day." He noted that several members of the Friends were "agreeable" to the notions of the more extreme reformers, and allowed the implications of their motion for reform to rest on that note. In short, Pitt believed that reform in a time of domestic agitation would serve only to create a desire for more reform. Those who advocated such a policy in good faith should study the example of France before proceeding.[19]

Fox's defense of Grey's motion was worse than no defense at all. Hamstrung by a desire to preserve unity among his political associates, yet desiring to advance what he considered English liberties, his speech straddled the fence, producing an argument that supported Pitt more than Grey. He implied that one of the best features of the constitution was its ability to change to meet different circumstances, not that the change in circumstances demanded reform. By overpraising the constitution, in fact, he removed any impetus that might at least have worked toward a compromise. By calling Paine's works libels on the constitution, he went even further than Pitt in preparing members of the House for measures designed to hinder their circulation. Trying to please both wings of the Whig party, he ruined any chance that Grey's notice would lead to any steps, however slight, toward redressing the discontents expressed out of doors.[20] Perhaps because Fox had not yet decided whether the unity of his party and his subsequent chance for office or the support of his principles was more important, his control of his considerable talents was shaken.

By April 30 the government, aided by the majority of the opposition, had a policy or the beginnings of a policy vis-a-vis the domestic reformers and revolutionary France. It did not imply any drastic action on the diplomatic scene, but it did suggest that the tolerant attitude toward artisans' clubs and the circulation of seditious literature had ended. It was under these circumstances that Pitt and his ministers, working carefully with the Duke of Portland, the nominal head of the opposition, drew up the May Proclamation, which created the conditions for the first appearance of the English loyalists.

As expected, the Commons and Lords voted addresses of thanks to the king for the proclamation on May 25 and 31. From that moment, addresses to the king began to trickle in from various parts of the country. This trickle soon amounted to a flood. Evan Nepean, the undersecretary of the Home Office, had performed the usual duties of his office by sending copies of the proclamation to all the lord lieutenants in the counties, with a covering letter asking them to distribute copies to the high sheriffs, mayors, and magistrates within their counties. The proclamation had to be read to all subjects. It is possible that a circular letter was also sent asking the local officials to call meetings in their areas of jurisdiction in order to draft and vote on addresses of loyalty.[21] If this were the case, the volume of the loyal response could be easily explained. The circular letter, if there ever was one, has not survived. At that, the actions of the local officials, as I shall demonstrate, did not follow any sort of plan. While it would have been a great propaganda advantage to the government to have had some means of controlling or magnifying the strength of the response, there is no real evidence that the government attempted such a thing or had any preconception of the power in the political community they were tapping.

There was no need, on the other hand, for official efforts to spread the news and concerns of government. England was admirably served with a network of newspapers in which the proclamation was printed. London alone had at least thirteen morning, eleven evening, and nine weekly newspapers, many of which were sent out to the larger county towns.[22] In addition, every larger town or city had one or more newspapers of its own. Using but a small sample of loyal declarations made later in the year, for instance, I have found over sixty of these provincial papers, and undoubtedly there were many more. The news they reported invariably included official releases taken from the organ of government, the *London Gazette,* news releases from other London papers, and debates in Parliament and in the various institutions which governed France. In general, newspapers offered Englishmen the opportunity of keeping well informed about national and international events. The public was well prepared for the proclamation before it was issued.

These newspapers, especially those in country towns, served other purposes. They informed Englishmen what other Englishmen were thinking. They reported local news, the usual vital statistics, and unusual or spectacular accidents or deaths. Some, however, gave opinions about national and international affairs and printed letters of opinion sent them by readers. Clubs or associations presented their declarations and purposes merely by buying advertisements, which could appear in practically any part of the paper. Another purpose served was broadcasting the opinions of the editors, which were likely to refect the opinions of the readers. Newspaper income stemmed from sales and advertisements, and those likely to buy or advertise in the papers were wealthier members of society, persons accustomed to taking an active part in local affairs. By using a small sampling of these weeklies, one each selected from the east, south, north, and west, it is possible to gather some idea of the opinions of people throughout the nation.

A few more qualifications should be noted before this analysis. Because their sources of information were so similar, these newspapers' ranges of opinions were relatively circumscribed. One can deduce the opinions of individual editors by noting the choices of news to be printed. Their correspondents in London and Paris also submitted many rumors, and we can glean an idea of the sentiments of the editors by noting which rumors they chose to print. The most revealing evidence, however, is their comments or lack of comments about events. With these qualifications in mind, therefore, we can gain not only an idea of the framework of facts available to the public into which they could inject their evaluations, but also, from the opinions of the editors, some idea of the evaluations themselves.

From the beginning of 1792 until hostilities began between France and the Empire in late April, the news columns of all four chosen newspapers were filled with stories of war preparations in the respective countries and rumors of moves made by each side to encourage or avoid war. All agreed that, should a war break out, France did not have a chance of winning it. Furthermore each editor based his conclusions upon evaluations of French weaknesses rather than upon Imperial strengths. These weaknesses, they all agreed, were a result of the inadequacies of the French constitution. The *Berrows Worcester Journal* and the *Chelmsford Chronicle* did not elaborate on this matter, but the *York Courant* held that the incompetence

of French leaders and the awkward workings of the constitution had not only ruined French finances but had
managed to promote a spirit of resistance in the outlying
provinces. The editor of the *Courant* believed that either a
civil war or counterrevolution would lead to an early
French caputulation. Regardless of the outcome, he believed "that the Annihilation of the Power of France will
prove a permanent Peace in the End to Europe, whether
Monarchy be restored or Democracy triumphs."[23] The
editor of this northern newspaper was more hostile to the
anarchy of the Revolution than to any ideological dangers
it might offer to its neighbors.

The *Sussex Weekly Advertiser,* on the other hand, while
agreeing with the *Courant* on some of the effects of the
French constitution's deficiencies, blamed most of the
divisions of the country on the activities of the "jaco-
bines." Admitting that the finances of France were in a
deplorable state and that the members of the National Assembly did not seem to know what they were doing, the
Advertiser pointed to the inexperience of the leaders and
men of the French armies, as well as the arrest or resigna-
tion of most members of the Executive Council, as reasons
for the probable failure of the French in the coming war.
The editor of the *Advertiser,* William Clachar, in spite of
reporting more completely than the other newspapers the
riots and killings in Paris and the insurrections in the
provinces, still hoped for a French victory. He revealed the
reason for these hopes when he commented that, after
observing the French for four years, "there is much to admire and not a little to condemn" in these struggles for
liberty.[24] Clachar realized the potential of the Revolution
and was willing to overlook mistakes.

Up to the time fighting began, therefore, these newspapers emphasized the beneficial or harmful effects that
the deficiencies in the new constitution had upon the
French people. This emphasis was deepened after the first
battle of the war on April 24. Three of the papers reported
a long succession of French defeats, routs, and panics.

Particularly shocking to the editors was an incident which occurred after the defeat of the French at Tournay. At Lisle, where the French halted their retreat, the soldiers put to death their commander, General Theobald Dillon, and seven others for alleged treachery. Not satisfied, the soldiers then hacked off their heads and limbs and danced with them around fires. These war stories undoubtedly sold newspapers, but the editors invariably explained French reverses by pointing to inadequacies in the constitution which, guaranteeing equality, prevented French leaders from controlling followers on all levels. Referring to the dangers of trying to lead French troops, the *Advertiser* commented: "The French commanders seem all likely to die in the field; but some distance from the ground."[25] Lacking constitutional restraints and enjoying their rights, French soldiers demonstrated the anarchistic behavior which was the larger problem of French society. Equality produced indiscipline; indiscipline, anarchy.

Constitutional analyses of the French led inevitably to comparisons between the French and English constitutions. Contrasted to stories of the bankruptcy of the French were news items that, because of a flourishing treasury, the English government was reducing the army, setting aside sums to pay off the national debt, and lowering taxes. These differences between the two constitutions were especially magnified when news stories of the massive drive to end the slave trade were printed next to stories of French atrocities. Even in the matter of the war itself, the cabinet's decision to remain neutral and uninvolved was taken as a sign of wisdom produced by the English system of government.[26] By comparison with printed reports of French activities, therefore, the English constitution and the beneficial effects it produced were much on display. From this perspective, it is not surprising that Paine's pamphlets were not well received.

The *York Courant* and *Berrow's Worcester Journal* mentioned Paine only by reporting that informations were being filed against him "for some passages contained in his

Publications." The *Chelmsford Chronicle* and the most reform-minded of these four newspapers, the *Sussex Weekly Advertiser,* however, ridiculed Paine and his ideas on every available occasion. The latter paper was especially annoyed by Paine. On February 13 the editor commented, after a discussion of Paine's notion that Englishmen had no constitution, that "the more the British Constitution is known, the more zealous in its defense and support will become the body of the people; till at length its *speculative innovators* shall be awed into silence." By April 16 the editor's increased hostility to Paine was evident. "John Bull sits, at present, under his fig tree, surrounded with as many blessings as can well fall to the lot of human nature. Fully sensible of this, John will not easily suffer a new gang of *Rights of Man* Robbers to plunder him of his happiness." Before the issuance of the proclamation, the editor had reached the conclusion that English reformers were somehow connected with the French. "The *Ca Ira* Reformers allege, that Errors are crept into the Constitution and that therefore the whole frame of Government ought to be taken to pieces."[27] Thus before the government alerted Englishmen to the potential dangers of the spread of Painite principles, newspapers had already taken sides on the issue.

Englishmen who kept up with the news had therefore had several months to think about constitutional issues and also had had the opportunity to reflect upon the causes of French miseries. If these newspaper comments were any indication of the conclusions they reached, French methods and examples had made a poor showing. Theoretical perfection, if one could find that in the French constitution, seemed to have no relationship either to effectiveness or to humane government. Not only was the government of France mishandled by incompetents allowed positions of authority by the principles upon which their constitution was based, but those very concepts themselves were endangered by the limitations of governmental power designed to protect them. In contrast, the

English constitution in practice served the purposes of government and protected individuals within the state. Moreover, those in England who proposed perfecting or improving the constitution upon theoretical grounds could be viewed, however mild their proposed changes, as advocating that the English should embark on the same path traveled by the French. If anyone needed materials for arguing against any change, the French supplied them daily.

The May Proclamation, therefore, did not appear as a bolt from the blue but only as an indication of the degree of seriousness the constituted authorities placed upon the danger of the spread of doctrines proposing constitutional modifications at that time. Like the editor of the *Advertiser,* the proclamation also hinted that the government had reason to believe there might be some connection between the people who were spreading these doctrines and others in "foreign parts." It is most probable, therefore, that the proclamation's success was due to its reflecting the opinions held by a large majority of Englishmen. The measure of that success was the timing, the numbers, and the inclusiveness of the respondents.

Unfortunately there is no accurate way to date the various loyal addresses from areas outside London. The addresses themselves have not survived, and reports of meetings held to approve them appear in the local newspapers as news items, usually with no dates appended. At that, a local newspaper could report a meeting held earlier as if it were a current item of news. The *Chelmsford Chronicle,* for instance, reported the Northamptonshire meeting and address on July 2, while the *Sussex Weekly Advertiser* had noted the same meeting on June 4. The *London Gazette* noted the presentation of addresses to George III, but merely mentioned the total number presented, not the dates of their composition or even their origins.

Added to this complexity in timing were the diversified methods by which Englishmen chose to testify their loyalty. These ranged from highly structured step-by-step procedures to spontaneous gatherings. The proceedings at the city of York and those at Doncaster are good examples of these extremes. On June 11 the *York Courant* printed a notice by the Lord Mayor of York, R. Dodsworth, that, because of the requests of 19 gentlemen, whom he listed, he was calling a meeting of the inhabitants of the city to give thanks to His Majesty for the late proclamation. The *Courant* reported the meeting in full, noting the comments of the major speakers and printing the address itself. The address, with signatures, was then sent to the members of Parliament from York, Richard Milnes and Sir William Milner, bt., to be presented to the king. The Doncaster gathering, on the other hand, was reported as a meeting of the principal gentlemen of that town, with no further news of the fate of the address.[28] Some meetings voted to publish their addresses in the local and London papers, but most did not. Of the 151 provincial meetings I have been able to discover, less than 30 went to the expense of advertising their loyal sentiments in the newspapers.

The first meeting was held in Northamptonshire on June 4, but from that date the frequency increased weekly. The crescendo was reached in the last two weeks of June, seventy-seven addresses being presented to the king on a single day. The rate descended slowly from that date. Evan Nepean at the Home Office received notices about the reception of addresses as late as August 1.[29]

Not all meetings proceeded smoothly. At the first Sheffield meeting the proposed address was negatived, for whatever reasons, by a "great majority." Another, however, was approved at a subsequent meeting. At Nottingham the mayor refused to call a meeting to endorse a loyal address, but the inhabitants called one on their own. At the Surrey county meeting, held at Epsom, Horne Tooke, a prominent member of the Society for Constitutional Information, and Sir Joseph Mawbey opposed the address as unnecessary, but they were overruled by a "large majority." Some attempts to vote down loyal addresses may have succeeded. As mentioned before, ten counties and eighty-one cities and towns did not respond to the proclamation, although the reasons are not known.[30] Presumably Nepean's tabulations was of those addresses actually presented to the king, although he may have used the slim resources of the Home Office to examine the reports of meetings which did not result in the sending of an address. Whatever the reasons for the silence of some counties, cities, and towns, the impression generated by those who responded was overwhelmingly favorable. At each stage of the loyal address movement, the local newspapers applauded loyal activities of any kind. The *York Courant* on June 4 praised both the proclamation and its favorable reception in Parliament as "the surest Proof of the Unanimity of the Nation in endeavouring to suppress those Seditious Meetings and Publications which have thrown the Kingdom into a Ferment." At the very height of the presentation of addresses, the *Chelmsford Chronicle* commented that this was "highly gratifying to every lover of his country. An ardent and steady spirit of loyalty and patriotism seems to pervade the whole Nation—such a spirit as must banish sedition from the land." As the magnitude of the loyal response to the proclamation became evident, the *Sussex Weekly Advertiser* noted that "this shows the disposition of the people to support the Constitution and Government of the country against those who would wish to undermine it under the specious word of reform."[31] These comments about the origins, climax, and implications of the loyal address movement afford us the opportunity to understand how these editors, and perhaps the public generally, evaluated the issues brought up by the May Proclamation. For this was viewed not as a struggle between conservatives and radicals, but as a clash between loyal and disloyal portions of the population; not as a trial between the corrupters of the constitution and reformers, as Paine depicted it, but as a contest between patriots and traitors. The conclusion inferable from the creation of these dichotomies is that the champions of change, the French revolutionaries, had discredited reform in England to the extent that the great majority of Englishmen wanted nothing to do with the minority who wished to imitate the French.

An outburst of loyalty on this scale, paradoxically, posed some dangers to internal peace and threatened one of the reasons for praising the constitution in the first place. The third anniversary of the Bastille approached, and if loyalists, carried away by enthusiasm, attempted to demonstrate their loyalty by actions, as some suggested they had done the previous year at Birmingham and other towns, the government's inability to govern, a primary charge against the French, might be dramatically demonstrated against the English. Taking no chances, Nepean ordered Colonel Oliver DeLancey, the assistant adjutant general, to station three troops of dragoons at Sheffield, Nottingham, Birmingham, and Coventry each, four troops at Norwich, and a full regiment at Manchester. These precautions, however, proved unnecessary. On July 15 Henry Dundas, the home secretary, informed George III that July 14 had not been the occasion for more outbreaks of violence.[32]

There is no doubt that the government assumed the proclamation to be a success. Grenville, the foreign secretary, who had assisted his brother, the Marquis of Buckingham, in the latter's plans for an address, assured him that "our addresses are going on swimmingly." On July 19 he wrote Lord Gower, the British ambassador at Paris, that "we have nothing but peace and prosperity at home, and no other concern in the miseries and misfortunes of other countries than what humanity calls for. I am sure you have seen with particular pleasure the effects of the proclamation." Later, when the problems of internal peace once again concerned the government, he admitted that he had thought that the loyal response to the proclamation had "completely quelled" the seditious movement.[33]

In this manner, and over this issue, the English loyalists made their first appearance. How many loyalists there were, their stations in life, and their political attachments are impossible to trace. Without the documents themselves these questions cannot be answered. Advertisements of the meetings were generally signed by the persons chosen to chair them. Some editors commented about the large numbers of people attending, but usually they described them as the inhabitants of this or that borough or parish, or as the freeholders of a county, the clergy of a diocese, or the noblemen and gentlemen of the surrounding area. In only one instance did I find mention of the "inferior people" being involved,[34] but whether they were there out of curiosity or conviction is impossible to state. The usual practice was to place copies of the address at convenient locations where all people could sign them, but how many took advantage of this opportunity is unknown. The issue, however, was the identifying mark of the loyalist. Here was his first opportunity to stand by the constitution, and in 71 counties and 315 towns and cities he did just that.

It is a striking commentary upon the unusual climate of opinion of the times and upon the convictions of the loyalists that no commentator remarked about the extraordinary proceedings that transpired between May and August 1792. To be sure, addresses of support, opposition, and thanks for contending sides in practically every important issue in Parliament had been eagerly sought by politicians for some time. Referring to the opinion of the public at large was no innovation. What made this movement unusual was the nature of the question. The proclamation had only asked the subjects of the crown to "avoid and discourage" tendencies toward social disorders, yet every address was a pledge of loyalty to the existing constitution. It was as if the political community of England was ratifying the constitution by open voting. From a cold twentieth-century perspective, it is not unthinkable that perfectly loyal subjects could vote addresses which stated that they would indeed obey the law, which is all the proclamation requested. The confidence of those who ruled in breeching this question must lie in the fact that the community of intersts was comprehensive and strong enough to allow them to undertake a project of this sort with few misgivings. Paine's analysis of the existing relationships between governors and the governed was therefore so completely wrong as to be ludicrous. If this was so, why the alarm over the spread of his doctrines? Again the answer must lie in the English analysis of events across the Channel, of the ferocious activities of people formerly out of the political community who had managed to acquire a voice in their own government. The confidence of the governors of England, therefore, was not shaken but merely challenged. Their response was mild but definite. The methods of the loyalists in demonstrating their opinion deserve some notice also. The focus of their loyalty was the king. The monarchy was the symbol of their patriotic sentiments. This was in keeping with tradition and was perhaps necessary, for the expressions necessary to explain the feelings which animated their support of the nation had not yet been invented.

The English loyalists first appeared, therefore, as a result of a challenge to the constitution by reformers in England, a challenge made practical and threatening by events in revolutionary France. The loyalists' actions were muted and their composition, in its entirety, was unknown. Their chief significance was the demonstration they made of their willingness to stand forward and be counted. They effectively gave a vote of confidence to the constitution when it was under attack. Whether or not their appearance reversed tendencies toward a radicalization of the English public or merely illustrated that there were other sides to the question of the timing of reform, a new group of Englishmen had appeared on the political stage.

CHAPTER II

THE CRISIS OF 1792

The alarm which prompted government to issue the May Proclamation had been generated by the appearance of propaganda, and of propaganda-distributing groups which may or may not have been in contact with persons in "foreign parts." These groups, whether or not their activities were curtailed, attracted little attention between July and September 1792. From the latter month through December, however, their renewed activities, or a reawakened sensitivity to their activities, generated a new concern in the public and among members of government that far overshadowed the "ferment" that had led to the first appearance of the loyalists. More alarmingly, government received reports from various sources which could have been interpreted to mean that an armed insurrection was planned, to be supported by French soldiers. The combination of ministerial findings and the intense concern about the activities of the artisans' clubs by the population generally produced the crisis of 1792, which was to be the direct cause of the loyal association movement, the second appearance of the loyalists and their supreme effort before war began with France.

Although the government assumed that the volume and extent of the loyal response to the proclamation had ended the dangers posed by the artisans' club movement, the growth of these clubs had continued throughout the summer. The Sheffield Society, which had claimed a membership of 2,000 in March, collected 10,000 signatures on a petition for manhood suffrage in May. In September it attracted "5-6,000 in a street *mascarade.*" By August the Norwich Revolution Society claimed 48 affiliated clubs and an "associated brethern [*sic*]" of 2,000. Hardy's London Society claimed a membership of 2,000 by July.[1] Because these were not secret societies, information about their growth was easily available to the public and officials in government. In spite of this, Home Office records indicate that few wrote the government to express their concern and that the members of the Pitt ministry ignored the clubs altogether. There were probably several reasons for this.

The first was undoubtedly the satisfaction felt by members of government and the political community in general about the favorable response to the proclamation. In a "tryal of strength," and allowing for political manipulations by Fox and his adherents, practically the whole community had expressed its approval of the existing state of things,[2] and those in power now thought that discontent with the constitution was the feeling of but a few persons of the lower class. In addition, there was no indication of any relationship between these domestic signs of discontent and the radicals in France. Confident of their strength, the government and the public generally believed they had nothing to apprehend from the activities of a few thousand artisans.

The second reason for this unconcern might be traced to the activities of the artisans themselves. One of the provisions of the proclamation called for justices of the peace to transmit to the government information about the publishers, authors, and distributors of seditious literature. In reality, this provision was aimed directly at Paine's *Rights of Man.* There is a possibility that these clubs curtailed distribution of that pamphlet during the summer, and indeed other activities which might excite disapproval. The continued growth of the artisans' clubs does not indicate that Painism was on the rise. It is reasonable to assume that some sort of impression had been made upon the artisans' spirits by the outpouring of loyalty in June. After all, theirs was essentially a propaganda campaign, and the negative results they had achieved must have been disheartening. One can admire their tenacity in continuing their efforts, but a dogged determination to continue in spite of social disapproval breeds actions and attitudes quite different from those born in enthusiastic anticipation. In this instance perhaps the "quelling" of the seditious people by the first appearance of the loyalists may really have been only a severe dampening of their spirits.[3]

An important influence upon the dampening of the artisans' spirits, and also upon the sensitivity of the public and those in power to their activities, was the continuing transformation of the image of their inspiration, the Revolution in France. For just as the Revolution—the flame of liberty—could warm the hearts of liberty-loving people everywhere, so could it also consume its adherents. As the Duke of Brunswick advanced into France, French soldiers deserted and French towns opened their doors to him. Battlefield atrocities of the French upon the French indicated that the supporters of the Revolution were infected with a desire to injure themselves. For if the dynamism of the ideals and aspirations of the French Revolution could, in the first instance, inspire imitation in other countries, other characteristics, such as self-destruction, lack of will, and cowardly desertions on the battlefield, could paralyze these same imitators. These manifestations could be observed not only on the battlefield, but also in the actions of French politicians and the French mob in Paris.

On August 10, after absorbing the news of a series of defeats and frustrations on the battlefield, a mob stormed the royal residence, the Tuilleries, massacred the Swiss Guards, and imprisoned the royal family in the Temple. Hundreds of suspected royal supporters were killed and thousands more thrown into prison. A provisional government was established which assumed dictatorial powers, and the Terror began. As Brunswick continued his advance into France, the executive government expelled all refractory priests, over 2,000 of whom found refuge in England. Finally, after the fall of Verdun, the last major stronghold between Paris and the advancing army, Parisian mobs killed over 1,400 people in a series of atrocities known later as the September massacres. Revolutionary ardor seemed to lead the French to vent their ferocity upon themselves. With no other results than an extended panic, there was little inspiration to be derived from French actions by those Englishmen who wished to support the cause of revolution.

The English press responses to these events were varied and confused. Nothing like this had been seen since the struggles over religion in the seventeenth century. The *Morning Chronicle,* the organ of the reforming Whigs, attempted desperately to maintain its pro-French policy by printing the excuses offered for these atrocities by the French Assembly and later by the Executive Council. *The Times,* a government newspaper, thundered its shock at French misdeeds and castigated domestic reformers for wishing to follow so malevolent an example.[4] Provincial papers editorialized less but printed letters from their correspondents in London and Paris describing what was happening across the Channel. Through September little that could be called inspirational was discernible in the activities of the French. Indeed, it seemed to most that the Revolution had but a short life ahead.

English politicians responded similarly. Writing to Grenville, Pitt ascribed fear and punitive will as the causes of French behavior. "You will hear from the Office the shocking accounts which have been received this morning [September 7] of fresh horrors at Paris. They are probably near their term from the approach of the Duke of Brunswick, but the last paroxysm of fear and rage will be dreadful." Fox had excused the August 10 activities in Paris as the result of the Duke of Brunswick's manifesto of July 11, in which he promised to put the revolutionaries to the sword if the royal family were harmed. Fox abandoned this strained causal explanation when he learned of the September massacres. His letter to Lord Holland illustrates the untenable position occupied by pro-French politicians after that event. "I had just made up my mind to the events of the 10th of August, when the horrid accounts of the 2nd of this month arrived, and I really consider the horrors of that day and night as the most heart-breaking event that ever happened to those, who, like me, are fundamentally and unalterably attached to the true cause. There is not, in my opinion, a shadow of excuse for this horrid massacre, not even the possibility of extenuating it in the smallest degree; and if one were to consider only the people of Paris, one should almost doubt to whom one should—[the rest of the letter is torn off]."[5] Fox, like the artisans, had found a true cause, but the methods of achieving that cause in France revealed tendencies in the body politic that were less than ideal.

The insensitivity of the government and the population at large to the growth of the artisans' clubs was explainable, therefore, to some degree by the changing image of the clubs' champion in the summer of 1792.[6] Moreover, what support the artisans might have received from other sections of society was threatened by their interpretations of French behavior during that time. To those who ruled, it appeared that the life of revolutionary France was nearing its end and that as long as there were no connections between radical Englishmen and radical Frenchmen, no danger need be apprehended from that quarter.

The defeat of Brunswick by Dumourier at Valmy on September 20 reversed the military fortunes of France and halted the pessimism of French adherents in England about the power of freedom. Indeed, Brunswick's defeat, occurring simultaneously with the meeting of the National Convention in Paris, marked a new phase in the revolutionary process which was to be different enough in its manifestations to be labeled a new French Revolution. Vitality and dedication, so noticeable by their absence during the summer, now were visible in practically every action of the French.

From September through December the French armies appeared irresistible. Spier, Mainz, and Frankfort on the Main fell to General Custine. Dumourier won the victory at Jemappes and virtually conquered the Austrian Netherlands. Savoy and Nice were annexed and the Scheldt was declared open to commerce. Developments on the French political scene matched these stunning victories in their rapidity and audacity. The monarchy was formally abolished on September 21 and France was declared a republic. On November 19 the Convention declared universal revolution by offering the assistance of French armies to all peoples who wished to follow the French example, and Louis XVI was put on trial for his life. Even plans to change the calendar were adopted, the new era dating from the meeting of the National Convention. Goethe's remark on September 20, "Here [Valmy] and today begins a new age in the history of the world,"[7] was literally valid for France, and by inspiration and example, perhaps figuratively for the rest of Europe.

This phase of the Revolution redefined the concept itself. The sovereignty of the people had often been expressed as a justification for constitutional and political changes in the last half of the eighteenth century. The realization of that sovereignty in practice, however, had been attempted upon accepted, perhaps disliked, theoretical constructions of the state. The republican and representative form in the example of the United States, or the mixture of representative and traditional in the British and, from 1789, the French constitutions, were two of the old methods devised to achieve that end. After September 1792 the will of the sovereign people was to be expressed by a government with ill-defined or nonexistent limits of power in order to guarantee the continuation of the process which had led to its own creation.

Preservation of the Revolution now became the *raison*

d'être of the state. There would be no theoretical barriers
to power which might determine the goals or the use of
governmental powers save that of preservation. The "will
of the people" and "reasons of state" were combined
to such an extent that a government of men and not
laws became almost inescapable. Modifications in the lives
of Frenchmen would depend upon either apprehended
dangers to the Revolution or the willingness of French
politicians to experiment. The Revolution, now the voice
of the nation, had unlimited power and goals which could
not be predicted. For the next year and a half the Convention would be the constitution of the state, in spite of its
completion of a written document in 1793. General will
would be expressed without regard to form. In terms of
extreme change, the Revolution of 1792 set the standards
for all future revolutions and was truly the acme of the
revolutionary process in France.

The response to these activities in France by different
groups in England created the crisis of 1792. The inspiration of the new Revolution stimulated an increase in the
activities of radical clubs. The nonchalance toward their
activities ended. Now that revolutionary stimulation no
longer depended upon an almost-defeated folly, those who
sensed danger were sensitized to the echo of French activities in England. The domestic tranquillity created by the
May Proclamation ended, to be replaced by an anxiety
that the mysterious forces operating in France had been
exported to England and that a revolutionary situation was
rapidly growing. After three months of rising tensions, Pitt
and his ministers, along with a sizable portion of the political community, concluded that revolution was possible
and that steps to counter it had to be taken.

The government took these steps on December 1 by
issuing proclamations calling out the militia and convening
an emergency assemblage of Parliament. The government
explained this new state of affairs in the militia proclamation. "And whereas we have received information that in
breach of the laws, and notwithstanding our royal procla-

mation of the 21st day of May last, the utmost industry is still employed by evil-disposed persons within this kingdom, acting in concert with persons in foreign parts, with a view to subvert the laws and established constitution of this realm, and to destroy all order and government therein; and that a spirit of tumult and disorder, thereby excited, has lately shewn itself in riots and insurrections."[8] Here was the crisis of 1792. Domestic subversives, acting in concert with foreigners, were seen as attempting to overthrow the government. Moreover, their efforts were believed to have been partially successful. Because these steps were the occasion for the second appearance of the loyalists, how government reached the conclusions upon which they were based deserves some attention.

The ministry based its conclusions upon evidence laboriously compiled in September, October, and November. It learned not only that the activities of the artisans' clubs had increased, but also that there were three new domestic developments produced by the new French Revolution whose effects on domestic peace had to be evaluated. The number and intentions of the emigrants who fled to England after the August and September massacres, the location, number, and intended use of arms privately bought, and, more ominously, the intentions and activities of known and suspected French agents suggested a relationship between domestic radicals and their French counterparts which could not be ignored with safety. From scanty evidence, the ministry concluded that all of these pointed to the possibility of an insurrection supported by a French invasion.

The government applied its various means of obtaining evidence to two tasks. The first was the gathering of verifiable data which could be used to construct an overall picture of the situation in any of the areas mentioned above. The second task was more difficult. Because the covert struggle between England and France during these months involved the capturing of English public opinion, the government had to discover some means of counteracting pro-French activities and, if possible, of building a loyal platform upon which stability could be maintained. In this latter effort the government had to gauge the effects of the activities of those who were attempting either to create discontent or to foment revolution, and to discover means of counteracting those attempts. This latter task, partly because of the ineffective tools possessed by government, proved later to have commanded the major part of its resources and ingenuity, and, in the last analysis, was perhaps never completed. The loyalists once again stood forward, but whether the government called them out or whether they were aroused by purely patriotic motives, stimulated by their own experiences, is impossible to state. In the end, however, the loyalists did almost exactly what the government wanted done.

Perhaps if the government had had time enough to investigate alarming reports sufficiently to collect evidence for prosecutions, the normal processes of law would have been sufficient to end the seditious activities. Events moved too quickly for this. Faced with the possibility of widespread insurrection or rebellion, and aware of the inadequacies of its intelligence-gathering resources, the government collected information about seditious activities which could have been interpreted in a variety of ways. Under these circumstances the government had no choice but to act as if the most alarming interpretations were valid, and to take precautionary steps to meet any threat to the constitution. To discover these threats, however, the government had to use information sources which were scarcely adequate to the task.

The government had to rely upon a bureaucratic organization designed, or evolved, to perform tasks entirely different from the impossible job of discovering intentions and motives from speeches and statements given by individuals under these new circumstances. Even the terms used to describe what government wanted to know were vague and understandable only in degree. "Disaffected" and "seditious" were the most used and, as could be expected, were relative to the moment and amenable to many interpretations. As in the days of religious strife, how much in vain did the suspect have to take the Lord's name before blasphemy was reached? Faced with these complications, customs collectors, postmasters, and magistrates sent information to the Home Office which varied in importance and reliability. These and other members of the governing structure of England were unable in most cases to give the government the information it most desired: news of the activities and intentions of the artisans' clubs. To obtain this much-desired information, the government used secret agents.

Government agents were used to infiltrate the radical clubs as early as the autumn of 1792. A "Mr. Lynam" was either the coordinator or the infiltrator himself who informed the government of the activities of the London Corresponding Society until November 1793. He was not, however, privy to the secrets of the Committee of Delegates, the executive branch of the society. Lynam was followed by "Mr. Metcalfe," "Graves," and "Taylor." Reports from seven other individuals, using either a cipher or no identification whatever, arrived at the Home Office in the latter months of 1792.[9] Even at that, the information they contained was suspect. It was likely that some of them manufactured evidence in order to maintain their income.

The most unusual agent used by the government at this time was a woman in the Austrian Netherlands who dined with Dumourier and reported regularly to Dundas from December 1, 1792, until January 19, 1793. "Ever Anonymous," "Ever Yours," or "E.W." posed as a pro-French advocate and a lover of Dundas intent on convincing him of the desirability and necessity of a French-English alliance. In the course of stating the reasons for such an alliance, she managed to identify the chief French agent in Britain, hinted at a plot to overthrow the government, and finally gave Dumourier's estimate of the number of Englishmen (40,000) who were willing to join the French in the event of an invasion.[10] Most secret agents, however, were assigned the task of verifying information received by the government from other sources or were instructed to attend meetings and report the nature of their discussions.[11]

Occasionally individuals in or out of the governing structure informed government of the activities of French spies or of estimates of the size and intentions of the disaffected in England. Although the reliability of information obtained from this source varied, Pitt and his ministers did all they could to encourage these sources. The methods used by the Home Office in dealing with information volunteered by Thomas Curry, a magistrate at Gosport, illustrate how the government tried to squeeze out every drop of information gratuitously supplied. Curry wrote the Home Office on September 12. Seizing this opportunity, Home Secretary Dundas replied the following day in this manner:

> I have been favoured with your letter of yesterday's date. So far from thinking your addressing me on a subject of the nature mentioned in your letter an intrusion, I consider myself particularly obliged to you for the information it contains.
>
> It is very desirable at this moment, that every degree of intelligence respecting the number and description of People arriving from France should be obtained—and you cannot render a more essential service than by a further attention to this object whenever any other opportunity should present itself.[12]

Dundas did not remind Curry that he was doing his job, but instead flattered him and stated the interests of government. All the Home Secretary could hope for was that Curry would respond with more of the desired information. In this case Dundas was successful. Curry responded on September 28, and his information, as I shall demonstrate later, was put to use.

Information gathered in this manner was expensive in time. Because it was impossible to determine the reliability of the correspondent, whether he wrote as a private citizen, as a member of local government, or as an official of the church, the information supplied had to be evaluated in the light of known facts about the situation existing in the area of the letter's origin. Moreover, if the informer was unclear or indefinite, a reply had to be sent which clarified the government's needs. Between September and December, all the important members of government—Pitt, Grenville, Dundas, Nepean, and Long—had a hand in collecting information by this method.[13] Although restricted in scope, it formed a valuable supplement to the data collected by other means.

The Customs and Post Office, local governmental officials, chance informants, and hired intelligence agents, therefore, were four recognizable sources of information which can be readily identified by the investigator of the period. Much information was transmitted orally, and except in those rare instances when such conversations were mentioned in office memoranda or letters,[14] is impossible to trace. Even though governmental business was not yet affected by the unrecorded information transmitted by telephone, the small numbers involved in policy decisions made the verbal sharing of views and information relatively easy. By September, when refugees began arriving from France, this intelligence network was put to use.

Political exiles from revolutionary France began to arrive in England in large numbers after the Executive Committee of the French government ordered all refractory priests banished on August 25, 1792.[15] Reports of boatloads of French emigrants, private citizens as well as clerics, arriving in England prompted the government to try to determine their numbers and intentions.[16] Because legal restrictions regarding aliens were vague and unclear, not to be clarified until the passage of the Aliens' Act in January, this sudden influx posed a serious problem for the government. Sympathy for the plight of these unfortunates clashed with apprehensions as to their intentions. On September 21, Dundas expressed to Lord Hood his qualms about the adoption of an official plan to help the emigrants. "I am afraid," he wrote, "that there are many who have mischievous intentions and ought to be a little attended to." Ten days earlier the first orders had been issued from the Home Office to customs officials in the major ports asking for strict accounts of all Frenchmen who arrived in Great Britain.[17] *The Times* voiced its suspicions on September 14. "Under the appellation of Fugitives, a multitude of insidious and evil designing persons . . . intrude themselves, with the intentions of raising a . . . disturbance in this kingdom."[18] Because no means existed to determine which of the emigrants were bona fide political exiles, this suspicious reception is understandable.

Others had different views of the clerical emigrants. George III wrote Dundas of his concern for these "fleeing clergymen" from France and later offered them lodgings in Winchester at one of his establishments. Burke began a subscription for their relief, which was copied in various cities and towns all over the kingdom. Dundas approved of this aid on humanitarian grounds but still believed that it should be the affair of private individuals. He feared that official involvement in the relief of these refugees and clergymen would only "offer an inducement" for more to come to England.[19] As it was, the government had all it could do to locate the Frenchmen already arrived.

In order to discover their locations and intentions, Nepean sent letters, similar in form to the following, to persons suspected of sheltering refugees:

> You are required to render an Account to the Secretary of State for the Home Department at his office in Cleveland Row St. James of the French Emigrants now harboured in your house. In three days from this date, you must attend in person and answer the following questions—Who are these people? What is their business here? how are they supported? Their Occu-

pations? And by whom they came recommended to you? The hours are from 10 'til 3—and if you fail, you will most assuredly answer for the consequences at your peril.[20]

Nepean was obviously trying to frighten the recipient, a "Mr. Rose [Ross?], Perfumer at Walworth," into informing on emigrants of whom he had knowledge. The legality of such a summons was questionable. The mere fact that the government thought such tactics necessary, however, indicated the degree of its concern. In October, reports from customs officials began arriving with assuring regularity at the Home Office,[21] which relieved the government of the necessity of using such extreme tactics in order to obtain information about the emigrants.

It was necessary, however, to learn more than the numbers and overt intentions of the emigrants. As early as September 1, the government received reports of a mission headed by an Abbé Noel and began its observation of as many of the French agents composing it as it had knowledge of.[22] The government had no knowledge of the size or intentions of Noel's mission, nor were the English counteragents able to supply definite details to clarify these points. W.A. Miles, for instance, reported on September 9 that "Mons. de Noailles told me yesterday that there were many of his countrymen here, very wicked men, for very wicked purposes and what I have heard this morning confirms what he said."[23] Reports of this nature, while confirming the suspicions of the government that French agents were active in England, added little to its knowledge of the extent and nature of French designs. Before taking countermeasures the government had to know not only the strength of its opponents, but also the measures they wished to oppose.

The government gained its first indication of the intentions of the French agents from information supplied by Thomas Curry of Gosport, Hampshire. On September 28, replying to Dundas's letter mentioned previously, Curry

informed the government of the activities of some Frenchmen in the Portsmouth area and warned, "I have reason to
fear that there are many suspicious characters, as some
have been seen in obscure places, taking plans of the harbour, Navy, etc. etc." Nepean sent this letter to Vice-
Admiral Lord Hood, a member of the Board of Admiralty,
on October 1, with a covering letter: "I have no doubt that
there are many people at Portsmouth and in that neighbourhood, employed in the manner Mr. Curry has stated,
and if any man should be caught in the act of taking plans,
there cannot, I think, be a doubt of the propriety of taking
him into custody." Nepean further warned Lord Hood of a
"Beaumarchais," a "dangerous, intriguing fellow." He then
wrote Curry thanking him for his information and suggested he send any further information he might have to
Lord Hood.[24]

This incident points out another difficulty the government faced in dealing with French spies. Even when
magistrates responded to the government's direction to
supply information, local officials were unaware of the
government's suspicions. Nepean, therefore, had to assure
them of the "propriety" of taking French agents into
custody. There were no existing laws, strictly speaking, that
would enable either officials or the local magistrates to
take such action on their own initiative. Nepean and other
members of the government must have been aware that
Curry's information was a fortunate accident, that it was
possible there were French agents in every port "taking
plans of the harbour, Navy, etc. etc." Under these circumstances, therefore, it was unlikely that the government
would be able to repress the French spies effectively. The
alternative was to attempt to nullify the effects of their
activities, one of which was the buying of arms.

On September 21, John Brooke, a magistrate in Birmingham, wrote Nepean that a Dr. Maxwell had placed an
order for a large quantity of arms, and a week later, on
September 28, he sent Nepean a copy of the order for
20,000 daggers "12 inches in the blade" to be delivered at

2,000 per week.[25] Brooke also sent a specimen, which may
have been the weapon used by Burke in his "Dagger
Scene" in the Commons during the debate on the Aliens'
Bill on December 28.[26] Maxwell's complicity with the
French was proved on October 2 when his brother, James
Maxwell, in an effort to clear himself, forwarded several of
his brother's letters to the Home Office. In them Dr.
Maxwell clearly indicated his adherence to the French
cause. In spite of Dr. Maxwell's stated intention of buying
these arms for French use, there was a possibility that the
Frenchmen who were to use them might already be in
England. These fears were proved groundless when, on
November 5, Mr. Newport from the Customs House at
Dover reported that the daggers had been shipped to
France.[27]

With a large number of newly-arrived Frenchmen within
England and with large purchases of arms by private individuals being reported, there was always the possibility
that those who wished to overthrow the government were
quietly arming themselves and their allies from France
right under the eyes of the government.[28] Moreover, the
danger existed that the orders placed with the arms manufacturers were intended to arm disaffected people in Ireland and Scotland. It was necessary, therefore, for the government to attempt to track down every report or rumor,
"however vague and uncertain,"[29] concerning the sale of
large quantities of arms regardless of their ostensible destination.

On October 21 Nepean sent almost identical letters of
instructions to agents of the government in Birmingham
and Sheffield, informing them that information had been
received by Dundas that arms lately made at those cities
were being sent to Ireland. Nepean asked these agents to
determine the truth of this information and instructed
them to investigate "by whom the Arms were made—The
quantity—By whose Order—To whom they were consigned—To what place—By what mode of conveyance—
And, in short, every particular respecting them." Not

satisfied with this, Nepean also wrote Arthur Onslow, the customs collector at Liverpool, for information about any arms which had been shipped to Ireland. Brooke, in Birmingham, hired "two or three" additional agents to assist in the search. On November 14, T. Galton, a Birmingham manufacturer, obviously responding to the pressure exerted by Brooke and his agents, wrote the Home Office that the arms were intended for France, not Ireland. Nepean, while awaiting the results of the investigation of Galton's activities, wrote to Brooke instructing him not to relax his efforts regardless of the results of this one investigation. Mr. Mason, one of Brooke's agents, finally corroborated Galton's story on November 14.[30] From October 12 through November 14, therefore, time, money, and ingenuity were expended by the central government and its agents in verifying information which proved to have been incorrect in the first place.

Nepean, after December 7, compiled a "List of areas, reports and numbers of arms collected for people not connected with government."[31] Twenty items were carefully arranged by the under secretary in an obvious attempt to determine how many arms had been ordered and consigned to areas outside Britain as well as how many had actually reached their destinations.[32] Nepean also attempted to learn the area of origin, and in this list Birmingham seems to be the principal area. "Arms for an Hundred and Thirty Thousand Men," however, are mentioned in an "extract from a letter from Maestricht," with no indication where these weapons had been or were to be manufactured.[33] From a tabulation of reports, orders for between 335,000 and 765,000 stands of arms plus 20,000 daggers and 1,000 pistols were placed with the Birmingham arms manufacturers alone.[34] It was clearly impossible to trace this enormous quantity of weapons through the ordinary channels of information available to the government. While the question of the location of these weapons continued to be a crucial one for the remainder of the year,[35] the government's main efforts in November and

December were focused upon the revival and increased activities of radical associations. The members of these clubs were deemed the most likely users of those weapons should any remain in Britain. This renewed sensitivity of the government to the activities of these clubs represented a complete reversal of its policy formed after the May Proclamation. After October 8, when Brunswick's defeat was certain,[36] the Home Office made a determined effort to discover how far the radical movement had recovered. In late October or early November, Nepean compiled a list of "Associations for relief of pretended Grievances." Included were fourteen cities in England where the government had knowledge of the formation of workingmen's associations.[37] From this moment through December, the government was to expend its major efforts in an attempt to counteract the effects of these clubs' activities.

While the threat of internal disturbances was obviously the most important reason for the government's concern about the growth of radical associations, a subsidiary effect of their existence was a limitation upon the government's diplomatic freedom. As that mysterious Mata Hari "E.W." cautioned, "How go to war, when at home all is tumult and plot?" Agents operating in England warned the government about the impossibility of sending troops out of England as "the measure of men's opinions" stands. Grenville, who was convinced that the radical associations were tools of French policy, put the matter succinctly in a letter to Lord Auckland, the English ambassador to the Netherlands. "It is clear to me that the French rely, in the present moment, on their intrigues in the interior of both countries [England and the United Provinces], and that they imagine they have brought us to a condition of inability to resist any demands which they may make."[38] While Grenville urged Auckland to do all in his power to resist, clearly the existence of an unknown number of disaffected persons at home limited the activities of the foreign minister. It would have been perilous to take steps in foreign affairs which would add fuel to domestic discontent. Domestic discontents, in the first weeks of November, however, assumed alarming overtones and revealed serious weaknesses in the structure of local government. Between October 31 and November 15 the government received reports of riots in four eastern ports. The ability of local governments to maintain order was put to the test and found wanting. Again, as at Birmingham and London, the military had to come to the aid of local authorities to prevent the central government's losing control of sections of England.

The riots, which broke out at Great Yarmouth, South Shields, King's Lynn, and Ipswich, were similar in many ways.[39] In each case, sailors demanded increases in pay before they would allow ships in the harbors to sail. In two cases, at Yarmouth and Lynn, the rioters were joined by other workers. The most remarkable similarity exhibited by the rioters was their disciplined and orderly behavior, within limits,[40] while they attempted to coerce ship owners into acceding to their demands. Correspondents repeatedly spoke of "riots" and "disorders" and continually referred to the sailors as "the Mob," yet in only one instance, at Yarmouth,[41] was there any street activity that could be called riotous by modern standards. While the term "riot" will be used in this book, it should be understood that these strikers were riotous only in the fact that they willfully defied the lawful authorities. The very discipline they displayed, however, seemed ominous to some observers.

What must have been one of the most disturbing elements in the riots from the government's point of view was the tardy reporting of the disturbances by officials on the spot. The first intimation that anything out of the ordinary was happening in the Newcastle area was contained in a letter from Lord Townshend on October 31. When R. Burdon, a county magistrate of Durham, finally reported the riots at South Shields three days later, he admitted that the sailors had been rioting "near 3 weeks." One reason for this tardiness was that South Shields, with a population of 14,000, had no magistrates. Burdon blamed the Newcastle magistrates for being "either diffident of their power, or unwilling to exert it." A ship owner, Thomas Powditch, wrote Pitt of the South Shields riots on November 3, but he had not felt obligated to do so until one of his own ships was seized by the rioters.[42] Apparently neither the officials of local government nor private citizens could be counted upon to inform the government of large-scale disturbances. The ports of South and North Shields as well as Newcastle had been out of control for at least two weeks before the government knew anything about it.

Once informed, however, the central government acted quickly. Grenville immediately informed Townshend, relative to Yarmouth, that he had full authority in the "event of any riot or disturbance . . . to call upon the military for assistance." Nepean answered Burdon's letter of November 3 on the day he received it, November 5, informing him that troops had been ordered to South Shields from the Tynemouth Barracks across the bay at North Shields. He had also ordered an additional ship of war, the *Martin,* to the Tyne to assist the civil magistrates in putting down the riots. Nepean also alerted the mayor of Newcastle as well as "Mr. Bulmer of Shields" of his actions. And Nepean wrote the bishop of Durham, the *Custos Rotulorum,* "to call upon the magistrates . . . to take all proper and legal methods" to end the disturbances and bring the culprits to justice.[43] Everything that could be done was done quickly.

In spite of this prompt response from the central government, the difficulties persisted. James Reedman, the mayor of Newcastle, upon receipt of Nepean's information that three troops of the regiment stationed at Tynemouth Barracks were to be sent to South Shields, called a "General Meeting of the Magistrates of the Counties of Durham, Northumberland and Newcastle" to discuss the "alarming Tumults." As a result of that meeting, the magistrates "prevailed upon" the commanding officer at Tynemouth

Barracks "not to separate the Troops under his Command" on the argument that dividing his force would weaken it. Reedman asked for troops "not already in the Neighbourhood" to be sent. Specifically, Reedman wanted troops from York as well as another ship of war and "three or four Companies of any Regiment of Foot."[44] As this was the first communication from the mayor of Newcastle concerning the riots, the degree to which he treated the seriousness of the situation could not help but magnify the government's concern over the disturbed conditions in the Newcastle area.

Nepean responded in the only manner allowed him. He informed Reedman that he had ordered "fresh" troops from York and the warships *Hind* and *Drake* with marines on board to Newcastle and had alerted the commander of the forces available at Edinburgh to be ready to march. He had no option but to accept the evaluations of those on the spot as to the number of troops and ships necessary to do the job. Nepean was obviously dissatisfied with the performance of the civil magistrates, however, and dubious of their rationalizations. On November 13 he sent Col. Oliver DeLancey copies of the letters he had received from them with these comments: "This information appears to be in many respects extremely defective and insufficient, particularly in regard to the reasons of the Magistrates for being unwilling to lessen the Force at Tynemouth Barracks, although no intelligence has ever been transmitted . . . of any disturbances among the Seamen at Newcastle. It is extremely necessary that some further information should be obtained." Nepean ordered DeLancey to Newcastle to take command of the troops there and to obtain this information. In the minor responsibility of supplying the government with information, the officials of local government in the Newcastle area had failed to do their job adequately and, more seriously, had failed to use the anti-riot forces at their disposal. The arrival of the frigate *Hind* calmed the situation, and the riot, although not the dispute over wages, quickly ended.[45]

There were several disquieting features of these strikes other than the inadequacies demonstrated by the local officials. The most important of these were the motives behind the closure of the ports. Correspondents indicated that the sailors claimed to be striking in order to increase their wages.[46] When the shipowners at South Shields capitulated to the original wage demands of the strikers, however, the latter refused their offer and raised their demands.[47] In the meantime the port remained out of control. Was this the real intention of the leaders of the strike? Had they used the pretext of raising wages to encourage ordinarily loyal seamen to take steps which, unknown to them, would endanger the security of the country? Had a French invasion fleet appeared during that period, the local authorities could have done little to resist the landing of French troops. Moreover, if the majority of the seamen were disloyal, they might have been willing participants in activities designed to overthrow the government. Indeed, several correspondents hinted that the reasons for the sailors' discontents lay deeper than a desire to increase their wages.

If the primary purpose of revolutionary propaganda was to lessen or destroy the respect for law held by individuals, the riots could be viewed as manifestations of that loss of respect. Correspondents indicated that the doctrines of revolutionary propaganda were in circulation in three of the four riot areas. T. Powditch, the ship owner at South Shields, warned Pitt of the "combustible matter" of "thousands of Pittmen, Keelmen, Waggonmen . . . strongly impressed with the new doctrine of equality," who could be ignited by the "least spark." J. Reynolds, at Yarmouth, reported that "many insidious and incendiary papers have been industriously distributed among the lower orders of the people in this Town and Neighbourhood by the Revolutionists and their Clubs." Townshend indicated that at Lynn "much paine [sic] is certainly taken to agitate the minds of the Common people by seditious writings which are read to them."[48] The attempt to raise a spirit of dissatisfaction with the existing order of things was certainly being made. While it was impossible to gauge the degree of influence this attempt had upon the sailors' riots, it was certainly an ingredient in the disorders that had to be kept in mind. Preventing the continued circulation of these doctrines, presumably by the artisans' societies, however, posed several problems for the central government.

On November 14 Grenville wrote Buckingham his evaluations of the reasons for the aroused activity of the radical societies. "The real fact is, that these people were completely quelled, and their spirits destroyed, till the Duke of Brunswick's retreat. Since that time they have begun to show themselves again." Grenville planned to apprehend as many of the authors, printers, and distributors of the inflammatory materials as possible by sending "persons into the counties to purchase these libels," but confessed "this is a thing that can be done but once, and could not be continued without an expense equal to that of the old French police." Grenville uncomfortably recognized the limited power available to the central government to meet the threat of rising sedition. The lessons of the sailors' riots were aptly summarized in his admonition to Buckingham: "The hands of government must be strengthened if the country is to be saved; but above all, the work must not be left to the hands of the Government, but every man must put his shoulder to it, according to his rank or station in life, or it will not be done."[49] More than force or the threat of force was needed. Grenville wanted a spontaneous demonstration by a large majority of Englishmen in support of the existing constitution. This seemed a solution, in that those attempting to cultivate a dissatisfaction with the existing state of things would be shown the hopelessness of their task. Unhappily Grenville at this time had no notions of the means for arriving at this solution.

Added to the specific information collected by government about activities in the ports was the arrival at the Home Office of letters indicating that many Englishmen were more than casually apprehensive about local affairs.

From Birmingham, John Massey reported that "Republican principles" were making hasty strides "in this part of the Kingdom . . . and I am really sorry now to say that since the French have been victorious—I can . . . declare that more than two thirds of this populous Neighbourhood are ripe for a Revolt, especially the lower class of Inhabitants." Massey attributed this state of mind to the circulation of Paine's pamphlets, "they being at the present juncture in almost every hand, and I believe without purchase." W.A. Miles warned Charles Long, one of the secretaries of the treasury, that a revolution "in men's minds" was building and that the time for argument was over. The Rev. W. Sproule, the vicar of Appleby, wrote the Home Office that "I think it necessary that Government should be apprised that the firment amongst the People in the North increases daily."⁵⁰ Moreover, there did not appear to be time to meet this threat by the ordinary application of law. Events moved too quickly. Dumourier's victory at Jemappes on November 6 was followed by the triumphant entry of a French army into Brussels on November 14. The French now occupied the Austrian Netherlands, and the sailors' riots, especially in their coincidental occurrences, took on a more ominous implication. If the French relied upon intrigues in their plans to conquer other countries,⁵¹ the pieces of that intrigue in England were slowly being revealed as a plot which had as its goal the landing of French troops in England to support an insurrection.

Circumstances had evidently reached the point where something had to be done. Only a week earlier Grenville had confessed to his brother that it was necessary "to nurse up in the country a real determination to stand by the Constitution when it is attacked, as it most infallibly will be if these things go on." While Buckingham repeatedly called for legal actions, Grenville believed that more comprehensive steps should be taken. "If you look back to the last time in our history that these sort of things bore the same serious aspect that they do now—I mean the beginning of the Hanoverian reigns—you will find that the

Protestant succession was established, not by the inter-ference of a Secretary of State or Attorney General, in every individual instance, but by the exertions of every magistrate and officer, civil or military, throughout the country." Grenville at first merely wanted every official of government to do his duty, but the idea proved so attrac-tive that by the end of his letter he wanted "every man, according to his rank or station in life" to stand up for the constitution.[52] To be sure, other steps would be taken, such as legal indictments for seditious libel and the calling out of the militia, but the real answer to the attacks being made on the constitution by the public at large could only be given by the public at large. Each of the precautionary actions, as well as the appeal to the public, however, was attended by several difficulties.

To take legal action against the subversives it was neces-sary for the treasury solicitors, Messrs. Chamberlain and White, to collect evidence against publishers, authors, and printers for presentation to the Christmas quarter sessions in each county. Yet, as Buckingham reminded Grenville, "the forms of law will allow . . . a traverse which cannot be tried until April." Legal delays, therefore, would largely nullify the possibilities of meeting the challenge with the law. Even at that, Grenville feared that English jurymen, unaware of the seriousness of the threat, would opt for the freedom of the press over the security of the state.[53]

The major task of the government was to awaken Englishmen to the dangers of the threat to the constitu-tion. Lord Auckland, from the Netherlands, evaluated the "pulse" of Englishmen beating right "though with some slight symptoms of fever." In the Burkeian analogy, while the silent cattle chewed the cud, the grasshoppers were making all the noise. Carrying the analogy further, it was the task of government not to stampede the herd but to direct it in a measured movement that would silence the "loud and troublesome, insects of the hour."[54] There never appeared any fear among governmental officials that the great majority of Englishmen were disloyal, yet, if this majority did not step forward to declare its adherence to the constitution, it could lose the battle by default.

The government, therefore, had to take positive steps to awaken this loyalty to action. Moreover, this action had to be in support of the existing constitution in deed as well as by profession. It would hardly serve the cause of order if loyalists took the law into their own hands, regardless of their intentions. Another Birmingham riot had to be avoided. In planning the counterattack, two considerations governed the steps necessary to bring about the desired response. A sense of alarm had to be created to awaken Englishmen to the revolutionary threat, and more importantly the energies created by that alarm had to be channelled into actions which supported the constitution. Because it was necessary to have the outlet prepared before the storm broke, the government anticipated its counterrevolution by attempting to create counterassociations.

Grenville wrote Buckingham as early as November 17 asking his opinion about the likely difficulties of founding a counterassociation in Buckinghamshire. Buckingham's reply indicated the first task contemplated for these loyal associations. "We can have no difficulty about the association; but as the quarter-sessions are so late, not 'till the 2nd week in January, I should think that, after has been circulated for a fortnight in the London papers, it might be advisable to get a certain number of gentlemen's and yeomen's names to an association in the same words, in the Buckinghamshire Herald."[55] Characteristically, Buckingham assumed that the associations would be used to defray the expenses of legal proceedings against the seditious. But Grenville's inquiry was indicative only of the initial steps in the government's overall plan.

The government had formed its plan of counterattack by November 17. On that day the prorogation of Parliament was extended to January 3, 1793, to give the ministry time to develop its domestic policy. On the same day Grenville wrote his brother for advice about the formation

of counterassociations and about any new regulations he
might suggest that could lessen the danger from subversives among the militiamen. To make sure that the government was kept informed about any increase in seditious
activity, Francis Freeling, resident surveyor of the Post
Office, sent a circular letter to his local postmasters on
November 18, enjoining them to report all seditious activities in their localities.[56] As early as November 17, therefore, the two major steps by the government had been
decided upon. Loyal associations would be formed to
channel the alarmed response of the British public to the
militia mobilization.

The sense of danger to the constitution generated by the
crisis of 1792 was based solidly upon a number of factors
disclosed to the Home Office by correspondents all over
England. There were logical reasons for assuming that each
of these had a sinister implication. The sailors' strikes, for
instance, appeared to be more than just wage disputes.
Arms bought by nonofficials were reported in such large
numbers that any intended use of them was possible. The
emigrants also included many who were not fleeing the
revolutionary chaos in France. Moreover, several general
developments on the domestic scene prevented the government from assigning innocent explanations to any of these.

The first general development was the existence and increasing activities of the artisans' clubs. Regardless of the
stated aims of these groups—that they merely wanted to
reform the constitution—what they proposed would have
transformed the state to such an extent that the results
would have been revolutionary. Where, for instance, in the
matter of change, does reform end and revolution begin?
Moreover, if the artisans were contemplating the use of
force, were not their natural allies the French, who were
generously offering assistance in the use of force for just
this type of organization? It would not have been reasonable to expect the artisans to reveal their plans to use
violence in public advertisements. Their declarations of
using peaceable means to achieve their ends, therefore, had

to be taken with a grain of salt. Here were organizations of Englishmen desiring exactly what the French were offering. This by itself was no reason for alarm. In spite of the fact that members of these clubs had been to Paris to address the Convention, hinting that some coordination of their efforts was possible, until the means by which this coordination was to be accomplished was discovered, the British government had reason only for concern. All that had been revealed by these activities was their motive. The means by which those motives might be realized were illustrated by the sailors' strikes. If nothing else, these strikes had revealed how easily French-supporting Englishmen could capture a port for the purpose of landing troops in England. The same events had also demonstrated the vacillations of local officials in taking steps to restore order when they had no knowledge of the implications of such a situation for national security. Motive and means existed for the possible invasion of England. Government had no alternative but to take steps to prepare Englishmen and to attempt to end the threat before a more favorable opportunity arose by which the disaffected could utilize these means to gain their ends by force.

The obvious first step was to alert Englishmen to the danger. Mobilizing the militia, with a proclamation explaining the reasons, would accomplish this. If the loyalists responded as they had in May (and there was no reason to believe they would not), Grenville's wish that "every man according to his station in life" would come to the aid of the constitution might come close to realization.

Associations were needed, however, not simply gatherings of loyal subjects voting addresses of support. The vulnerable part of any scheme to prepare the way for the introduction of French troops was the artisans' clubs. If these could be cowed into inactivity, the first steps in any coordinated plan would never be taken. To nullify their efforts, continuously meeting groups of loyal Englishmen had to be created with the primary objects of supporting the civil magistrates in their duties and counteracting any influence the artisans' clubs might have in seducing other Englishmen to join them in their seditious activities.

These, then, were the ingredients of the crisis of 1792 as interpreted by the government and those upon whom the government relied in those hectic days. It is apparent that the government was attempting to warn or even alarm the nation. It is also apparent that Pitt and his ministers had evidence that there was much to be alarmed about.[57] From our perspective it is not easy to fault their conclusions. This group of men were as competent as any England had in the eighteenth century to administer government. In no instance during these proceedings is it possible to find evidence of panic or of a quick jumping to conclusions. Indeed, quite the contrary conclusion has to be drawn. Pitt and his ministers were confronting, for the first time in modern history, the implications of ideological warfare and the possibility of a "fifth column" silently working to undermine the ability of the state to maintain itself. Perhaps their greatest error was in overestimating the power of ideas, yet in that regard they were no different from their contemporaries. With inadequate sources of information they took steps to meet a new kind of adversary never before encountered.

Everything depended, however, on the response of the public generally. Government, charged with the duty of protecting the state, was expected to be sensitive to any threat. Even with the evidence accumulated, there is a slight possibility that Pitt and his ministers preferred to err on the side of caution and perhaps believed that it was better to be ridiculed for panic than to allow a situation to develop in which they could be charged with negligence of duty. If the public responded in a manner large enough to silence sedition, this gamble, if it ever was considered such, would be justified. As matters turned out, the public response was more than the government had anticipated, not only justifying the correctness of the government's steps, but also ending temporarily the threat to the constitution.

CHAPTER III

THE LOYAL
ASSOCIATION
MOVEMENT

The loyal association movement which grew and flourished from November 1792 through February 1793 must surely have gratified the wishes of Grenville. Not only were all Englishmen made aware of the government's fears of the probability of internal disturbances, but also thousands took active steps to avow their determination to aid the civil magistrates in maintaining the peace and to work to "undeceive" those who might support the plans of the radical clubs. More germane to the thesis of this book, this was the largest peacetime appearance of the loyalists, who had been apparently only waiting for a signal to act and an example of the means by which they could express their loyalty. This movement was the largest and perhaps the most successful association movement in the eighteenth century.[1]

The ramifications of the appearance of the loyalists at this time are easier to understate than to overstate. Theirs was a preventive movement. Because they were successful in countering the rising excitement generated by the almost mystical fervor of revolution, their importance can only be judged imaginatively. What they prevented will never be known to a certainty, since it did not happen. Contemporaries believed that the loyal movement "saved" the nation. It is an old historical axiom that the realities of the past count less in explaining human actions than what were believed to be realities. Belief that a revolution was possible could have led dissatisfied individuals to attempt one just as easily as it led the loyalists to oppose the possibility. As the example of France illustrated, once begun, a revolution sets its own course. Any attempt to chart the consequences is impossible. If this moment in British history held the potential to be a turning point, the loyalists prevented the turning and, to a slight degree (much less than one would assume), turned the other way. If Napoleon later was defeated by an awakened nationalism in the countries he had occupied, the possibility of revolution was defeated by an aroused patriotism in 1792-93. These considerations were at first hidden by the enthusiasm and size of this, the largest association movement ever.

The outstanding impression one gathers from the comments of newspapermen and from the papers of private individuals is of unanimity. "The whole country," J. Bland Burgess exclaimed, "is forming itself into an association." Advertisements announcing the establishment of new associations appeared daily in the London newspapers, and, in some cases during the third and fourth weeks in December, had to be deferred in the provincial weeklies because of a lack of space. Grenville expressed wonder at the "miraculous change" that had occurred in only three weeks. Congratulations for the government's success were received from as far away as Russia.[2] It was as if the entire nation was rising and broadcasting its loyalty.

The first of the loyal associations announced its existence on November 23 in the *Star,* a London evening newspaper. That morning, however, the *Sun* had already noticed its activities and had given its approbation of this sort of action. "The better order of Britons are at length roused by the boldness of domestic enemies, and are forming themselves into Associations, for the purpose of repressing and defeating the pernicious doctrines now afloat in this country. The plan does infinite honour to the

Projectors, and we doubt not will be followed up with spirit and effect." On the following day, this association, entitled the Association for the Preservation of Liberty and Property against Republicans and Levellers (hereafter APLP), advertised in *The Times,* the *Sun,* and the *Morning Chronicle.* The advertisements in the first two papers were so lengthy (one and three-fourths columns in *The Times* and one and one-half in the *Sun*) that the Duke of Portland remarked that the APLP "seems to have spent all its energy in the endeavors to give itself existence." Resolution six of the APLP's first announcement called for the considerations of the Society to be printed "in all the public papers." If resolution six was carried out, advertisements were placed in over thirty-three London papers alone.[3] Portland was justified in noting the expenditure of energy, but quite wrong in believing this was all the organization had.

Whether or not this organization was founded directly by the government is difficult to decide, in spite of Grenville's and Buckingham's admissions earlier.[4] There are some reasons to believe that it was founded independently by John Reeves, a respected writer on British law and the former chief justice of Newfoundland. Three years later, when attempting to repeat his actions of 1792 and stimulate a new loyal movement, Reeves reminded Pitt that "I took this step . . . as on a former occasion, without any consultation or concert with anybody at Whitehall, for the same reasons, as on a former occasion, namely, that the government might have all the benefit of it, if it produced any, or none of the disgrace, if such was the fate of it." Earlier, when republishing the tracts produced by the APLP, Reeves claimed that "none of the King's ministers knew or heard of this association, till they saw the first advertisement in the public prints. It was planned without their knowledge, and has been conducted to the present [June 21, 1793] without their aid."[5] Grenville admitted that "we are preparing an association in London, which is to be declared in the course of next week," yet this admis-

sion was made November 25, five days after the first
meeting of the APLP. Furthermore, Grenville's association
was meant "to consist of merchants and lawyers," while of
the committee members of the APLP, only two were
lawyers and one a merchant.[6] The meeting held at the
Merchant Taylors' Hall on November 28, because of timing
and composition, may have been the "association" Grenville had in mind, although the latter, a far more respectable group, did not form itself into a permanent society.
Reeves may have been the independent originator he
claimed to be.

There are, however, compelling reasons to believe other-
wise. Reeves already served the government as paymaster
of the Westminster police judges. He was an intimate
friend of Evan Nepean and thus in a position to know, if
not the plans, at least the desires of government. Moreover,
how could Reeves, who depended upon government for
financial support, have paid the exorbitant fees to advertise the first meeting of the APLP in the London papers?
Added to this, the sheer coincidence that a person working
for government could do exactly what the government
wanted done without any "consultation or concert"
rather stretches the imagination. There are more concrete
reasons, however, for disbelieving all or part of Reeves's
claims for independence.

The discrepancy in timing between Grenville's admission
on November 25 of government's plans to form an association and the alleged date of the first meeting of the APLP
can be explained. Thomas Hardy of the London Corresponding Society later claimed that Reeves and his secretary, John Moore, were the only members present at the
alleged first meeting at the Crown and Anchor Tavern on
November 20, when the society was launched. Hardy's
claim was corroborated by Thomas Wright, a printer, while
giving evidence before a committee of the House of Commons on December 11, 1795. Wright even stated that John
Moore and Reeves were the same person.[7] Furthermore,
no announcement of a meeting "to be held," the usual

procedure in starting a society, is to be found in any of the major newspapers, nor is a list of those present at the first meeting inserted in any of the initial APLP advertisements. The correspondence of the APLP shows that the formation of the executive committee, usually among the first orders of business, was not completed until after November 29.[8] This week-long preparation perhaps explains why Grenville's admission to Buckingham on November 25 was correct. Until the permanent committee was formed, there was no association.

It is probable that Reeves both told the truth and lied in his preface on June 21, 1793. It is likely that he discovered from Nepean Grenville's intention to form an association, and attempted to gain favor with the government by taking the necessary first steps without informing anyone in the ministry, hoping that government would come to his aid once the advertisements of the association were printed in the papers. He was successful. John Heriot, conductor of the *Sun,* wrote Reeves on November 29 offering the services of his newspaper, and admitted that he had inserted the APLP's advertisement at the suggestion of Nepean.[9] Thus Reeves lied when he asserted that he had no assistance from government, but told the truth when he stated that government knew nothing about his plans.

Following this example and excited by the actions of government in calling the militia, Englishmen all over the country founded associations of their own. The great majority of the clubs were organized in conformity to the usual religious or governmental division of the nation. Parishes, hamlets, villages, towns, hundreds, divisions, and counties—all had societies, sometimes overlapping. Existing organizations formed for other purposes took this occasion to declare their loyalty and their determination to support the civil magistrates. Former constitutional societies at Manchester, Penzance, Wednesbury, and Rotherham changed their names to defenders of the constitution.[10] At least sixteen dissenting congregations made known their loyalty either by advertising in the local papers or by

joining, as a group, local loyal societies.[11] The Company of
Fellowship Porters, Billingsgate, the Underwriters at
Lloyd's Coffee House, the Worshipful Company of
Butchers of London, the Worshipful Company of Bakers,
London, the Stationer's Company, London, and the Guild
or Brotherhood of Masters and Pilots, Kingston-upon-Hull,
declared their loyalty and support.[12] Even debtors in York
and in the King's Bench Prison wrote addresses of support,
the latter professing "that neither the length of their imprisonment, nor the sufferings occasioned thereby, have
destroyed or in the least impaired those early imbibed
principles" of loyalty.[13] Englishmen everywhere responded patriotically to the government's call.

Typically a new association began with an advertisement
in the newspapers, inserted by either a local official or a
group of prominent individuals, of a meeting to be held to
discuss the alarming state of the country. At the meeting,
the first order of business was the selection of a chairman,
usually the person who had called the meeting or a respectable member in attendance. Patriotic speeches were given,
declarations of loyalty were agreed upon, and a committee, varying in numbers, was chosen. Then resolutions were
entered and debated. In practically every instance the
meetings declared themselves associated under various
titles to support the constitution by suppressing the activities of those attacking it. Subscriptions were sometimes
opened, normally with a limit of 10/6 or one guinea, and a
secretary and a treasurer were appointed. Finally resolutions were passed involving the opening of correspondence
with other loyal societies and naming the newspapers in
which the resolutions were to be printed. Most clubs chose
to advertise in one local and several London papers. There
were wide variations from the scheme I have outlined, but
generally, if some of the steps above were omitted in the
first meeting, they were taken in subsequent ones.

To examine the number of associations formed at this
time, the number of people who subscribed to them, their
growth and spread, and their ideals and purposes, one has

to begin with the collection of declarations and minutes gathered by John Reeves in the parent society. In resolution C of the APLP advertisements, Reeves welcomed all communications from societies directed to similar ends. Nearly 200 societies answered by sending him copies of their original resolutions, information about their activities, and requests for materials to distribute in their areas.[14] While these were but a fraction of the societies formed at this time and cannot in any way be considered a scientific sampling, one can add some validity to conclusions about the whole movement by supplementing the Reeves collection with newspaper accounts of club activities in four counties: Essex, Sussex, Worcester, and York. The pattern established in these four scattered counties roughly approximated that revealed in the Reeves collection.

There are several methods of estimating the number of associations formed. One can compare the number formed in these four counties with those making their presence known to Reeves, presume that this is a semi-valid ratio, and apply it to the whole country. For instance, of the thirty-eight associations formed in Essex, only nine reported to Reeves. This four-to-one ratio holds for York as well; of the thirty-four associations there, only eight communicated with Reeves. For Worcester and Sussex, however, the ratios change: eight to one for the former, and six to one for the latter. These two counties had fewer associations, however, and when added to the total of all societies formed in the four counties, and compared with the total of the four found in the Reeves collection, the ratio stands at roughly five to one. If this ratio held for the entire country, approximately 1,000 associations were formed from November 1792 through February 1793.

Another method of determining the number of clubs founded is to average the number of clubs found in the four counties and multiply it by the number of English counties. Since these four averaged twenty-eight apiece, multiplying that figure by forty-three (forty-two counties plus the Isle of Wight) puts the total number of associations formed at 1,218, a figure not far from the estimate reached previously. Contemporaries estimated the total to be much higher. Individuals as far apart in political sentiments as John Reeves and Richard Sheridan agreed that 2,000 loyal associations appeared at this time. There are reasons to believe that this was an inflated estimate, however, just as my calculations may be somewhat low. Undoubtedly the enthusiasm of the time led some observers to overestimate the loyal impact. This was exactly what most wished for— the larger the number, the more effective the impression the new clubs would make. My own calculations do not include those clubs reporting to Reeves but not advertising in the newspapers at my disposal. Indeed, there may have been many that were formed but neither communicated with Reeves nor advertised in the newspapers. It would be safe to conclude, therefore, that at the most there were fewer than fifteen hundred loyal associations, five hundred less than were commonly assumed.

In one respect the number of organizations was more important than the number of people who joined them. Each society performed two major functions. By advertising its existence, the society, if it did nothing else, sent a message to all who were discontented that theirs was a group dedicated to the preservation of the constitution as it was. The propaganda value of thousands of groups forming to oppose the relatively few organizations dedicated to opposite ends may have been decisive in itself in ending the threat of internal disturbances. The other function was much more practical. The standing committees selected at the formative meetings ranged in numbers from ten to above a hundred. Disregarding all other associators and counting only these as actively involved, all at once the size of the peace-keeping bureaucracy of government was increased by at least 15,000 individuals and probably many more, dedicated to seeing the task accomplished. To be sure, their efficiency and effectiveness probably varied widely, but their dedication and energy could not be questioned. The hands of government, as Grenville had desired, were indeed strengthened.

The number of people who joined the associations and signed the declarations of the clubs cannot be determined with any accuracy. John Heriot, conductor of the *Sun,* a government newspaper, predicted that over one million signatures would be collected by the end of December.[15] The source of this estimate, however, makes it questionable. Heriot may have deliberately overestimated the possibilities of the movement in an attempt to encourage individuals to join. Few figures are supplied in the materials collected by Reeves, only twenty-eight of the declarations mentioning specific numbers. The descriptions of the sizes of the meetings in the newspapers were rather similar; each was portrayed as at least a "numerous and respectable" meeting or a "very numerous meeting." Many were depicted, as was the Manchester meeting, as "a more respectable and numerous meeting than was ever remembered on any former occasion." The Rockford Hundred Association, for instance, was reported to be "the most numerous and respectable ever experienced within the District." The Middleham, Leyburn, Hawes, and Askrigg associations merely noted that their declaration was "signed by many hundreds, all descriptions of people, appearing eager and zealous to declare their loyalty."[16] These descriptions indicate an appreciation of size, but nothing upon which to base an estimate of numbers.

In some instances the secretaries of the associations mentioned to Reeves the numbers of people who signed the resolutions of their meetings. Peterborough, for instance, claimed 212; Weymouth, 492; Falmouth, 745; St. Albans, 1,129; Canterbury, 1,409; and St. Mary-le-bone, 1,659. The largest listing was from Bath, which claimed 5,033 members.[17] Heriot may well have been closer to the mark than he realized. If so, between a quarter and a third of the adult males of England participated in the loyal association movement. The conditions under which a few signed, however, might diminish the loyalty that figure represented. The usual method employed by the associations, after the declarations of loyalty and resolutions of support were approved by those in attendance, was to place copies of them at various locations so that those who had not been able to attend the meeting would have an opportunity to express their sentiments on the matter. For the associations representing large areas, such as counties, divisions, or hundreds, this was a practical and logical step to take. Some of the associations, on the other hand, took more direct action. Eight representing towns and parishes resolved that a copy of their resolutions would be taken to every house in their district for all to sign. The Pevensy Rape Society went even further. Not only did members of this group solicit every house, they also made a list of those who would not sign, with their reasons appended.[18] Social pressure of this sort would not reveal the sentiments of those shamed or coerced into signing. When one considers the enthusiasm of the times it is remarkable that this sort of coercion was used in only nine of the nearly two hundred cases in the Reeves collection. Much more common were appeals to "all good and loyal men," "all classes," or "all who love their country." The loyal movement did not need to resort to shoddy tactics to gain members.

While it is logical to assume that the May loyalists spoke out again in December, for various reasons it is difficult to point out where they did so. I was able to track down only 151 of the 386 addresses counted by government. These I found mostly in news reports which mentioned only the areas of origin. Here and there it was possible to see a loyalist, such as Robert Shirley at Kidderminster, convening a meeting to draft a loyal address on June 11 and calling another on December 23 to found a loyal association. The mayor of York, Ralph Dodsworth, did the same, as did Thomas Wilkerson, the mayor of Ripon. Henry Zouch, the magistrate at Wakefield, called the June meeting, but only attended and "encouraged" the December meeting when an association was formed.[19] These identifications are few, however, as the names of the May loyalists are generally lacking. Depending only upon locations, it is possible to state that 36 of the Reeves associations were preceded by loyal meetings earlier in the year, for a ratio of about one to five. This compares with a ratio of about four times as many associations as addresses. Part of this discrepancy might be explained by the different sort of areas represented by the associations and by the number of societies formed for other purposes which joined the movement. Regardless of these figures, it is still reasonable to believe that the May loyalists were joined by tens of thousands more in December, and that their patriotic feelings had not diminished in the six-months' interval.

An analysis of the timing and rate of founding of new societies reveals that the example provided by Reeves was followed by few loyalists before government mobilized the militia. News of the founding of the APLP appeared in the *Chelmsford Chronicle* on November 30, and a few societies, perhaps inspired by this example, appeared on December 6 and 7. On the latter date, however, the *Chronicle* printed news of the mobilization of the militia, and from December 10 onward the momentum rapidly grew. The same pattern holds for York, where the news of the militia, appearing on December 10, was rapidly followed by a rush of new societies. Sussex and Worcester conformed to these patterns, as did other societies reporting to the parent organization. William Smith, the mayor of Southampton, distributed a handbill on November 30 calling a meeting for December 4, and four other societies were formed which may have been planned before the militia was called out.[20] In all, the great impetus toward associating grew after the assembling of the national guard, although the example set by Reeves was generally followed once the gravity of the situation became known.

The government mobilized the militia piecemeal. The

December 1 proclamation called out two-thirds, or those actually trained the previous summer, of the counties along the eastern coast from Scotland to Kent, including Cumberland and Westmoreland. It was not until December 5 that the militias of the counties from Kent to Cornwall, plus Berkshire, Buckinghamshire, Hampshire, and Surrey were mobilized. This slow mobilization continued through December and January so that by January 29, 1793, only two English counties, Staffordshire and Rutland, along with nine Welsh counties, had not been called out.[21]

The growth of the loyal associations followed a different pattern. By December 8 most of the loyal associations had been founded in London and the surrounding counties and along the southern coast, with a few scattered in the west and north. In the week of December 9 through 15, they were still being founded mostly in London and the home counties, but the westward movement was more pronounced. From December 16 through December 23 the spread began northward through the midlands. By the end of the year the pattern was set, with new clubs founded as far north as Durham. The wave of clubs, therefore, began in the southeast, spread westward, then north and east. In January new clubs were founded in the areas already represented. Northumberland, Westmoreland, Cumberland, and Rutland, as far as I have been able to discover, had no associations at all, and Lincoln and Norfolk had only four between them.

Allowing that the militia mobilization was a major stimulus to the founding of the societies, this discrepancy between the stimulus and the response, between the areas where the militia was called out and the different areas where the earlier clubs were founded, is not easily explained. Initially one might argue that the government and the loyalists apprehended danger from opposite directions. Perhaps Pitt and his ministers viewed Dumourier's army in the Austrian Netherlands, an army representing the striking arm of the French Revolution, as the real threat. That portion of the coast opposite the Netherlands was not only the most exposed but also the scene of the sailors' strikes, which possibly had been instigated by pro-French Englishmen. The loyalists, however, had perhaps been gradually building their apprehensions in those areas more immediately fronting France before Dumourier succeeded in invading the Austrian Netherlands. For three months, loyalists in the southern areas had had time to develop general opinions on what had to be done, and when the crisis appeared, they were the first to form associations.

Even more puzzling is the small number of clubs founded in the areas north of Suffolk. Charles Grey's influence in Northumberland might be cited as a major cause of the lack of societies there, and, as we shall see, nearly prevented the founding of the important club at Durham. Lord Townshend, however, was a fervent proponent of loyal activities later, but his influence in Norfolk at this moment was not apparent. Whatever the political issues at stake, the mobilization of the militia was a serious step which should have been recognized by all. By law, the militia could be called out only in the event of threatened invasion or in cases of actual insurrection. One would imagine that news of such a step by government would have been sufficient to alarm the entire nation, especially in those areas where the militiamen were actually embodied. I must confess I have no explanation for this strange response.

While the mobilization of the militia undoubtedly played the major role in stimulating loyal activities, the particulars of the emergency which prompted it were magnified by rumor. The fortifying of the Tower led some newspapers to print rumors of a plot. The *Chelmsford Chronicle,* for instance, speculated that "Government had discovered an infernal plot, planned by foreigners, and certain unnatural incendiaries of native growth, to seize the Tower and Bank, and, after diverting the stream of the New River, to set the city in flames." On the following day, the *Sun* reported: 'We have reason to believe that a party of men here, among whom, we are sorry to say, are

many Englishmen, have been in correspondence with the
National Convention, for the horrid purpose of having over
here a body of armed Frenchmen, to enforce their notions
of Reform." Two days later the *York Courant* fleshed out
the circumstances which led to the discovery of this
alarming turn of events and concluded that "there were
5,000 People in This Country, who had taken the Oath of
Secrecy to be ready for an Insurrection—that the Tower
was the first place to be seized on, being the Deposit of
Arms; and that the Pipes of the New River were to be cut,
while some parts of the town were to be set fire to."[22]
Undoubtedly, these rumors had much to do with the rapid
growth of the loyal association movement. Even after its
growth, however, they persisted.

During late December and January, one of the more
widely circulated pamphlets sent by the APLP to sister
societies was entitled "The Plot Found Out." In the
preface to his collection of tracts used in combating the
radicals, Reeves noted that "a revolt [was] planned for the
beginning of December, when the Tower was to have been
seized." This revolt was, of course, "plotted in concert
with France."[23]

There was enough plausibility in such a rumor to keep it
alive. Englishmen who read their newspapers were aware of
the November 19 *Fraternite et Succours* resolution, offering the use of French soldiers to all people who wished to
seek their freedom. They were also aware of H. Gregoire's
November 27 salute to the new republic which was soon to
appear on the banks of the Thames. Common sense told
them that a French invasion without some English support
would be impossible, and the noise of the radical clubs
pointed to the sources of that support. News that the
Tower was fortified and that the National Guard was
mobilized may have confirmed their apprehensions. Indeed, it is difficult to understand how Englishmen could
have come to any other conclusion. As we have seen, this
sort of activity was deemed possible by responsible members of government.

Government, however, could never be sure of this possibility until the relationship between the radical societies and the French was discovered. J. Bland Burges, Grenville's secretary, reported from Holland as early as September 1792 that there was indeed a sinister relationship between the two. On November 4 he wrote Grenville that the French intended to use sympathizers in Holland to create internal commotions before invading and that "a similar design prevails with regard for England, where under various pretences, both fire-arms and daggers are fabricating, and where many Jacobin emmissaries, under the pretense of being emigrants, are busily exciting sedition." Burges stressed that this was but rumor and that he had no substantiating evidence. Yet Grenville was at that time busily collecting evidence that such might be the case. There was no doubt, furthermore, that some English radicals were in communication and contact with the French.[24]

On the other hand, contact did not mean collusion. The "design" spoken of by Burges implied a closer relationship, and perhaps a giving of allegiance unprovable by any evidence possessed by government. And this was the all-important point. As Burke put it: "As to the growth of this contagion within our walls, as a mere domestick Evil, and unconnected with a dangerous foreign power, I have ever had little comparative apprehensions; But combined with foreign forces—there—there is the danger."[25] The danger was equally applicable to the radicals should they be found out. Government, therefore, could expect this sort of relationship to be their most closely guarded secret. Maddeningly, government could never put its finger on this one item of proof that would have given it the legal right to crush the radical movement in the courts. No member of government ever doubted that the radicals were tools or dupes of French policy, yet proof of this belief, legally all-important, was never discovered.

Despite the legal difficulties, members of government were so certain of the malicious intentions of the radicals that they could refer to them without antecedents. For instance, Grenville attempted to explain the uncertain time of the mobilization of the militia to his brother "because we are desirous, before the thing [the mobilization] is known, to have troops enough around London to prevent the possibility of anything happening in the interval, which they would of course try if they saw an opening." Grenville did not mean that the troops would try anything, but was referring to a mysterious "they." A spy clarified this identity somewhat when he reported that "the disaffected are alarmed at the Resolutions of the persons of property, ... Is this which restrains them? I shall know—." When nothing happened on December 1, Grenville still did not name his enemies. "We have . . . secured the Tower and the City, and have now reason to believe they are alarmed, and have put off their intended visit; but we are prepared for the worst."[26] Clarification was not needed; government believed there was no doubt about the identity of their opponents, even if not all the evidence needed for legal convictions could be obtained.

The belief that internal commotions were tied to French plans to invade added weight to the hopes of the loyalists that a spectacular response of loyalty might lessen the dangers of the hour. The surest illustration to the French of the impracticality of such a coordinated attack upon England would be a demonstration that the great majority of Englishmen would oppose them. John Hiley Addington's hopes "that the improbability of internal commotion here may have the best Effect on the other side of the Water"[27] pointed to a practical justification for all concerned Englishmen to stand forward at this time.

Outshouting the radicals was only one round in the contest, although an important, and in an ideological sense an all-important, one. The demonstration that the people of England did not support the goals or principles of the radicals certainly would strike the latter at their most vulnerable point. If they were working toward the implementation of a democracy in England, their goals would be democratically denounced. What English politicians did, how they interpreted the events of the past few months, and the directions they would point English policies were the crucial issues. The loyalists gave those politicians desiring stability a tactical victory; how that victory would be exploited would depend upon parliamentary maneuvers. Parliament, compelled by law to meet within fourteen days after the mobilization, met December 13.

The king's speech on the opening of Parliament stated the ministry's case, and was surprisingly only slightly different from the proclamation calling out the militia. Those seditious practices which the May Proclamation had largely checked, it stated, had been renewed with increased intensity. Riots and insurrections had required the calling out of the military to support the civil magistrates. This renewal, moreover, had been caused by a conscious "design" by persons "in connection and concert with persons in foreign countries."[28] The government offered no particulars other than the above to justify the emergency measures. If Englishmen were waiting for details, the government did not supply them, although the mention of a design could support those who believed the rumors of a plot. The debate which began with this speech, however, marked an important turning point in English politics and determined whether or not the loyal movement would continue. There was a slim possibility that Charles James Fox, the most brilliant speaker in Commons, might wreck the movement.

Fox and his followers faced a real crisis at this moment. Knowing that the major portion of those normally following the leadership of the Duke of Portland agreed with the government's evaluation of the gravity of the domestic situation, and knowing also the temper of the times, they were faced with choices which would largely determine their political future. They could attempt to regain unity with their lost friends and silently watch Parliament approve the emergency measures, they could state their tentative approval until the government offered evidence that its claims of emergency were valid, or they could attempt to discredit the ministry and the loyal movement in general and win back the unity the Whigs had lost. To their credit, and consequently to the restoration of Fox's historical reputation, Fox and his followers chose the last course.[29]

Why a man who had demonstrated on numerous occasions his political opportunism should pick this moment to stand on principle is not easy to answer. Perhaps one of the major reasons was his view of the French Revolution. Unlike most of his contemporaries, Fox's views of the gravity of the domestic situation were softened, paradoxically, by his evaluation of the actions of the French. As one of the most enthusiastic admirers of the Revolution in its early days, he managed, while others took a second look, to maintain his admiration, much to the annoyance of his political allies.[30] The doubts that entered his mind after the September massacres had been banished by December.

Fox's views on domestic reform, colored by his opinions of the Revolution, had arrived at the position held by the Friends of the People. Fox had not joined the society in May, although he defended it in Commons, but in December he was ready to adopt its program and even go further than his political allies had proposed. Not only was he ready to extend the franchise, but he argued also for the repeal of the Irish penal laws and the Test and Corporation acts. He dismissed the activities of the radical clubs as "silly and frantic speculations."[31] Fox had found a cause and was prompted by it to use his enormous talents to attempt to turn the tide of opinion that threatened to split his party, to crush the new liberal spirit of the radical clubs, and to doom all hopes for constitutional reform.

A second possible reason for Fox's rediscovery of principles at this time was his distrust of Pitt. From the day of his ouster from office by Pitt, he had vowed to call a division on every measure Pitt proposed. His failure to shake Pitt out of office over the years had undoubtedly deepened his rancor. Because he now found nothing alarming in the domestic situation, he naturally supposed that Pitt had raised the alarm needlessly as a means of breaking the ranks of the opposition. With these thoughts, the issue was not the security of the country but a personal duel between two politicians, with the leadership of government as a prize. Fox's speech, the most brilliant delivered on the occasion, was marked for failure by the opinions outlined above. Regardless of how right or wrong Fox may have been in his evaluation of the ultimate effects of the Revolution upon the progress of liberty in France, his contemporaries disagreed. Where Fox saw the French as "animated by the glorious flame of liberty," his fellow politicians saw them as unchanged in their desire to humble England, although with altered tactics. Where Fox sought to calm discontents by redressing grievances, his contemporaries believed this to be impossible. As Dundas put it, after admitting that the proper mode of removing discontents was by removing grievances, "what conduct could be adopted . . . when the constitution itself was held out as a grievance . . .?" Dundas and the great majority of Parliamentarians did not view the activities of the radical clubs as "silly and frantic speculations." That basic disagreement divided the Foxites from the rest of the House. When the division was taken, they went down to a crushing defeat, Fox's amending motion losing 50 to 290.[32]

In defeat, Fox raised questions that would be debated continually in the future. His defense of the radicals on the grounds that they were exercising their right of free speech posed the dilemma the politicians would face for a decade. Are there any circumstances in which this basic freedom can be curtailed? It has taken years to decide that free speech extends only to the point where it becomes injurious to others, as for instance in the usual example of shouting "Fire!" in a crowded theater. In a sense, Parliamentarians viewed England as a crowded theater, as did the loyalists. Preventive steps to keep irresponsible people from shouting "Fire!" were not only prudent but necessary. To be sure, the measures taken by government and by private individuals were novel as Windham admitted, but he asserted that "there never has been such an occasion before."[33] And this was the heart of the matter. Never since the days of religious controversy had opinion mattered so much. Looking at France, Englishmen concluded that the cataclysm and chaos there were the results of ideas and that England's fate would be the same unless something was done. This belief in the power of ideas made the freedom of speech more of a problem than it might appear to moderns. We have had more than one revolutionary upheaval upon which to found our opinions. England was involved in the first of the modern ideological wars,[34] and paper bullets were the first to be apprehended.

Fox was not yet finished. Failing in his attack upon Pitt, he next turned on the loyalists. One of their publications, he discovered, could be libellous. *One Pennyworth of Truth, from Thomas Bull to his Brother John* contained sentiments which he thought could provoke riots against dissenters. Grey moved that the offending paper be read and that instructions be given the attorney general to prosecute, presumably the author, publisher, and distributors.[35] This was a difficult position for the Foxites to maintain, given their principled defense of the freedom of the press in the cases of writers, publishers, and distributors of radical tracts. But if some odium could be cast upon the loyal associations, their growth and spread might be lessened.

This maneuver, however, was a clumsy self-made trap for the Foxites. Not only could their own words be thrown back at them, but many of the members of the House were on the committees of loyal associations, and these men rallied to the defense of the clubs, producing, in effect, a vote of approbation from Parliament for the whole loyal movement. Robert Peel, a member of the committee of the Manchester loyal association, clearly pointed out that the main purpose of the clubs was to support the magistrates in maintaining order. Fox's support of Grey's motion was so inept that all possibility of blackening the reputation of the loyalists was lost. The motion was negatived.[36] Just as the supporters of the loyal movement had given Parliamentarians the public support to take preventive measures against the spread of radical doctrines, so the Parliamentarians had voted their support of the loyal clubs.

The stage was set. England and France, sliding gradually into war, were governed in a strangely similar fashion. The French Convention was supported and influenced strongly by organized public opinion in the form of Jacobin clubs, perhaps organized as copies of earlier English models. The English copied the copy and were now organized into clubs which represented English public opinion similarly supporting the English government. The difference between them was the extremes to which each government would go in order to enforce its opinions upon the public. The ideological war had first to be fought internally in each country, and until France declared the beginning of the hot war, both nations witnessed domestic cold wars. In France the Terror was building; in England a far different cold war began.

CHAPTER IV

THE LOYALISTS AND
THE COLD WAR

On December 9, two weeks before the wave of enthusiasm for founding new societies crested, the *Observer* optimistically commented that the loyal movement had, "in the course of ONE WEEK, triumphed over the evil machinations of a dangerous and deluded faction, which was too long permitted to disgrace this country."[1] Making allowances for the prematurity of the opinions of the *Observer*'s lead writer, to a degree he was correct. A victory of sorts was in the making, and before December was out, was rapidly turning into a rout of the enemy. Practically every person active in the political community of England was joining the ranks of the loyalists. Even Charles James Fox seconded a loyal address at St. George's Parish. If this kind of activity was the antidote to the "French poison," a large dose had been administered to the English body politic, and only time would reveal whether or not the patient was on the mend.

Moreover, the loyalists revealed themselves by standing up for the constitution. By all precedents (and consequents, as well) this was an unusual occurrence. Normally, it is the discontented, those who desire change, who speak loudest and are more noticed by historians. In this instance, those who were normally not heard of, those who were satisfied with things as they were and who generally did not have anything to complain of were the chief actors. The loyal movement offers us a rare opportunity to examine the thoughts and to analyze actions and their effects in a different section of society, differently motivated and with different goals. In addition, because the loyalists were the ultimate victors in the struggle, their influence upon the subsequent course of English history was of greater importance than that of their defeated opponents, and a study of them is imperative for any understanding of what was to transpire in the future.

There are limitations to such a study. The chief sources of information about the loyalists are their declarations and resolutions, either collected by Reeves or published in local newspapers. These relate to but a single event. Loyal activities were only occasionally noted by newspapers or were revealed only in the few minutes forwarded to Reeves. The records of the original society in London are fairly complete but should not be taken as representing the whole movement. In spite of this paucity of information, some definite answers about the loyalists in general can be ascertained. It is possible, for instance, to know to some degree who they were, why they joined the movement, their chief goals, and some of their methods of achieving them. It is also possible to state with some certainty what they failed to do and what they had no intention of doing.

The first question to be answered about the loyalists is: Who were they? About half of the meetings examined were chaired by members of the extended government of England in church and state. Forty-five mayors, aldermen, boroughreeves, sheriffs, and constables, as well as thirty-five rectors, churchwardens, vestrymen, and other church officials were called to the chairs at the originating meetings of eighty of the associations. Fourteen others were chaired by individuals in some official capacity. From this, one could assume that these were semiofficial organs of government organized on an ad hoc basis.[2] Whether these officials instigated or called the meetings on their own initiative and whether they controlled their eventual outcomes, however, is debatable. By chance, several notices of meetings to be held are included in the Reeves manuscripts, and in those instances the officials called the founding meetings in response to petitions by private individuals.[3] It is likely that many meetings, perhaps the great majority, were called as a result of urgings from the private sector. It would not have been wise even for those officials who acted without petitions to proceed without some intimations of support. As chairmen, these officials acted in the capacity of the Speaker of the House, theoretically maintaining a fair and impartial conduct, hence their control was severely limited in influencing the ultimate decisions of the meetings. At that, their elections to the chair were probably more a result of their status among those present than of any involvement they had in convening the meeting in the first place. The respectability of the meeting, hence its effectiveness, was largely determined by that of its chairman, so it was natural for ardent loyalists to advance their cause by electing whatever person was most likely to enhance it. The selection of noblemen, members of Parliament, and wealthy private individuals points to the same conclusion. Indeed, in function these associations were semiofficial organs of government, but not because governmental officials founded them.

The names of the members of the societies show no clear demarcation of classes. To be sure, "respectable" individuals were usually elected to the committees, but again this was a matter of effectiveness. This was a movement based upon something broader than status or property. It was based upon emotion, a deeply felt relationship between the individual and his nation which as yet had not invented all the phrases to explain itself, as it was to do in the following century. Nor was it unique to England. Just as Frenchmen could rush to the colors to defend *la Patrie,* so Englishmen could join hands to defend the constitution as the best representative of what was unique and satisfying to the native Englishman. However much one might love the application of rational principles to governmental systems, however beautiful the concept of Liberty, Equality, and Fraternity might appear to some individuals, they took second place to love of country. English liberty, English equality, and English fraternity were far more desirable than any imports from across the Channel, simply because they were English. From these feelings of native patriotism few Englishmen were immune. With this perspective, one can understand the inclusion as loyalists of Friendly Societies, Methodist, Quaker, and Dissenting congregations, liveried companies, manufacturers, insurance agents, innkeepers, and even (making allowances for their desperate plight), the inmates of prisons. They were expressing, at a time of national stress, the emotion which would dominate the next century. This emotion knew no class boundaries. The loyalists were nationalists of England in all ranks of society.

The motivation which awakened this patriotism was a sense of the threat to the constitution. Whether apprised of this threat by the newspapers, by official proclamations and actions, or by their own experiences, the loyalists met the threat directly. Some groups, such as those in Dudley, Birmingham, and Bury St. Edmund, were willing to take on all opponents. The Dudley associators resolved to protect the constitution "against every attempt to subvert it." The Bury St. Edmund loyalists resolved it to be their duty "to counteract the designs of wicked and mischievous men." Birmingham was even more general; the associators there resolved to oppose "*whatever* attempt under *whatever* pretext" to disturb public order in order that they might preserve "their country." The Deal association resolved to suppress "all Incendiaries, whether foreign or domestic," pointing to a danger perhaps recognized by the great majority of the associations.[4]

The loyalists were but little troubled about absolute proof that the domestic radicals were allied with the French. Whether they believed the allegations of the Militia Proclamation, or, after December 13, the declarations of concern in the king's speech to Parliament, or the subsequent debates in Parliament, there never appeared any doubt to the loyalists that the radicals were leagued with the French against their own country. The Blything associators, for instance, declared themselves, not associated to silence sedition, but joined together against "the abettors of the Designs of France, against this Country." Hounslow and Heston justified their association because "the Internal Enemies of the Kingdom have formed a Conspiracy with its Adversaries Abroad."[5] The same sentiments were echoed by the great majority of the associations, but the statement of "detestation" of this sinister connection which seems to summarize best the general sentiments is that made by St. Mary's, Islington. Conscious of the blessings they enjoyed under their mild and benevolent constitution, they united "in its Defense against the subtle and seditious Attacks of wicked and designing Men, who, enjoying its Freedom and living under its Protection, in concert with its open and avowed Enemies, are meditating its Destruction."[6] In this circumstance the arguments of the radicals, whatever their merits, were moot. Fundamentally this was not a constitutional debate, it was a patriotic campaign against enemy collaborators who wished to destroy the constitution.

The object of this fervent loyalty, the constitution, was not described in many ways by the associators. Some, perhaps a quarter of those listed in the Reeves manuscripts, having had practice writing declarations of loyalty in May, and emphasizing the wickedness of their enemies, painted a picture of the constitution in vivid colors. One can almost hear the majestic notes of the *Doxology* as these documents describe an instrument from which "all blessings flow." These statements were pro forma, usually issued by those associations which immediately got down to the business of protecting the constitution with little or no flourish. Somewhat fewer made no attempt to describe the constitution, but pointed to the wealth and prosperity of England as proof that the constitution was sound. Their justification for action, if they needed one, was that the constitution was being attacked and it was the duty of all good subjects to defend it. These pragmatists, especially the associators at Bath, seized the opportunity to contrast the conditions of England and France and to deplore the conditions of the latter as a result of the foolish application of theoretical principles which were unsound in practice.[7] A few, however, attempted in the short space allowed them to define what the constitution was.

The associators at Horbury in the West Riding were the most theoretical. They asserted that "the Government of these Realms, consisting of a King, Lords and Commons, in whom are combined the advantages of *monarchy, aristocracy,* and *democracy,* is the most perfect form of all governments: uniting in it the powers of dispatch, wisdom, and responsibility, as well as possessing, at all times, the competency of internal regulation and redress." Pontefract, also in the West Riding, said that the constitution answered "every Good Purpose of Civilized Society," for under it "No Man can be deprived of his Personal Liberty without Cause assigned, and that Cause liable to a Speedy Discussion in a Court of Justice. The Poor Man enjoys his Cottage by as sure a tenure as the King his Crown.—No exclusive Privilege is known, And even the Labouring Class, may by honest Industry not only live in Plenty, but according to their Talents attain WEALTH and HONOURS." The Woolwich Association, however, managed to sum up the various descriptions of the constitution in the fewest words: "We further declare, That our Principles are equally abhorrent from Despotism and Anarchy: that all Extremes in Government are equally bad: and that National Felicity is in the Medium, of which the British Constitution is the admired Prototype."[8]

These descriptions reveal no ideological reaction to domestic and French activities. Indeed, in their emphasis upon efficiency, equality, and moderation, there is no anti-reform or anti-improvement bias whatever. Here is an important clue as to the practical ideology the loyalists supported, if only given in passing. Had they faced opposition, perhaps their views might have been defended at length, so that what they stood for might have been more easily seen. As it was, I could find only one instance when the patriotic enthusiasm of the moment was checked and such an explanation had to be offered. This occurred at Durham. The mayor of Durham called a meeting for December 20 in order to put forward several resolutions, among which were the usual one about the necessity to repress seditious writings. The majority of those present voted them down. The minority of eighty-six, however, withdrew and held another meeting in which the original resolutions were carried. These associators addressed the majority in the following words:

> We avow ourselves most zealous adherents to the present Constitution; nor fear the imputation, that an avowed, unequivocal declaration of attachment and adherence to the Constitution, is inconsistent with a disposition to improve it, where it can readily be improved: an imputation which is not less unjust than its opposite, that a zeal for reform, necessarily includes disaffection to the Constitution. . . . We declare ourselves friends to the reformation of any real defect in the Constitution; but do not think this is the season for publically discussing them: most ardent friends to the principles of reform, but as decided enemies to a spirit of innovation, where the good is not clearly ascertained, and the consequences are indefinite and uncalculatable.
>
> We conceive the question, at the present crisis, is not, Shall the government be reformed; but, shall it be maintained?[9]

By being forced to clarify their sentiments, the loyalists at Durham brought out the essential nature of the loyal movement. It was not a conservative reaction, nor the beginning of a White Terror, but an attempt to maintain the most liberal constitution in Europe. As pragmatists they were not concerned about the indirect effects they might have upon the nature of the constitution by their defense of it. Whether freedom of speech would be damaged by their denying that freedom to people whom they assumed would abolish freedom of speech never entered into their resolutions. The constitution they pledged to maintain was depicted as a system of laws and conventions which, in their operations, produced the practical freedoms under which they lived. Moreover, this constitution contained within itself methods of self-improvement. Of the fifty or so declarations from those associations which bothered to explain, even in glowing tones, what the constitution was, thirty-one stated that it had the means and energy to correct its own defects. The loyalists intended neither to support moves toward despotism nor to allow anarchy.[10] They were the true holders of that middle ground Fox had attempted to preempt.

These were some of the sentiments and goals expressed by the loyalists. What must be examined now is what they did, for, however nobly they pictured themselves, the test of the validity of their principles can best be derived from their actions. To be sure, they were confronting a situation new to their generation, perhaps new to their century, in which they faced the puzzle of trying to defend the constitution without wrecking it. Their solutions to this puzzle, if they were solutions, accomplished some of their goals and managed, in an unusual sense, to leave a legacy which was, as we shall see, both a strength and a weakness for England during the long war years.

It should be noted at the outset, however, that loyalist activities rarely involved violence. In contrast to the efforts of their Jacobin counterparts in France, English defenders of the constitution used little or no physical coercion to accomplish their ends.[11] This might be explained by the fact that they were an organized majority, backed by the law of the land, which was administered by an efficient and vigorous ministry. Extreme tactics were not necessary, perhaps unlike the case in France. Even so, the magnitude of the support they received from politicians and the press could have backfired, leading individuals to throw off their usual restraints and vent their enthusiasm upon a decidedly outnumbered enemy. That this never happened to any great extent is a tribute to the excellent leadership of the various units of the movement, or to the traditional respect of Englishmen for the law. Except for minor incidents, such as that at Manchester when a street procession threatened the leader of the local radicals, and a dunking given some London radicals by some watermen of the Thames,[12] the loyalists attempted to prevent and counteract radical activities with social and legal pressure and with counterpropaganda calculated to "undeceive" the deluded.

The effects of or the methods used to exert social pressure can never be known, except that some associators vowed that they would use whatever means they could to show their abhorrence and "detestation" of the radicals.[13] In close-knit communities, where social approval could mean not only economic advancement but also enhanced status, this may have been the most effective weapon available to the loyalists against the carriers of the new doctrines. How it was accomplished, however, is not, and perhaps could not, be revealed in the available evidence. Social ostracism can be a fearful weapon, as the upholders of Victorian "respectability" were to demonstrate in the nineteenth century, or as "sending a man to Coventry" demonstrates in the twentieth. We can only guess at the methods and results obtained in the eighteenth.

Social pressure might dull or delay the effectiveness of radical propaganda, but the activities of those radicals and the distribution of their literature more or less determined the preventive measures taken by the loyalists in the next instance. The laws of sedition were clearly on their side, and they resorted to threats to put the law into operation. Forty of the associations in the Reeves collection warned or threatened publicans, victuallers, and innkeepers with the possible loss of their licenses if they allowed seditious meetings to be held in their houses. Only one association, that at Deptford, actually investigated reports of seditious meetings at pubs in its area. Oddly, the association, founded December 13, 1792, had not included a warning to publicans in its original resolution. In the report of its investigation on December 31, however, it found that on November 14, twenty members of the London Corresponding Society had held a meeting at the Unicorn, where Paine's works were read. The publican there had refused them permission to hold another meeting. The investigators reported another meeting, on December 3 at the George, where a "movable club" of about forty people had held a secret meeting and nailed a bough of laurel, representing a tree of liberty, to the wall. The publican there also refused them permission to hold another meeting. After hearing the report, the Deptford associators voted their thanks to the publicans for their patriotic actions and offered rewards for information about other seditious activities: £10 10s. for any seditious meetings, £5 5s. for proof of seditious papers read, and 10s. 6d. for information about anyone defacing loyal posters.[14] In all likelihood, since there was no attempt to discover the identities of those attending these meetings, the publication of the investigation was intended as a threat to prevent other publicans from allowing such meetings to take place, or to discourage the radicals from attempting to meet in public houses.

Some publicans, however, either for economic or for patriotic reasons, or perhaps both, had already taken the initiative. On October 26, a month before the loyal association movement began, the *Chelmsford Chronicle* reported that "resolutions of Publicans, not to suffer any seditious club or meeting to be held at their houses, are extending fast through the kingdom."[15] The editor probably noticed the beginnings of a movement among publicans which, either because of self-interest or patriotism, pointed to steps which would later be taken by the loyalists. In all likelihood the associators were prompted by the actions of the publicans themselves to suggest, ask, or warn other publicans not to allow such meetings at their houses. After the loyal movement began, and after warnings were published in the local newspapers, several groups of publicans, victuallers, and innkeepers formed associations of their own to announce their intentions. At Bath on December 20, 111 innkeepers and victuallers vowed they would not allow meetings, clubs, or language on their premises which "tended to disturb the public peace" without giving information to the civil magistrates. They also thanked the Bath Association for Preserving Liberty, Property and the Constitution "for their judicious recommendations of a Line of conduct which had been anticipated." At Market Marlborough the victuallers of the area attended the founding meeting of the association and pledged to "discountenance" all seditious activities in their places of business. At Hinckley 34 innkeepers and victuallers promised the same, but also entered a subscription to print notices of their intentions to be posted in their places of business. In Somerset, the Frome Association of 84 innholders, which included all the innholders of the hundreds of Frome and Kilmarsdon, formed their own loyal association promising not only to prevent subversive activities in their inns but to assist the civil magistrates in combatting subversion anywhere. The largest group I have found of publicans declaring similar intentions was 680 in Sussex. The publicans and innkeepers of England were not immune to the wave of loyal enthusiasm which swept England.[16]

The most difficult and the most criticized task of the associators, however, was apprehending the subversives themselves. Here they were acting in a quasi-legal capacity, self-assumed, which from this distance smacks of vigilantism. Moreover, by offering rewards for information leading to the arrest of the radicals, they seem to moderns to have been appealing to the avarice of their fellow countrymen. Only five of the associations in the Reeves collection posted rewards for this service,[17] yet all that promised to aid the civil magistrates in the performance of this task had to depend upon information given them by witnesses. With our modern distaste for informers, these activities seem to dim the glow of patriotism which activated the associators.

This point of view, however, evaluates the loyalists out of context. To work within the law, to make the constitution its own best defender, the loyalists resorted to the usual practices in apprehending legal offenders. These practices were those used by constituted officials throughout the kingdom and by those private citizens who had joined protective associations long before the loyal association movement began. These earlier associations had been organized for various purposes—to catch horse stealers, to apprehend and prosecute felons or thieves, or simply to protect property in general. Their usual practice was to advertise rewards which would be paid for information leading to the recovery of lost property, sometimes noting the members' names and estates which were joined in the society.[18] Lacking a police force, the English legal system had to rely upon informants in order to function. Because only legally constituted bodies could indict lawbreakers, private associations had to file informations. These local associations merely aided the civil authorities by using the powers granted private individuals by the constitution.

The only association which informed Reeves of this sort of activity was one lackadaisically established at Mansfield, Nottinghamshire. The association was founded on January 1, 1793, and in its founding meeting merely issued a declaration of loyalty and passed resolutions to support the civil magistrates in suppressing sedition. No standing committee was formed, nor was a subscription opened to defray the expenses of publishing their resolutions. The Right Honorable Frederic Montagu, who was later elected to Parliament from Huntingdonshire in 1796, defrayed these costs out of his own pocket. Compared to the enthusiasm exhibited by the great majority of societies, the associators here, in the rather lukewarm resolutions they presented, seemed only to be doing their duty, as indeed they admitted in the preamble to their declaration of loyalty.[19]

This semi-lethargy was jolted when the association was given information on January 29 that a Benjamin Ward, a George Eaton, "and divers others persons resident at Sutton-in-Ashfield" had been involved in seditious activities. Reconvening the subscribers to the original resolution, the meeting appointed a committee of investigation headed by Hayman Rooke, Esq. This committee examined witnesses (paying their expenses and an allowance) and the accused themselves, finally deciding on February 4 that both should appear at the ensuing Nottinghamshire sessions. In the process, the committee reconstituted the association, establishing a permanent committee and opening a subscription to defray all expenses.[20] It was undoubtedly this late burst of enthusiasm which led them to send their minutes of proceedings to Reeves. They had not informed Reeves of their original meeting. Faced with a challenge, Mansfielders responded with gusto and exhibited in microcosm the underlying strength of the social organization and constitution of the English.

That strength lay in the willingness of the leaders of society, on whatever levels they were found, to take the initiative and use the existing system in order to achieve their ends. A glimmer of that strength can be surmised from the various protective societies already spoken of, where the same willingness to make the system work can be observed. Indeed, the whole loyal association movement is a manifestation of it. One might argue that the constitution of England was a living thing, composed of far more than the statutes, precedents, conventions, and administrative organization of the layered powers of civil and religious government from Westminster and Canterbury to the parish. Its versatility and flexibility allowed room for the inclusion of every member of the political community as the need arose. Tom Paine's argument that the English had no constitution was completely wrong. If he weighed constitutions by the number of written words on parchment, he was looking at the wrong evidence. This brief crisis offers us the opportunity of observing that the constitution included not only the legal and administrative apparatus, but also the basic social organization of the English nation.

There were, however, large elements of the English population not included in the political community. The campaign of the loyalists can be viewed as repressive in that it worked, by threats and in some areas by the application of law, to keep out portions of the population attempting to force their way in. The argument was about means, not rights. The political community was not a closed caste, and the opportunity to enter it was available to all. Its badge of membership was birth, ability, or wealth, and, as this was the period when thousands, perhaps tens of thousands, of individuals were converting the basic economic foundations of the state, when the "take off" into economic growth had already occurred, the opportunities of meeting the standards of political participation were multiplying daily and would increase in the future. These conditions of political participation were as much a part of the English constitution as any other and were defended by the loyalists just as avidly. The possible destruction of the system, however, lay in the numbers of the politically unenfranchised who might support the radicals. It was to these that the loyalists directed their counterpropaganda campaign.

This campaign can be divided into three different activities: advertising in the newspapers and distribution of handbills, street processions and banquets, and finally distribution of pamphlets and tracts which argued against radical propaganda. In each of these activities, however, the intent was to reach those portions of the community deemed most likely to be susceptible to radical promises.

Here was the real battleground of the cold war. The ultimate struggle was over the opinions of the great mass of Englishmen, both sides attempting to convince or persuade them either to rally to the constitution or to wreck it. There was little coordination of the loyal activities, although Reeves managed to assist some associations by sending them batches of pamphlets. The expenses and the decisions about which tactic would be most useful depended upon the initiative of the various societies.

As I have noted previously, the almost universal practice of the loyalists was to publish, both in local and in London newspapers, their declarations of loyalty and their intention to support the civil magistrates in the performance of their duties. Several associations, however, included transcripts of the patriotic speeches given at the foundation meetings. The Peckham Association in London ordered that George III's accession speech be printed in handbills and distributed to every inhabitant in the district.[21] Some kept the association's activities in the public eye by publishing accounts of their meetings when sister associations, inspired by their example and founded in nearby towns and districts, vowed their intention to cooperate in every way.[22] To a reader of the daily papers in London or the weekly papers in the counties, every issue in the months of December and January carried news of the patriotic activities of his countrymen. One such activity was always the occasion of a town festival—the burning of effigies of Tom Paine.

The local newspapers made no special effort to report the numbers of burnings. The *Chelmsford Chronicle,* for instance, after noting the activities surrounding the burning of an effigy at Crowden, mentioned only that there had been many similar happenings "in different parts of the country." As the lead writer of the *York Courant* put it, "The Effigy of Tom Paine having been so generally hanged, gibbetted, shot, etc. shows the sincere loyalty of the Public at Large. To recapitulate the Ceremonies observed at the different Places would be somewhat humerous, but yet too tedious to our Readers." *Berrow's Weekly Journal* excused the lack of this activity in Worcester by explaining that, "as the *original* is not worth powder and shot, neither is his portraiture worth a halter."[23] Yet in spite of the attitude expressed by these disclaimers, news of thirty-two such events appeared in the four local papers at my disposal.

Whatever the opinions of newspapermen, these events, ludicrous in comparison to the grim methods of legal repression, were significant and perhaps as effective a means for preventing the spread of sedition as any other adopted by the loyalists. They demonstrated the ambivalence of the loyalists who, motivated by an idealism to preserve their national identity, nevertheless adopted practical means to that end. In making a mockery of the writer of the most influential tracts used by the radicals, they matched, in symbolic propaganda, his own methods. If Paine hoped to ridicule the constitution and destroy the respect which supported it, the loyalists gave him tit for tat, and ridiculed not only his ideas but Paine himself. For a brief period he was probably the most burned-in-effigy personality, excluding Guy Fawkes, in English history.

The ceremonies surrounding the burnings varied. The effigy, usually with a pair of stays in one hand and a copy of the *Rights of Man* in the other, was either paraded through town in a carrion cart on on an ass, or dragged behind a cart or with his face stuck to a horse's tail, and was whipped through town. In Tunbridge Wells a man concealed in the cart "bellowed out lustily at each stroke." At Scarbrough the effigy was made to appear to cry by concealing a wet sponge under its hat. An attendant squeezed the sponge at each blow.[24] A band usually followed the procession, playing the "Rogue's March" or some other mournful ditty. At the place of execution the effigy was hanged on gibbets of various heights, that at Snaith being the highest, at fifty feet, before it was burned. As the effigy burned, the bands usually played "God Save the King," which was sung by all present, and the festivities began. Food and drink, paid for by a general subscription, were distributed and the town or village had a banquet. It was during these occasions perhaps that the greatest danger of violence existed. Supported by the local authorities in showing their disgust for those who expressed radical principles, the leaders of such a ceremony could have lost control of their followers, and physical abuse could have replaced the hootings and hissings that were reported as the usual crowd responses. On one occasion, at Sible Headingham, an effigy of Priestley was burned along with that of Paine. More ominously, the inhabitants at Shipley burned an effigy of the parish clerk "before his own door, for having publicly stood forth in defense of Paine's Rights of Man."[25] The violence, however, never materialized or was not reported in any newspapers.

The most extensive, and the most expensive, activity of the local clubs was purchasing and distributing loyal propaganda. While thirty of the loyal associations declared this to be one of their intended activities, there is no evidence of how many more were involved in it, or indeed of how many of these carried their intentions into effect. Four wrote Reeves thanking him for the pamphlets he had sent them,[26] but as these notes of thanks were included in the original transmission of their resolutions, it is likely that letters sent later were not kept by Reeves. Nor is it probable that these local associations received the overwhelming offers of money, materials, and encouragement that the parent society received in London. The ability of all the interested loyalists to be directly involved in the local association, something not possible in the metropolis, probably meant that all the available manpower was being utilized. Their activities after the founding of the associations, with the few exceptions already noted, can only be guessed at. The propaganda activities of the Reeves association in London, however, are fairly well documented.

Volunteers contributed most of the propaganda materials to the APLP. In some cases individuals informed the

London society that they had already distributed copies of their own works in their districts. Others submitted pamphlets and money for the use of the society as it saw fit.[27] In still other instances, the society reprinted selections of earlier works which were thought to have the proper values. Excerpts from Hume's *History of England* and, with his permission, Archdeacon Paley's *Reasons for Contentment* were reprinted and distributed in this fashion.[28] But the most effective literature distributed by the society was that written especially for the occasion. A good example of how this material was created and sent to the society is *Village Politics* by Hannah More.

The Bishop of London, Bielby Porteus, approached Hannah More on the subject of writing "some little thing tending to open their [the lower orders'] eyes under their present wild impressions of liberty and equality." More responded, and "on one sick day" she produced *Village Politics, by Will Chip.* The Fulham APLP published and distributed the tract in the bishop's district, where it achieved some success.[29] This success prompted Porteus to send a copy to the attorney general, who forwarded it to the London society with the comment that it was "better calculated for the understanding of the lower classes of the people than anything that has [y]et been published. If your excellent so[ciety] chuses to distribute it, it is at your service."[30] The society chose to accept it and sent copies to sister societies in other parts of the kingdom.

More's case was not unique. Many pamphleteers offered hundreds of copies of their works to the society for distribution, and some donated money to defray the costs of additional printings. To administer this volume of work, the works submitted were divided into two classes. The first were "such Publications as the Society ordered to be printed, after they had been perused and approved by the Committee." The second were tracts edited "by a person in whom the Committee confided. This person directed his attention principally to provide for the lower class of readers."[31] In this manner at least twenty-five tracts were printed and distributed by the London society alone, and many hundreds more were distributed after being contributed to the society by private individuals.

Regrettably, I have been unable to discover the identity of the person who edited the pamphlets intended "to provide for the lower class of readers." A person who may have been considered for the position was the Rev. William Jones from Nayland. In a letter to Chief Justice Lord Kenyon, King's Bench, Jones hinted that he was connected with the publication of one of the most successful series of the lower class tracts, the "Thomas–John Bull" letters. "I must inform you, in confidence, that I am in a great bustle, under the character of *Thomas Bull*. By the blessing of God . . . I have hit upon a mode of address which has gained the ear of my countrymen, and may be of great use at this critical time. . . . In consequence of this . . . I have a summons, in such terms as I must not resist, to attend a meeting on Thursday [December 6], at London, where nothing effectual can be done without me."[32] As the last of the "Thomas–John Bull" tracts was dated December 6, it is possible that Jones spent his time editing the works of others rather than continuing to produce his own. The results of the meeting, however, are not known and Jones remains only as a person who may have been a candidate for the job.[33]

The society had three sources of income to finance the publishing and distribution of these works: the membership dues of five shillings, voluntary contributions from patriotic citizens, and the government itself. As soon as the Executive Committee was formed on November 29, John Heriot offered the services of the *Sun* "as a fit paper for your Advertisements to appear in." Heriot explained that the "first two advertisements from the Crown and Anchor I inserted in my paper by desire of Mr. Nepean to whom I have the honor to be well known."[34] Obviously more than advertisements were paid for by the government. Heriot received £232/14/9 in two payments from the Secret Service fund on December 28, 1792, and March 10, 1793, for "pamphlets and advertising."[35] Apparently the London society never had any financial difficulties. With these funds the APLP carried out its propaganda campaign. The literature it had printed varied in composition and specifically intended purpose. In many cases the form of the pamphlet was as important as the message itself. The tracts intended for the lower classes, such as *Village Politics,* appeared as contrived situations. Hannah More used a dialogue between Jack Anvil, a blacksmith, and Tom Hod, a mason. In this manner both sides of the controversy could be presented, with the loyal argument, of course, winning out.[36] Some of these tracts appeared as letters, several of which were between Thomas Bull and his brother John. In this series each could tell the other how foolish the French and those who wished to imitate them appeared.[37] The fourth letter from John Bull was addressed to every Englishman. In it John Bull presented himself as a personification of all things English, who had risen in the past and "kicked out James II" and who had arisen again to reject the attempt of the French to impose another tyranny.[38]

Of the eighteen tracts "approved by the committee," ten are reprints of earlier works. Selections from Hume's *History of England,* various charges to grand juries, *Lord Loughborough's Speech on the Alien Bill,* and even *Cautions against Reformers* by Lord Bolingbroke, were intended to support the resolve of those who respected authority, whether literary or judicial.[39] Of the remaining eight tracts, four were anonymous, two were by John Bowles, a paid pamphleteer of the government, and two were by individuals arguing against the necessity of reform.[40] These last, written especially for the occasion, contain essentially the same message as those written for the lower orders, and taken with the reprints represent the argument the APLP thought best calculated to strengthen or awaken loyalist sentiments.

Because the strongest inducement for the feasibility of radical changes in the state was simply the existence of a revolutionary state, the basic argument of most of these tracts accepted this fact and insisted that the effects of radical change were not desirable. Since France could not be ignored, a picture of France was created which made revolution appear as a destructive and self-defeating act that only the simple-minded would approve of.[41] Against this depiction of the results of revolution, the blessings of English order and stability were contrasted, with various degrees of astonishment, incredulity, and anger expressed at the thought that the French, and some Englishmen as well, wished to reduce England to the level of French misery. As Thomas Bull told his brother John, "You and I are now to learn everything from these conceited monkeys, the French. Nobody knows anything now but they, and some Englishmen at home, who hate this country as bad as the French do."[42]

Aside from the general attempt to demonstrate the dire consequences of revolution and exhortations to support the constitution, no other generalizations can be made about the messages contained in the pamphlets. Tom Paine was refuted quite ably by Bowles's *A Protest against T. Paine's Rights of Man,* and the same author refuted the charges against the APLP and the intentions of the Friends of the Liberty of the Press, including in his pamphlet a plan for the formation of more APLP clubs. Five charges to grand juries by various individuals were printed and circulated, all warning the public to be on guard against the "poison" of seditious literature. It is apparent, therefore, that massive retaliation, rather than unity of message, was the aim of the APLP.

As has been demonstrated, the associators were not directing their energies against reformers and were, in many cases, reformers themselves. The crucial dividing line between reformers within and without Parliament was their evaluation of the gravity of the domestic situation. Those joining the loyalists, the great majority, regarded the situation as critical and, while not disallowing constitutional reform forever, argued that it should await the resolution of the domestic crisis. They were not opposed to reform in general but only to the necessity of constitutional reform at this time. It was the minority, those who insisted upon immediate constitutional modifications, who cast the issue in black-and-white terms. For instance, as Malone, a former reformer, wrote to Earl Charlemont, "The question is not now whether we shall have this administration or the other, or whether this king is a good or bad one, but whether we shall have any king." On the other hand, F.A. Sayors, a reformer who refused to delay reform, exaggerated the aims of the loyalists. "I cannot but condemn the Conduct of those persons, who class all men as Republicans and Levellers, who are not like themselves, *inclined to destroy every freedom of opinion* and to execrate and punish every man who may not be inclined to subscribe the same declaration or test of attachment with them."[43] (Italics mine.) If Malone exaggerated the threat posed to the constitution, which is a matter unprovable, Sayors exaggerated the consequences of a movement to preserve the constitution of England. The loyalists were not out to destroy every "freedom of opinion." Those reformers insistent upon immediate modifications of the constitution, decidedly a minority of a minority, lumped all of their opponents together, regardless of the practical reasons they gave for their stance. It was they who refused to see any opinion but their own.

By February 20, 1793, after France had declared war on England, the estrangement of this group was complete. A former "friend to reform," a Mr. Mullarton, wrote Windham his evaluation of the choices left open to Englishmen. "Circumstanced as this country is at present I trust that the distribution of men can be but into two classes—Those who would hazard their existence for the defense of this happy Constitution under which we flourish and those desperate subversives who would overturn the glorious fabric and involve this country in all the horrors of Anarchy, Pikes and Guillotines."[44] Fox and his few followers were condemned to years of hopeless opposition because Fox's "centre point" was really not the center of opinion at all, but a view shared by only a few reformers, impatient of restraints. The cause of reform, awakened by French events in the first place, was delayed, by its affinity to those events, to some unknown time in the future.

This delay was caused, paradoxically, by the success of the loyalists in preserving the structure to be reformed. For if we judge the movement a success because it kept the spread of opinions hostile to the constitution to a minimum, we must admit that in doing so it also froze the constitution into a form which would take years to thaw. By recoiling from extremes, by holding fast to the moderate position, constitutional mobility, either in structural reorganization or in emphasis, was made impossible. By nailing the constitution to a fixed position, by declaring that reform was laudable but untimely, the loyalists may well have avoided some or all of the horrors of the French experience, but they also made it impossible for the constitution to retain that flexibility which had allowed it to adapt to differing circumstances.

In a sense the struggle between the loyalists and the radicals had all of the ingredients of a Greek tragedy. Both sides, by professing and acting upon what they believed to be the highest motives, created conditions that would ultimately produce much grief in the body politic. The radicals, by jumping on the French bandwagon, created the loyalists, who worked to oppose their progress. To do this, however, the road had to be permanently blockaded, so that all movement in constitutional terms had to be blocked, as well. Continued efforts by the radicals to achieve their goals only intensified the loyalists' desires to stop them. By the time the radicals gave up, the habit of immobility had sunk in too deeply to be changed, and it would be almost thirty years before the state would make any meaningful changes to adjust to constitutional conditions that had developed in the interval.

There were, however, many chances yet that this im-

mobility might only be temporary. There was the slim
chance, for instance, that the bustling activities of the
loyalists, their arguments against the goals of the radicals,
and the social and political approval of their activities by
practically all the spokesmen in society might convince the
radicals that perhaps they were wrong, or that their desire
for constitutional change should be put in abeyance, or
even that the radicals might become so despondent that
they would cease their activities altogether. As the editor
of the *Sussex Weekly Advertiser,* in a state of ignorant
bliss, put it: "The moment the doctrines of the French are
stopped in their circulation, their reign is at an end. . . . It
is pleasing to anticipate, that the French will be more
speedily defeated by the operations of reason, than those
of arms."[45] Reading radicals for "French" in this quota-
tion, this view represents the beliefs of the loyalists. If
there were no longer any radicals, the dangers to the
constitution would be over. There would then be no
reason to shun the normal game of politics, and the *Advertiser* could once again speak out for reform. This was
whistling in the dark, or perhaps a general misunderstand-
ing of the nature of the battle between the loyalists and
the radicals. For, as long as the bright promise of the
French Revolution shone across the Channel, as long as the
impetus toward a new world existed within France itself,
the English radicals would continue their efforts to be a
part of it. Their deepest desire, as Gwyn Williams has
simply but eloquently expressed it, was for "recognised
manhood."[46] This desire could not be dampened by debate, social ostracism, or legal prosecutions. While representing the last large movement for equality of rights in
preindustrial society, the radicals sounded a note of
modernity which was to characterize later movements by
demanding rights justified by existence alone and not as a
special reward because of behavior, status, or value to the
community. Men could not be argued or intimidated out
of that dream.

And so the radicals persisted in their efforts. At the very

height of the loyalist movement, when the excitement of founding loyal associations was sweeping the land, the *Advertiser* noted that the "stubborn weeds of sedition" had not yet been killed: "Two men with large wallets at their backs" had been observed selling cheap editions of Paine's *Rights of Man* "in several villages in the Eastern part of this county." Dundas admitted to the lord mayor of London a month later "that the check which has lately been given to the spirit of sedition . . . has not been so effectual as could have been wished." On February 14, 1793, the government received information that the Friends of the Liberty of the Press were attempting to support the artisans' efforts. Once again reports arrived at the Home Office of meetings of seditious clubs, although a new, or perhaps an old, tactic was now observed. "The clubs are now much more cautious in their proceedings than formerly, and make their professed object the Reform of Parliament—but their leading people are the same as formerly assembled."[47] This change in tactics occurred, however, after war had been declared by France on February 1, 1793, and, as we shall see, the war changed everything. It began, however, on the heels of the victory of the loyalists. Although they had not stamped out sedition, they had curtailed the spread of doctrines which might have influenced people to be seditious.

The loyal association movement, therefore, can be interpreted in a narrow sense as the largest sustained vote of confidence ever given by the English public to their constitution up to that time. If the goal of the reformers in Parliament or of the artisans' clubs was to extend the franchise so that the public will could be expressed, they witnessed, whether they knew it or not, just such an expression of that public will. The loyalists voted with their signatures, their contributions, their participation in patriotic events, and their declarations of support, just as surely as they would have in a ballot box, their decision that the constitution was more than acceptable, that it was worth defending when attacked. If the artisans simply wanted to enlarge the democratic portion of their constitution, they succeeded by provoking a democratic rejection of their proposed methods.

In a speculative sense one can view the loyal association movement as a major reason why England avoided at this time the French precedent of resorting to revolution to effect change. Whether the artisans intended a revolution or not, the goals of popular movements are not easily managed by their instigators. As matters turned out, the radical artisans' movement was the last peacetime possibility of a French-style revolution taking place in England. Elie Halevy has suggested that England avoided a revolution because the individuals most likely to have taken part in it were finding outlets for their desire for improvement in the revitalization of religion. E.P. Thompson suggests that, while the radicals did present a revolutionary threat, their intended reforms failed because the government panicked and introduced repressive domestic measures.[48] Both of these arguments may be part of the explanation. The militantly loyal outburst of sentiments expressed by this movement, however, cannot be ignored as another major explanation. Revolutions are indeed "made" by minorities, usually against a disorganized or apathetic majority. The radical artisans were a militant minority, but they faced an aroused, organized majority, equally militant. In this sense the loyal association movement was a successful counterrevolution and a major reason why England did not have a revolution.

But the contest between these two groups was not over. The war between France and England merely broadened the arena of conflict. A successful revolution after war began would no longer be the spontaneous, indigenous, forceful reform of the constitution and society that reflected only those impulses already existent in English social values. For war with revolutionary France made those supporting the principles of the French Revolution blatant allies of the declared enemy. If French armies supported and allowed domestic radicals anywhere to achieve their goals, the result could not be called a revolution—it would be a simple conquest.

CHAPTER V

THE YEAR OF INDECISION

The wave of loyalty swept into wider channels after the beginning of hostilities between France and England, and as a consequence lost much of its momentum and identity. Now Englishmen focused their attentions upon a greater variety of objects and goals, so that the single-mindedness of the loyalists, which in spite of the lack of any concrete organizational structure had led to their easy identifications, was merged into a larger stream of activities in which the loyalists acted not in control but in cooperation with patriots devoted to winning the war. Undoubtedly many of the personnel were the same, since the prewar loyalist movement involved most of the political community of England, yet matters directly involving victory or defeat attracted many to causes other than combating disaffection at home. Primarily, therefore, the first effect of the war upon the loyal movement was to dilute it. Winning the war was now the object which created patriots, not just maintaining domestic peace.

This is more than just a play on words. Loyalists were created not just by the appearance in England of individuals who wished to alter the fundamental character of the state and society, but also by their suspected alliance with the revolutionists in France who possessed the practical means by which this could be done. Before the war, the danger perceived was that the English Jacobins might encourage disaffected Englishmen to revolt or oppose the government to the degree that the French would respond with aid sufficient to overthrow the government and establish a republic. Whether this danger was real or not did not matter; enough Englishmen believed it to be real so that they took action to oppose the first steps of such a scheme. After the declaration of war, military operations against France took center stage. Englishmen supporting the French were not now merely exercising free speech; they could be flirting with treason. Moreover, any possibility of cooperation of the French with English radical plans would be determined by French successes on the battlefield. Old-fashioned conquest was now the primary danger and revolutionary resistance in England was viewed as a tool, not the object, of a French invasion.

This change of perspective affected loyalist activities in many ways, and indeed confused the nature of the term loyalist itself. Contemporaries used it to describe every action which assisted the government in prosecuting the war. The people under examination, however, were those who supported the existing constitution ideologically, and were defined by their voluntary activities in that respect. Because defeat would mean the certain destruction of the constitution, the loyalists naturally merged with those who were defending their country. Artificially, therefore, I shall use the term patriot to describe the wartime loyalists, although the line separating patriots and loyalists was rather thin, or in some cases nonexistent. Had events not transpired in 1794 which called for the reappearance of the peacetime loyalists, I would now be at the end of my study, as all but a few Englishmen were by that date loyalists. There are, however, some activities in aid of the war effort in which we can see the loyalists in action, and the tempo of these activities was in direct response to the fate of the Revolution and the French military effort. For, as the initiative on the battlefield passed from the French to the allies and back again to the French in 1793, so radical activities in England decreased and increased. Loyalists joined patriots in many activities in that year, but the longest joint effort was the subscription drives.

The subscription drives of 1793 did not represent a new feature in English life. The same willingness to assist the nation in times of emergency which lay at the roots of the loyal association movement existed throughout the eighteenth century and manifested itself in whatever ways were thought necessary at various times. Its essential characteristic was its voluntary nature—the offering of unasked-for aid. During the first year of the war, loyalists joined others in responding to this inclination in three large money-gathering operations: the subscription drives in February and March to raise bounties to encourage the enlistment of seamen, the collection of funds from March to July to relieve the widows, orphans, and other dependents of servicemen killed in the war, and the drive for collections to purchase clothing and other necessities for the soldiers in Flanders during the winter of 1793–94. Because the recruiting of soldiers and sailors might cause discontent, and also because the families of recruits might resent inadequate treatment of those servicemen, each of these subscription drives can be viewed as an effort to prevent dissatisfaction with the government. Simple generosity and especially humanitarianism, now developing into a marked feature of English society, undoubtedly played a large but unmeasurable part in these efforts as well.

The English method of obtaining men for naval service could only be described as barbaric. Press gangs, armed with warrants to draft quotas of men, could force individuals, regardless of their situation, into service. "Protections" were often ignored with impunity by the press gang. If the individual resisted, he could literally be kidnapped with no legal recourse. Understandably some English sailors would desert if given the slightest opportunity, and this propensity had much to do not only with the harsh discipline aboard naval vessels, but also with the maritime problems which arose between Britain and the United

States during the war. Surprisingly, once impressed into service many accepted their lot and, more than any other factor, were the real reason for British naval superiority. British seamanship, not technology or numbers, was the decisive factor in winning sea battles. The method of impressing, however, was viewed with repugnance by practically all sectors of society, including, it appears, the government. It was continued apparently for lack of any better method of obtaining individuals trained, or partially trained, in the exacting science of sailing the complicated ships of the period. Voluntary enlistments, on the other hand, would decrease the number who needed to be impressed, so bounties were offered as inducements to enlist. These usually consisted of a general bounty by government and additional bounties from the major cities and the ports where the ships were being staffed. This is another instance of the English propensity to make existing laws work, although it produced, in this case, less than desirable results.

When Pitt called for increasing the number of sailors in the navy by 20,000, cities and towns all over England offered bounties to encourage enlistment. The general bounty offered by the government, called the king's bounty, was five pounds, and additional sums offered by the various corporations and towns increased that amount to various levels. Seamen enlisting in London, for instance, received thirteen pounds: five from the king, two from the city, and six from various organizations within the city. By March 10, when the bounty was discontinued, 1,550 seamen had been encouraged by it to enlist at that city.[1] Not only was this a means of avoiding the injustices of impressing, it also appeared to several loyal associations as a means of supporting the civil government.

The first loyal club that I have been able to discover which offered a bounty was that at Lewes, chaired by William Campion. By January 28 the club had already opened a subscription to that end. Moreover, the idea spread to the loyal associations at Portsmouth, Portsea, Southampton, Haverford, "and several others." On February 11 the Newcastle association was reported to have collected £235 4s. for the same purpose. Throughout February, as the goal set by the government was quickly reached, loyal associations scattered around the country subscribed funds for the purpose of "augmenting" the bounties for the sailors. The Manchester association was the most successful, attracting "upwards" of 1,700 enlistments.[2] The idea of subscribing money to aid the government in the war caught on and different sectors of society responded.

At Ashburnham, where there had been no loyal society, a special meeting of the inhabitants was called on February 16 to assist the government by raising money to pay bounties to seamen and also to provide a fund for the wives and children of soldiers and sailors killed in the war. Other towns and counties which had not announced bounties now did so. Wealthy individuals also contributed to the war effort in this manner. At Rochester a Mr. Nicholson, ship builder, offered a bounty to all seamen who would enter the frigate *Tartar,* which he had built. The "Gentlemen of Stockton" offered five pounds to every seaman entering the *Assistance,* and Lord Darnley offered three pounds to the first fifty able and the first fifty ordinary seamen to enlist from Gravesend.[3] There is no doubt that this assistance helped man the fleet, but it also pointed the way for the next effort of the loyalists.

It became apparent during February that the sailors' grievances about the system of impressing stemmed less from its injustice than from the practical effects it had upon their families. The resistance of the seamen at Newcastle, for instance, pointed to this problem. When the press gang visited the Newcastle area they were met by a united resistance from the seamen, who attempted to justify their position in a handbill published on February 2. The local loyal association, they said, in order to encourage them to enlist, had offered them a bounty of one guinea above the king's bounty, and by doing so admitted that the pay of sailors was insufficient. The sailors argued

that twenty-two shillings per month, the naval wage for
able-bodied seamen, was not enough for a "single Man to
live upon," but how were men with families going to meet
expenses? This sum was "not Half" what was received "in
the Merchants' Service." On such a salary "our Children
and Dependents are neglected: They are exposed to all the
Miseries of Poverty, and are hindered in their Course of
Life by Want of Protection and Education." On these
grounds the sailors were determined not to allow themselves to be impressed into the navy.[4]

Undoubtedly the seamen in the Newcastle area had
learned their methods of opposition in the strikes of
November 1792. At that time they successfully bargained
for a rate of four pounds per voyage to London and back,
a trip which usually lasted about six weeks. Their peacetime pay, therefore, would average about fifty shillings a
month. The emphasis in their demands, however, was upon
their concern for their families after they left. In the subsequent efforts to end the resistance, which were reported in
all the newspapers, it appears that this concern alone was
understood. Here the loyal associations and other groups
and individuals concerned with maintaining the peace had
an opportunity to take action of the kind which might
have helped avert the mutinies at Spithead and the Nore in
1797. A movement to raise the pay of sailors was not
beyond contemplation at that time, nor were suggestions
to that end lacking. Instead the associators became involved in a subscription drive to help the dependents of
servicemen.

As early as February 4 a fund was opened at the Crown
and Anchor Tavern in London for the "Support of the
War." The committee which administered this fund was
appointed by the parent club of the original loyal movement, although the leadership of this association had
passed from John Reeves to William Devaynes. Devaynes,
a London banker who had been added to the executive
committee of the association on November 29, 1792, pre-
sided over the association through 1794. As chairman of

the committee, Devaynes received and disbursed funds for various purposes throughout the next two years. The fund's first purpose was to relieve the wives and families of soldiers and sailors killed in the war. By February 4, 1793, nearly £1,000 had accumulated in the support fund.[5] It is likely that the founding society, under new leadership, was the first to raise funds specifically designated for dependents of servicemen.

The movement grew quickly. On February 24 the Trinity House in London offered a monthly pension for the duration of the war to the wife or aged parents of every seaman who enlisted before March 31, and a monthly pension for life if the seaman was killed or wounded. The Brighthelston loyal society on February 25 informed other loyal societies that moneys collected for bounties could be better spent on dependents, and promised to raise a fund for that purpose. By March 10 the movement was so widespread that the *Observer* could remark that it was an "irrefutable attestation of the general approbation" of the war itself. Lewes, the city of London, "Ladies of Fashion" everywhere, "Philanthropists" and members of the nobility joined the movement.[6] In York, when the Bradford loyal association donated fifty guineas to the London fund, the *York Courant* predicted that this was "so laudable an Example . . . that it would be followed by all other Associations in the Kingdom." Two new funds were noted by the editor, "The Patriotic Subscriptions of the Ladies for the Relief of the Widows and Children of such Sailors and Soldiers as may fall in the Present War," which had collected £5,000, and "The Subscriptions of the Noblemen and Gentlemen" for the same purpose, which had also collected nearly £5,000. The patrons of the latter fund were the dukes of York, Clarence, and Gloucester.[7]

Money and subscriptions for these three funds as well as for direct payment came from other sources, as well. The "Gentlemen at Eton" subscribed £100, the 38th Regiment of Foot gave a day's pay, various congregations took up special collections, and even a benefit play was given in

which £11 13s. was collected for the fund. Beginning on
May 13, the *York Courant* kept a running account of the
subscribers and their donations, remarking that the outpouring of care must console those dependents who had
lost someone in the war. By July 8 the fund at the Crown
and Anchor had grown to £18,000 in spite of regular dis-
bursements.[8]

Not all loyal associations jumped on this bandwagon. In
Manchester, for instance, a meeting was called on March 4,
after the seaman's bounty drive ended, to decide upon the
most effective means of assisting the government "in the
present emergency." The associators decided to raise "a
Corps" of marines and subscribed £5,000 on the spot. By
May the associators were collecting money to assist those
unemployed because of the war and had already subscribed "upwards of £1,000." Collections for this purpose
were also received at Manchester churches, where £94 1s.
was donated at one meeting. These funds were given to the
unemployed, upon application, in the form of checks
which could be exchanged for food. The editor of the
York Courant estimated that "thousands" were relieved of
misery in this way.[9]

While the mania for subscribing money to aid the war
effort in various ways subsided during the summer of
1793, when victory seemed all but assured, it revived again
as winter approached. The object of this new subscription
drive at first was to send flannel waistcoats to the soldiers,
and it was first noticed by the *York Courant* on October
14. A month later, a John Brookfield of Sheffield wrote
the Home Office that he had opened a subscription for
that purpose but now needed directions on how to get the
waistcoats to the soldiers. He also asked what other articles
were needed, "as I have reasons to believe our Subscription
will be much increased and we are apprehensive, for the
Zeal manifested in different parts of the Kingdom that the
supply of waistcoats will be greater than needed." The following day, November 14, a Richard Baugh from Wolverly
near Kidderminster wrote Nepean that he had collected,

without advertising, £10 in one day for the same purpose and wanted to know where to send the waistcoats.[10] From that date until January 19 the movement skyrocketed.

By November 18 the *York Courant* noted that subscriptions for flannels were being opened all over the kingdom and that at London 9,040 waistcoats, 1,640 pairs of hose, 1,438 caps, and £816 had been collected, exclusive of 5,000 waistcoats sent from Edinburgh. Various articles of clothing and money were collected at practically all the larger cities and towns, so that by December 2 the editor of the *Courant* estimated that 10,000 waistcoats had been sent to the Duke of York's army and 20,000 had been given to the soldiers in the Earl of Moira's army. This money was usually sent, as formerly, to William Devaynes in London, who graciously thanked each group donating. Balls were given to raise funds, and the "rage of the land" for "ladies of quality" was making waistcoats, but blankets, shoes, and even old linens for bandages were contributed, as well. By January 28, 1794, John Lodge, the secretary of the society at the Crown and Anchor, estimated that the value of the donations added to the cash in hand amounted to £35,000.[11]

This willingness to contribute to the war effort and the general approval of the war were frequently remarked about in the local press throughout the year. The *Sussex Weekly Advertiser,* not averse to criticizing the ministry when occasion presented itself, remarked on March 4 that "never was there a war in which the spirit of the nation seemed more roused and interested than the present." By September the *York Courant* confidently stated that "the internal situation of this country at present is such as every friend to it could wish—tranquil, prosperous, and happy."[12] In its first year, the war against France was popular. The last subscription drive has been interpreted as resulting from pressure from members of Reeves's committee "as an auxilliary means of testing loyalty."[13] The evidence demonstrates something quite different. It shows that the Reeves (or Devaynes) committee did not have that kind of power. It is more likely that the generous donations of the English people were a result of their patriotic or humanitarian willingness to do what they could to alleviate some of the usual miseries and discomforts of war. Other patriots and loyalists were willing to assume some of those discomforts themselves. The loyal society at Dover, for instance, initially formed itself into a paramilitary organization to protect Doverites from harassment by passing French ships as well as to aid the civil magistrates in maintaining the peace.[14] Not only did gentlemen organize "Patroles" to avoid being surprised by landing parties from marauding French ships, but individuals and groups of various sorts, volunteer fishermen, anti-smuggling merchants, and even the entire male population of coastal cities organized themselves to protect their lives and property. It was not until May 11, 1793, that the government attempted to give some regular organization to these people, but by that time all of East Kent and much of the west was ringed with paramilitary organizations composed of groups volunteering to assume some of the responsibilities ordinarily reserved to government.[15]

Many individuals, two of whom are notable, volunteered much advice to the government during this period, as well. Jeremy Bentham, for instance, prefacing his advice with the declaration that he was not a republican nor at that moment a reformer, offered his assistance to government in many areas. His assistance in the war against the Revolution, however, consisted of plans for a rapid communications device which he called a "crytophone," which he thought would be useful in the event of a riot or of invasion. James Mill, writing under the pen name of "Pro Bono Publico," gave assessments of public opinion and advice on how to fight the war. William Devaynes at the London APLP urged government to look to the needs of the poor. And a Mr. Goring of the Essex Loyal Society imaginatively sketched a plan for sending out agents or ombudsmen to all parts of the kingdom to discover exactly what griev-

ances might exist so that they might be redressed before
they accumulated.[16] Many other suggestions were made,
illustrating the involvement of Englishmen in the war, but
these decreased during the summer. It appeared to many
by then that France was defeated and that peace was near.
They were mistaken, of course, but it is now time to assess
what these efforts were all about.

Compared to the loyalists' prewar activity, the efforts
described above were laudatory and highly respectable but,
upon analysis, passive and rather aimless. Facing the enemies of the constitution and society boldly in the prewar
period was an action worthy of note. Saving old bed
linens, holding knitting parties to make waistcoats, or even
at social meetings pledging to pay a few pounds to support
recruiting or console the dependents of killed servicemen
were actions of a different order. Loyalists who actively
fought a vague possibility before the war were now
passively responding to possibilities on a different level. In
short, the loyalists, while still eager to assist the government, lacked direction. Their aimlessness and confusion
can be seen at the center of things—the government at
Westminster. For it was here that the confusion originated,
and it rested upon the ministry's inability or disinclination
to clarify England's war aims.

Pitt had struggled to define these even before he knew
of the French declaration of war. In a speech on February
1 he recognized that the likely enemy was fighting a new
kind of war, one which involved control of the opinions of
men as well as the usual kind of war involving ships, soldiers, and perhaps subsidies. The ideological assault, Pitt
insisted, had been launched formally by the French on
November 19, when they declared that French soldiers
would be used to assist people attempting to gain their
liberties, and that French principles had been imported
into England specifically so that the English might make
such an attempt. On February 12, after news of the beginning of the hot war arrived in England, Pitt repeated

these sentiments, stating that, because of French pro-
nouncements and actions, the English were indeed, involved in a "war against opinions."[17]
It was at this point that Pitt stumbled. He had perhaps
overdrawn the planning and directed actions of the French
in the ideological war, but basically he was quite correct in
the assessment that England was faced with two kinds of
war, or perhaps two kinds of enemies: a rival state and the
Revolution itself. The appeal of the fundamental doctrines
of the Revolution to the politically underprivileged of
Europe was such that conscious attempts by the French to
spread them by decrees, pamphlets, and other means were
necessary only in those countries in Europe which lacked a
free press. Englishmen did not have to read radical
pamphlets; they normally could read the speeches of
French politicians in the Convention in their local papers.
Moreover, because of the style affected by French speakers
of that day, practically every minute action proposed in
the Convention was backed in argument by reiteration of
the philosophy of the Revolution itself. Ideological war
was carried on as much by the news of the activities and
speeches of the revolutionaries in Paris as it was by radical
pamphlets, speeches, and meetings. English radicals were
the effects, not the primary causes, of the spread of revolutionary ideas in England, although they in turn could
assist the spread in various ways. And herein lay Pitt's
dilemma. How to fight such a war? Was the primary enemy
the Revolution or France? To be sure, the conventional
war would be fought at first conventionally, but what
could be the war aims of the English: the defeat of France
or the destruction of the Revolution? Pitt did not answer
these questions.

This was an important omission. The same enthusiasm
which supported the revolution in France was evident in
England. Indeed, as has been demonstrated, the eagerness
or zeal in defense of constitution and country which sustained the loyal associators was the kind that sustained the
French in defense of *la Patrie* and the Revolution. Nor did

it evaporate with the beginning of war. Without direction
from the top, Englishmen—loyalists, patriots, and radicals—were quite willing to subscribe, to volunteer, and to
sacrifice for the good of their country, however they saw
it. In short, like the French they wished to participate in
the national life of their country, by supporting or attacking the constitution, by working for or against peace, by
removing or creating discontents. What was needed was a
focus, a channel into which this zeal could be directed. To
be sure, it went without saying that the English would
defend themselves in the war, and Englishmen eagerly
sought to do this. But defense is passive and in the long
run is the killer of enthusiasm. What was needed was an
active war policy which would allow the nationalistic
fervor of the English population a measure of expression.
Pitt indeed failed to formulate such a policy at the outset
of the war; when opportunities arose later to recast the
war into a national crusade, he failed to take full advantage of them. The result was a continual bewilderment
about the object of the war and a considerable waste of
intellectual effort and time in Parliament trying to explain
its nature.

Charles Fox, in the debates of February 1, for instance,
immediately noticed and deplored Pitt's omission of war
goals. "Of all wars he dreaded that the most which had no
definite object, because of such a war it was impossible to
see the end." Other Parliamentarians began to see the light
shortly thereafter. Lord Beauchamp noted on March 15
that "this war had peculiar features belonging to it, which
set at defiance all attempts at comparisons with former
wars." To describe those peculiar features, Parliamentarians in the next four years exhausted hyperbole. The war
was fought, they said, to preserve the fortunes, liberties,
and lives of all Englishmen, the security of Europe, the
causes of justice, humanity, and religion, and the safety of
the world. Jenkinson said it was a war of necessity, Burke
that it was a "war of perfidious rebellion against honourable loyalty, infidelity against religion, of robbery against

property, of murder against humanity, of barbarity against social order." The Earl of Abingdon exceeded all others' attempts to explain the magnitude of importance he placed upon the war when he described it as a "war with original sin; . . . with the enemies of all mankind . . . and with the enemies of God and nature." By November 1797 Lord Gwydir finally confessed, "The powers of language have been so often employed to describe the complicated nature of this war, that words have lost their effect by repetition."[18] This confusion as to what the war was all about can be laid directly at the feet of Pitt and his ministers. There were, however, extenuating circumstances.

The first of these was the possibility that France would be defeated quickly. Pitt, a great financier, believed that wars were fought with money, and he assumed from the outset that France was practically bankrupt. The French navy and army, democratized by the Revolution, were not a threat at this time. As matters developed in 1793, these assumptions seemed accurate. The slow, methodical advance by the Imperial armies, with the small British contingent on their extreme right, seemed unstoppable by the untrained levies the French threw against them. By midsummer the British navy had effectively cleared European waters of French naval vessels and privateers. In a sense the scenario of 1792 was being replayed. Just as Brunswick's advance into France the previous summer had been met with desertions from the French army and the opening of the gates of cities lying in his path, so in 1793 large sections of France disavowed allegiance to Paris, and several cities—Lyons, Marseille and Toulon—declared for Louis XVII. Just as the radicals in Paris had overawed the National Assembly as defeat appeared certain in August 1792, so did the radical faction of Robespierre, supported by the Sections, gain control of the Convention in July 1793. Just as the government in England could ignore the continued growth of the artisans' clubs in England during the summer of 1792, so could it ignore the reawakening of the same clubs in the summer of 1793. In 1793, therefore,

Pitt could conclude that there was no reason to clarify England's war goals.

The repetitious drama, however, continued. Just as Dumourier's victory at Valmy electrified the radicals in France and England to greater exertions, so the French recapture of Toulon gave new hope to and revived the spirits of the same radicals. The allied advance halted at the borders of France, to begin its year-long retreat over the same ground as its previous year-long advance. From the perspective of the twentieth century and many experiences of ideological conflicts, it is clear that by 1794 it was too late for Pitt to announce new war goals. To be sure, Pitt had George III proclaim that England would make peace with any section of Frence deserving it,[19] but this, given the circumstances of the day, was not a declaration of what the war was all about, but rather an attempt to take advantage of a temporary situation. By not speaking out in time and by not finding some time to speak out, Pitt left the English without a clarification of the positive objects of the war.

Leaving aside public utterances by politicians, which are frequently unreliable in defining their motives, the question of Pitt's views on the real nature of the conflict still remains. I propose that, from the outset of the war until its conclusion in March 1802, Pitt's view of the war is best explained by the title of a song composed by George Canning for his birthday in May 1802: "The Pilot that Weathered The Storm."[20] In this analogy, Pitt's actions during the long war years are clarified somewhat. If we take the storm to represent both the Revolution and the war, Pitt's efforts to keep the ship of state watertight, to plug the leaks through which revolutionary principles could invade, and to take advantage of any opportunities that might occur at the whim of the storm, make sense. This means that Pitt viewed the Revolution as something uncontrollable, something which must be endured. Perseverence and steady control would be at a premium, so that any wartime opportunity to injure the enemy had to be waited for and quickly acted upon, but the storm must wear itself out. It meant, in essence, that Pitt had no offensive plans at all and intended only to fight a defensive war. To be sure, a defensive war involved opposing in any way possible the occupation of the Low Countries by any great maritime power. It meant offensive actions against overseas possessions of the enemy, not only for use as bargaining chips at the peace table, but also to deny the enemy wealth with which to fight the war. It meant launching a fleet large enough to gain control of the sea, and pursuing an active policy, as far as possible, of blockade and interdiction of all of France's coasting and international trade. Had the allies on the continent pursued the war against France with single-minded determination, perhaps this policy of pruning the branches while the allies cut the tree might have worked. European problems, however, were never that simply solved. Poland was too tempting to Prussia and Russia, and the emperor could not view the acquisition of new territory and people by his major rivals with composure. The allies, England included, lacked the single-mindedness necessary for success, and the defensive policy of Pitt and the allied leaders meant only that a long war was in the offing, that tens, perhaps hundreds of thousands of men would die needlessly.

Domestically this defensive mentality helped insure the continuation of the war. The only offensive arm of the English military establishment was the regular army. If England was to take part in the defeat of France, the regular army would be the only instrument to do the job. The confusion and chaos in the organization, recruitment, and operational plans of the regular army remained with but little alleviation for the whole of the war against revolutionary France. Despite the efforts of the Duke of York after the complete defeat of the allies in the Flanders campaign in 1795, the problems of the army and the failure of the government to solve them mark this as one of the major failures of the English system of government during this time.[21] There were, however, other consequences of the ministry's defensive mentality.

Using conventional methods against radical agitators domestically meant the application of law against the disturbers of the public peace. English law was singularly, perhaps happily, unequipped to do this. Fox's Libel Law, passed at the time when the May Proclamation of 1792 was issued, allowed juries to decide questions of guilt or innocence in seditious libel cases which involved their judgment on the intentions of the defendents. Faced with this responsibility, when the cases of authors, distributors, or publishers of matter charged as seditious came up, juries frequently decided that this or that person was guilty of publication but not of seditious libel.[22] The problem was deciding just exactly what sedition was. Daniel Eaton, for instance, was tried three times for seditious libel. In his second trial the jury first found him "guilty of publishing." Lord Kenyon refused the verdict and sent them back. Their second verdict was "guilty of publishing the pamphlet in question." Kenyon accepted this as a verdict of not guilty. In Eaton's third trial for seditious libel as the acknowledged author of *Politics for the People or Hog's Wash,* the jury found him simply not guilty.[23] The inexactness of the laws of seditious libel, however, are best illustrated in a trial at the Leicestershire assizes. The first verdict was "guilty, but with no evil intent." When this was not accepted, the jury reported, "Guilty, but with no wish to injure the King." As this also was not accepted, the final verdict of the jury was "Not Guilty."[24] The imprecise nature of the law, but more importantly the jury's paramount power to decide motives, led to a weakening in this conventional weapon for waging domestic warfare against alleged subversives. While some individuals were convicted, the relative power of the government in controlling public opinion in this manner was unpredictable and depended upon many variables, not the least of which was the sense of alarm felt by the jurymen themselves.

Thomas Briellat, a pumpmaker from Shoreditch, and Dr. William Hudson were both convicted of seditious utterances before December 9, 1792, while rumors of the plot and fears of internal subversion were at their height. The acquittal of three printers and proprietors of the *Morning Chronicle* and Daniel Eaton's second and third trials occurred after December 25, 1792, and before February 28, 1794—in other words, after the victory of the loyal movement and before the crisis which occurred over the possibility of invasion in 1794.[25] This was a time of security when domestic radicals seemed to be defeated and when their allies, the French, had not yet assumed the military initiative on the Continent. Given latitude, English jurymen were not vindictive or punitive, a fact which Jeremy Bentham knew quite well, and which, one might assume, was known by others in the legal system as well. This inability to obtain convictions could only encourage radicals and defeat the government's purposes in waging a war against the Revolution in England. Even when English politicians in 1794 confronted new features of the ideological war in England, as we shall see, serious doubts were expressed by the ministers as to whether the system should be changed so as to obtain convictions, because necessarily the new statutes would alter the constitution that the government, the loyalists, and the patriots were struggling to defend. The danger in 1793 did not warrant more extreme actions. This relationship between external and internal events was illustrated in the latter months of 1793 and the early months of 1794 when the radical movement revived.

The radical movement which reawakened in the summer of 1793 was a transformed movement. During the spring and early summer all of the clubs, with perhaps the exception of the Sheffield, suffered losses of membership as their inspiration across the Channel seemed incapable of countering the allied pressure on the northern and northeastern fronts. It was at this time, May 30, that Hardy proposed a three-month moratorium on the London club's activities.[26] As news trickled into England of the radical measures being taken in Paris, however, this decline was at first halted, then reversed. Let us look first at the picture of France created by the press to account for this new turn of events.

On July 7 the *Observer* noted the reorganization of the French executive which was taking place. Although it overstated and misinterpreted its extent, the *Observer* correctly evaluated its probable consequences. "The dissolution of the National Convention was a desperate measure, which must accellerate the downfall or establish the Republic of France." The editor suggested the former consequence because of the "madness and civil war that agitate the Convention." A week later, the editor noted that the Committee of Public Safety had merely replaced the Executive Committee, but held to his opinions about the probable consequences, for now the Terror had begun and the astonishing number of people who were reported killed and imprisoned caught the editor's attention for the next few months. This behavior added disgust to the reporting of events in France, and in general began the final alienation of those intellectuals who might have excused French misdeed before. The revolutionaries now became the "Dogs of Hell."[27]

By September this disgust became a regular feature of news reporting on France. The *York Courant,* for example, when speaking of the *levee en masse,* called it the last act of "madness and despair" as the French continued to run "from absurdity to absurdity." The *Sussex Weekly Advertiser,* which once had cautioned its readers to reflect on the good that had come out of the Revolution, now capitulated. "The whole history of the French Revolution has been a regular descent from bad to worse. At first there were certainly men of abilities employed . . . in attempts to frame some sort of governance. . . . [But] in the general turbulence the lowest filth rose to the top, and there [they] have continued."[28] That human beings could act in such a manner was treated as a matter beneath contempt, as several of the papers reported body counts and other enormities at Paris and other cities without comment. If individuals wanted to find reasons to condemn France morally, the papers furnished more than enough. On the other hand, if individuals wanted to find reasons for hope in the French example, these were offered as well. The French leaders now threw off all restraints, all deferential attitudes, in their attempt to preserve the vitality of the Revolution. Those imprisoned or killed could be viewed by sympathizers in England as the betrayers of the Revolution who had caused the internal weakness of France in the first instance. The important point was that the revolutionary leaders were now taking the initiative and were doing all they could to avert defeat. Moreover, the policy seemed to work, as rebellious cities—Lyons, Marseille, Rennes, Caen—were brought back into the authority of the Convention. By October rumors of possible French invasions of England to relieve the military pressure on France were reported in the English papers.[29] Once again the phoenix of the Revolution seemed to be rising. The surrender of Toulon, reported in September, was, in spite of the joy it brought to ministers, a temporary setback, for there was no way the allies could take advantage of it. The French navy in the Mediterranean was captured, but one could not invade France with ships of the line. In short, France did not appear to be in danger of defeat, and the life of the Revolution, despite French hardships, was secure.

This news from France and the ineffectiveness of the legal assault against the radicals were not the only reasons for the resurgence of radical activities in England. For now, whatever restraints on their behavior may have been exercised by the Society for Constitutional Information were lifted. The coordination of the movement passed to the London Corresponding Society. By August it was in contact with societies in Derby, Manchester, Stockport, Nottingham, and Coventry. There was also a new emphasis. Painism was no longer the creed, and while the old themes of purifying the constitution were spoken of, these were incorporated into the new goals of removing economic and social grievances. The identification of the societies and France now became more evident as the artisans appeared obsessed with the imitation "of French example, forms of organization and address." Caught up in this spirit, when the Scot radicals proposed the calling of a Convention at Edinburgh on the French model, the London Corresponding Society accepted.[30] It seemed, for a moment, that the new day had arrived.

The London Corresponding Society held its first public meeting on October 24 and elected Maurice Margarot and Joseph Gerrald as delegates to the Convention. These men, after much posturing and rhetoric, were arrested, tried, and convicted, but this did not dampen the enthusiasm of the Society. Even the moribund Society for Constitutional Information "came back to life and on 17 January, 1794, voted to oppose tyranny by the same means by which it is exercised." If the sentences imposed on the delegates represented the "tyranny" spoken of, we may assume the Society for Constitutional Information planned to put the Scottish judges on trial and sentence them to transportation, although the means by which this was to be done were not mentioned. The Society for Constitutional Information did, however, order 40,000 copies of a "fiery Address" to be sent into the provinces, which Williams claims caused a rebirth of many of the clubs. Membership in the London Corresponding Society, with forty-eight divisions, supposedly grew to over 5,000.[31] Here was an enthusiasm and a recklessness that had not been seen since the autumn of 1792. In addition, there was a militancy about the radicals which had not been seen before. Not only were the speeches of the radicals harder in tone, but some of them advocated that arms be secured. The English radicals copied not only the principles and forms of organization of the French, but also French militancy, which under Robespierre was increasing daily.

The government was aware of the growth of the radical movement. As early as July, Nepean sent additional spies to attend "the various Clubs or Associations which are inimical to and mean to overthrow the Government of the Country." James Greene reported in August the activities of the clubs in the north, warning that sedition was "rising daily." C. Stuart and James Colquhoun, the latter a magistrate, gave accounts of the elections of delegates to the Scotch Convention and the proceedings which transpired.[32] Copies of some of the new radical publications were remitted to the Home Office. The most complete report, however, was compiled sometime after the Chalk Farm meeting in April 1794.

This report, or a rough draft of it, is fourteen pages long with nine appendices, which have disappeared. In it Nepean attempted, without success, to abstract the messages of agents who had attended all of the meetings of the London Corresponding Society since August 1792. The organization, the membership (which he estimated at between 1,200 and 1,900), the type of members, the subjects of discussion, the activities, and the plans of the London society are dealt with at great length. Nepean admitted "that the candour, and liberality of the law of England is not a match for the boldness and frequency which these attempts against the peace of society are practices." He noted especially the reluctance of Middlesex jurymen to convict individuals for seditious activities because they consisted of "ordinary persons, who do not feel a pride in giving their best attention to the business of the Country." He suggested new laws, which were indeed passed in 1794, but had no other recommendations. This was a report for information, and while it noted accurately many features of the London Corresponding Society, there is no urgency of tone or alarm expressed in it.[33] A similar lack of concern can be found in the government's reception of news that a new type of counterassociation, The Society of Loyal Britons, was being formed.

The parent organization of this new loyal movement

was founded in Southwark on October 10, 1793, by Grove Taylor, who may have been the "Taylor" mentioned in Nepean's report coordinating the spying activities on the radical clubs. It resembled the Reeves association of former years and was quickly copied by eight similar societies in and about metropolitan London. In December Taylor wrote Dundas that he intended to found societies in "every City and principal Town in England," to be called the General Association of Loyal Britons. Taylor included lists of the places, broken down in counties, where these societies would be located, intimating that this network of clubs, tied closely together, would perform a service the government needed during the present crisis.[34] Had the government wished to apply the same remedy to the radical movement as it had in 1792, here was one opportunity that it could have taken advantage of, regardless of its belief in Taylor's competence to carry out his plan. That the government did nothing reveals much about its true apprehensions and its changed evaluation of the goals of domestic radicals.

For the situation had changed since 1792. Then, the government took the relationship between the domestic radicals and the French at face value. The radicals would "invite" French soldiers into England, after providing a port at which to land, in order to gain their assistance in establishing a republic. Without any knowledge of the strengths of either the radicals or those who were willing to support them, the government acted wisely and moderately, with considerable success. The strength of the proconstitutional forces was clearly revealed to the government, to the radicals, and indeed to all of Europe. If the radicals merely wanted "reforms," the impossibility of achieving them by massive public support was demonstrated.

The rout of the reformers in Parliament, upon the failure of Grey's proposals, indicated that the cause of reform was temporarily lost. It should have been clear to everyone that the goals of the radicals were unobtainable for the foreseeable future. Yet the radicals persisted and were growing bolder. What conclusions could be drawn from this? Were their activities a result of natural English tenacity? Did they still propose to work toward the reform of Parliament in spite of the decided votes given against them? Or were they revolutionaries for revolution's sake intending to ride the wave of what they considered the future? The relationship between the radicals and the French, their true goals, and the possible consequences of both were matters of concern to the government in the latter months of 1793 and the early months of 1794, for it appeared that the French, against all odds of success, were contemplating an invasion.

The French had hinted at invading England even before the war began, and to a degree this kind of talk had been expected by the English. As the only way the French could conquer the English, threats and preparations for invasion had been a feature of all the wars between the two countries in the eighteenth century. Because invasion has never succeeded in modern times, we are apt to believe it was impossible, or so difficult that various French leaders gave it up after estimating the probable failure. In the days of sailing ships, however, the only difficulty normally faced in contemplating invasion was that of supplying the forces once they landed. The defending navy could not be counted upon to stop an initial landing, as the wind that brought the invading fleet to England would, in all probability, prevent the English navy from intercepting it, as happened when William arrived in 1688. With naval superiority, however, the enemy could be prevented from supplying his troops after they landed. Without friends in England, William's "invasion" would not have succeeded. Until the autumn of 1793 the superiority of her navy gave England insurance against logistical support after invasion. After that date a party of French friends appeared to be building. Moreover, from various sources government received news that plans for some sort of landing were in progress.

On October 13 the Duke of Richmond responded to an inquiry by Dundas as to the likely place of an invasion and the amount of force he thought necessary to meet it. The Duke suggested that the most likely spot would be around Brighton, Sussex, as there were nine turnpike roads nearby, and London, the likely target of such an invasion, was only sixty miles away. He ruled out any place in Kent or Hampshire because the former could be seen too easily and the latter, because of the ships at Portsmouth, was too well defended. While he made no estimate of the probable number of enemy soldiers that would be landed, the duke believed that "14,000 Infantry and 1,500 Cavalry and we mean effective Rank and File" would be enough to defend the Southern District. Since his force was 3,000 infantry and 700 dragoons short of that amount, he asked to be brought up to strength. He did not mention the units by number, so it is only a guess that most of these were militia, except perhaps for some regular troops at Portsmouth and all of the cavalry. He omitted altogether the various volunteers manning shore defenses. The duke also called Dundas's attention to a delicate problem. "It is a political consideration for you to determine how far such Preparations . . . may cause an alarm in the Country."[35]

What prompted this inquiry by Dundas at this time is not clear. It may have been a routine question, one that the home secretary was expected to make. On the surface the French seemed in no condition to take the offensive anywhere. Furthermore, the Southern District included the only threatened coast, as the French held no bases in the Low Countries at that time. The newspapers, to be sure, printed rumors of desperate plans by the French to invade England as a means of relieving pressure on the northern front. This would be a nuisance landing, involving the loss of many French soldiers and the probable destruction of much property, but not one which held much chance of success. Nevertheless the rumors persisted through October, the places of landing changing from time to time.[36] A spy, "X.Y.Z.," reported on November 4 that there was a "general feeling" that the French, who were making preparations at Dieppe, Cherbourg, and other places, "portend an invasion, probably at Portsmouth or Gosport," both of which were ill-prepared and lacked troops. X.Y.Z. suggested that the government investigate those ports.[37] With no hard information, however, the government did nothing.

Newspapers continued to print rumors of invasion after the turn of the year. Through February and March 1794, as the French preparations on the continent for the spring campaign grew to enormous proportions, the nature of the rumored invasion changed. Whereas in October and November the crossing had been viewed as a desperate measure by an almost-defeated enemy, now the supposed intentions of the French changed to a carefully coordinated attempt with the object of rallying all pro-French individuals in England and supporting their attempts to overthrow the government. In a sense this was a repetition of the "plot" rumor of the previous year, but this time there was more evidence to support it. While newspaper editors struggled to assess the validity of the "reports" they heard, the gvernment also attempted to evaluate the validity of the new information it received. By the time government believed an invasion possible and announced as much in Parliament, the newspapers had prepared the English public with enough speculations, facts, and rumors to make government's conclusions seem valid.

At first the papers attempted to meet rumors head on and squelch them before they got out of hand. On February 3 the *York Courant* first reported French preparations for a "descent upon England" by large forces. In this account the editor did not speculate upon the validity of the report, but merely mentioned rumors of the accumulation of large numbers of flat-bottomed boats at Havre de Grace and the assembling of numbers of troops in the area. Two weeks later the editor presented a more detailed plan involving 50,000 men, and the place of the probable landing, in this case Hastings. The *Courant* also noted that while the French might attempt such a project, it was more probable that all these preparations were meant to alarm Englishmen and force the government to concentrate its forces at home. Noting on February 24 the boasts of some French leaders that the landing in England would take place within the month, the editor dryly commented that this was just more French braggadocio.[38] Before the French spring offensive demonstrated the effectiveness of the "reforms" of Carnot, the editor of the *Courant* was skeptical about the possibilities of invasion.

The same skepticism can be seen in February in the *Chelmsford Chronicle*'s reports of these rumors. The editor of the *Chronicle* did note, however, an ingredient in the invasion plans missed by the *Courant*. "Private accounts from Paris mention, that the convention make a boast of having *men in this country,* who are assisting its views; and that it daily expects a deputation from hence, to concert the plan of securing the descent of the French in England." Printing continued reports of the impending invasion in subsequent issues, the editor offered several explanations of their authenticity, pointing either to deliberate attempts by the French to create alarm or to those of "the gentlemen of the stock-exchange" and their stock manipulations as the principal reason for the continuation of the rumors. While the editor noted that the government was interested and had some reasons to believe "that the threatened invasion will take place," he cautioned his readers to "discountenance everything like panick and dismay." Finally, noting the various estimates of the number of soldiers to be landed and their probable landing spots, the editor still tried to calm apprehensions, to assure his readers that "every means that prudence can dictate or policy devise, will of course be opposed to so desperate a maneuver," and to cast doubt on the probability of the invasion by printing an extract of a letter "from an Officer on board his Majestys Ship Serpent" which reported no invasion preparations in some French coastal cities.[39]

These laudable attempts at good journalism, tinged as

they were at times with "whistling in the dark" tones, were outdone by the complete nonchalance of the editor of the *Sussex Weekly Advertiser.* Here, in the area most often mentioned as the likely site of an invasion, one might assume panic would be greatest. Yet until February 24 the editor printed nothing about it. On that day, after a casual statement that in London bets were down that the French would invade by Lady Day (March 25), the editor commented: "The *poor cocknes* are so confoundedly alarmed at the threatened invasion of the French, that the Country Bumpkins on our coast here, are often seen to amuse themselves at their expense, by laughing 'till their sides are almost cracked at their *effeminate and foolish fears.*"[40] In February, therefore, while reporting rumors of the danger of invasion, the editors sensibly tried to keep those rumors in perspective. Other members of English society drew their own conclusions and were not hesitant to inform individuals in positions of power about their concerns and their suggestions as to what should be done. Most were agreed that the French planned an invasion.

During March evidence compiled by government supported this assumption. Indeed, government seemed more intent on investigating the means by which such an attempt, whenever it might be made, could be met effectively, and which particular weaknesses in its organizational structure could be exploited by the enemy, than on the validity of the rumors of invasion themselves. Government had been informed as early as January 27 that the French were collecting flat-bottomed boats at Cherbourg, Gravelines, and Havre de Grace.[41] The purpose of this activity, of course, could only be guessed at. Military affairs on the continent took a decided turn for the worse for the allies after the beginning of the spring campaign, and the comfort and security of 1793 were definitely over. The French had won the initiative, and their threats of invasion, laughable when they were losing, now had to be considered in a different light.

Of all the received suggestions of plans for defense,

some in response to requests by members of government, others offered gratuitously, and of all the possibilities suggested in the correspondence on invasion, one generalization holds true. None of the writers believed that the French would invade to conquer. Such an undertaking, given the English command of the sea, was never taken seriously at this time. But most agreed that the French might invade in order to precipitate a revolution. Here was the plot in reverse. The French, now that they knew that the people of England would never have a revolution of their own accord, would attempt to unify all disaffected Englishmen by landing a suicide force of at least 50,000 men to capture London.[42] News of this would encourage uprisings in all parts of the country, which, while ultimately doomed to failure, would so weaken the country that England would be forced out of the war and would later be subject to invasion for conquest. Judging by the later actions of government, the two reports which bore the heaviest weight and which seemed to combine all the warnings sent to the Home Office by private individuals were written by one author, a "W. Ogelvie." His analyses of the situation and proposals to meet it were very close to the steps taken by government later and may give us some insight into official motives.

Ogelvie sent his first report, entitled "On Military Associations," to Henry Addington, the Speaker of the House. When Addington brought it to the attention of the government is not clear, although it must have been before March. The merit of Ogelvie's suggestions lay in his analysis of the difficulties facing an invading army, which he assumed would be so great that if the country were "quiet," 100,000 Frenchmen landed anywhere could never reach London. If the country were "distracted," quite a different conclusion would have to be reached. "*Here then,* and at this point I conceive actual Danger to begin: guard against the Possibility of Riots and Confusions at Home, and I should despise the utmost Efforts of a foreign Enemy." The real enemy, to Ogelvie, was the disaffected people in England. He urged as an antidote paramilitary "Voluntary Associations for Mutual and General Defense" to stamp out any disturbances at their onset, before they could grow. "Such Military Associations . . . would answer . . . the different purposes of *Defense against a foreign invasion* and *Security against Sedition and Riots within.*"[43]

The dual nature of these associators, as anti-invasion forces and as internal police, was elaborated upon in Ogelvie's second report, dated "March, 1794" and entitled "Observations on the means of repelling Invasion." It is likely that Addington sent Ogelvie's original report to someone in government, probably Henry Dundas, who asked the author to expand upon his views. The result was this analysis, which was the most comprehensive of all those submitted. The draft retained in the Home Office records was copied by at least three identifiable hands, which might suggest that several hurried copies of it were made for a study by a committee or perhaps the cabinet. Ogelvie's analysis of the domestic situation of England, and his proposals, most of which were implemented, attest to the importance of this document in gaining insight into the motives of government in instituting the "Plan for the more completely providing for the Security of the Country" submitted to Parliament on March 25. Because this plan was the occasion for the reappearance of the loyalists, Ogelvie's views deserve some attention.

In effect, Ogelvie urged government to heed the lessons the French had taught in the past three years. One could not count on internal difficulties preventing the French from achieving their goals, as the French seemed capable of anything. The English, therefore, should prepare for the worst. Because the Revolution had divided "mankind into two Parts, the *Rich* and the *Poor,*" or those who had a stake in the country, from the largest landholders to the smallest housekeepers, and those who had nothing to lose, it was imperative that government arm the former and disarm the latter. These "military associations would at once *repress sedition, check innovation,* and overwhelm those *affiliated Societies* which the *Promoters* of *Mischief* are endeavoring to introduce into this Kingdom." Ogelvie argued that the English should beat the French at their own game by organizing and arming the loyalists to defeat the radical societies before it was too late.[44]

Here, then, was an analysis of the situation, a prediction of possibilities, and a solution offered at length by a private citizen. His proposals, to be sure, did not suggest the methods by which all of this could be brought about. They did, however, point out a justification and a means by which the government could tap the reservoir of patriotism that had prompted the loyal association movement and the scattered loyal activities of 1793. More than that, Ogelvie's proposals seemed an answer to problems confronting government of which the author had no inkling.

The first of these problems was highly practical. As the possibility of a quick victory over France vanished in the winter of 1793, the policies of the government had to be revamped, especially in the matter of raising men for the army. This was a problem never solved adequately in the revolutionary and Napoleonic wars. In the first instance, service in the regular army was rightfully viewed as something scarcely better than incarceration in prison. The soldiers enlisted for life or until they were unfit for service. Their pay, at one shilling a day, had to meet their victualling costs plus the replacement of clothes and equipment, so that it was barely enough to allow them to survive. Coupled with the harsh discipline exercised, these features of army life usually attracted individuals who could hope for nothing better in life, or individuals fleeing from the certain prospect of imprisonment.[45] In a time of rising opportunities, very few men enlisted.

Grenville, in order to keep discontents at home to a minimum in 1793, had suggested alternate, time-honored ways of raising men for service based upon the "recruiting for rank" principle. This merely meant that individuals who raised corps of soldiers would be given rank dependent upon the number of men they raised. If a person raised a regiment, for instance, he would be given a colonel's commission; if a company, a captain's. There were two major types of soldiers enrolled in this manner, those in Independent infantry regiments or companies, and those enlisting as cavalry units in the "Fencibles," the former to be incorporated into the regular army and obligated to serve anywhere, and the latter for domestic service only. In this respect the Fencibles served as a "select militia" and augmented the Home Guard. The Independent companies, however, were totally inadequate for the purposes they were to serve. Of the fifteen regiments raised in 1793 and the two in 1794, many were commanded by boys, many were ill-clothed, poorly trained, and deficient in equipment. They seriously weakened rather than strengthened the British contingent on the Continent. It is significant that one of the Duke of York's first reforms after his appointment as commander-in-chief in 1795 was to tighten the regulations governing the raising of Independent corps. Poor in quality as they were, however, these offered the quickest and the least dangerous way of rapidly building the regular army.[46]

As the growth and spread of the radical clubs became evident and the possibility of domestic unrest grew during the winter of 1793-94, the sending of even these poor replacements to the Duke of York came in question. The soldiers might possibly be needed at home. This problem was apprehended by others and many solutions were offered to the government, some rather imaginary, some far too conservative. A few, however, seemed to fit the occasion and the needs of the government, and, placed in the context of the government's experiences in this new kind of war, had some effect on the ultimate decision reached.

Suggestions about raising or increasing the forces retained in England began arriving before war was declared. "Amicus" wrote the Home Office on January 24, 1793, urging, instead of independent companies, the doubling of militia allotments and the raising of "Royal Gendarmes," who would serve at their own expense and only when needed. This emphasis upon voluntary assistance continued through the year. Oliver DeLancey, the assistant adjutant general, wanted volunteer cavalry, or Fencibles, to relieve the regular cavalry for other duties. As it was, the first coastal volunteers included cavalrymen and artillerymen.[47] John Barwis from the Isle of Wight reminded the Home Office that at the beginning of the century the government had issued weapons to the townsmen there to defend themselves, and he wanted "about fifty Musquets." The demand that government allow Englishmen to defend themselves became so great that by May 11 the king approved a plan whereby the lord warden of the Cinque Ports and the lord lieutenants could approve the raising of certain volunteer companies.[48] But this first movement toward the establishment of volunteer paramilitary organizations ended when the prospect of peace seemed bright during the summer, and was in most respects merely a movement to assist the regular forces. While some suggestions were made that these volunteers could assist the civil magistrates in the event of riots or other disorders, they were mainly intended to protect the property and lives of Englishmen on the coasts against marauding French ships. With the prospects of invasion a new, or rather the old, enemy reappeared in the winter of 1793–94—the radical artisans.

On February 2, 1794, Buckingham wrote Grenville about some of the difficulties facing the government. Because the English cavalry had scored notable successes against the French in 1793, it was likely that all the remaining regular cavalry would be sent to France. This left the problem of replacing them, and apparently Grenville was thinking of adding cavalry to the militia. Buckingham suggested an alternative: using "the young idle gentlemen of the country, foxhunters and sportsmen, who might be induced to form units under officers chosen by themselves." He reminded his brother that the Yorkshire

Rangers in 1746 were composed of such sorts, "and they did what might truly be called *Yeoman's service* on that occasion." This suggestion was explored further by Dundas. He asked Lord Amherst how such voluntary bodies of troops might be organized, and the old soldier responded on February 13. Amherst suggested three different types of volunteer organizations: the companies of infantry manning the batteries on the coasts already agreed upon, volunteer companies to be added to the existing militia battalions, and volunteer troops of cavalry of about one hundred men, armed by government but providing their own horses, saddles, and bridles. Amherst also suggested that recruiting-for-rank be used to determine officers.[49] Here was the nucleus of the plan which, with some modifications, was to be implemented by government in March.

Before any hints of the government's plans leaked to the press, others suggested additional points about the methods of raising such men, the possible uses to which they could be put, and their probable effectiveness. William Devaynes, who had helped in so many of the subscription drives of the previous year, conceived that the war was now "of a new and alarming description" and suggested that the government allow the parish of St. James to raise, "at its own expense, Men for the service of the Army." Devaynes proposed opening a subscription for that purpose. J.M. Bingham, guarding 2,000 French prisoners at Gosport, suggested that government arm the townsmen or at least "such as are known to be well affected to the present government." In the event of an invasion, the soldiers presently guarding the prisoners could "march against the common enemy" while the townsmen guarded the prisoners.[50] The use of private subscriptions to pay the costs of the volunteers, and the auxilliary uses to which they might be put and thereby release more soldiers for duty were suggestions later acted upon.

The news which probably helped the government decide that the proposed volunteers might be an effective arm of the service was that transmitted by James Fremenheere, the captain of the Penzance Volunteers, formed on April 11, 1793. The collector of customs at the port of Penzance, faced with a band of smugglers he could not control, requested the aid of the Volunteer Company Associated for the Defense of the Town, and Fremenheere responded. The smugglers were entrenched in King of Prussia's Cave and were not only armed but had a battery of cannons for defense. The volunteers, under cannon fire, charged the cave with bayonets, capturing the cannons and the goods of the smugglers (which turned out to be liquor), but were unable to capture the smugglers. The smugglers, regrouping, counterattacked but were driven off. Fremenheere related this rather lengthy account because he wanted the government to supply him with two field pieces in case a similar problem arose in the future.[51] If the government had any doubts about the effectiveness of volunteers, this instance should have made them think twice. Volunteers already were aiding the civil magistrates in enforcing the laws.

All of the ingredients were there for the recall of the loyalists: the new and perhaps more ominous invasion plans of the French with unknown connections to an enthusiastic and growing radical movement, the experience of the willingness of Englishmen to subscribe for patriotic purposes, and the eagerness of the loyalists to volunteer their services if called upon. These last were the key—if government requested their aid and only a lukewarm response was their answer, this would be exactly the wrong message to send the French or to reveal to the domestic enemies. Yet more would be lost, as Ogelvie reasoned, by doing nothing. In March, Pitt put his plan into operation.

CHAPTER VI

THE LOYAL
VOLUNTEERS

In March 1794 the loyalists of England quit the realms of debate and entered into full-fledged physical opposition to their enemies, the radical artisans. In the belief that invasion was inevitable sooner or later, and convinced that the radicals in England were not only assisting the French in preparations for that invasion but planned to join the invaders once they landed, the loyalists stepped forward to offer their money, their exertions, and finally themselves as defenders of the internal and external security of the nation. The loyal volunteers grew to a force of over 300,000 before peace was concluded in 1802, and when war was resumed against Napoleon the same number volunteered again. This was the third and climactic effort of the loyalists and was the most successful in its desired results. Until the vague threats of the French were clarified, indeed until the French proved their competence to execute those threats, the volunteer movement grew sporadically, stimulated more by supposed dangers to internal peace posed by domestic radicals than by the possibility of a military confrontation with French soldiers. At last there was an attempt to direct and control patriotic and loyal emotions into a channel which would satisfy the aspirations of the people and demonstrate their determination to get on with the job. The indecision of 1793 was over.

Prevention continued to occupy the major place in loyalist activities. As with the addressors in May 1792 and the associators in November 1792–January 1793, the success of the loyal volunteers makes it difficult to evaluate their services to the nation. Moreover, as the inspiration of the radicals burned itself out in Paris, and as some of the English radicals continued their emotional commitment to overthrow the state long after any such possibility existed, the role of the loyalists changed also. Originated with a dual purpose, protection of the internal and external defense of the country, as the internal threat died away the external took prominence until the loyalists were gradually transformed into patriots.

At the beginning of this analysis, it would be wise to clarify the use of the term volunteer. Until 1794 it was used in the normal sense by government officials, newspapermen, and correspondents. It meant simply anyone who offered his services to government in any capacity. Some of the earlier independent regiments "raised for rank" in 1793, for instance, called themselves volunteers. The 82nd Regiment of Foot, raised by Charles Leigh in September 1793, preferred to call itself "The Prince of Wales Volunteers." Lord Paget's 80th Regiment of Foot styled itself "The Staffordshire Volunteers," George Nugent's 85th Regiment called itself "The Buckinghamshire Volunteers," and so on. Enlistees in the army or navy, regardless of the amount of their bounties, were often termed volunteers in 1793. In that sense, in spite of the press gangs and crimps, one might argue that England had a volunteer army and navy. Conscription was confined to the militia, but even here those men drafted by ballot could hire a substitute to serve for them, and at least one regimental clerk had difficulty deciding whether or not to call these substitutes volunteers. The volunteer companies organized for coastal defense in 1793 pointed to the activities which later would be used as criteria for the use of the term.

After March 14, 1794, when the "General Orders for the Security of the Country" were released, a technical meaning of the term evolved.[1] The orders issued by the government called for the addition of men to the existing militia organization by two methods: by raising volunteer companies to add to the regiments as units, or by raising individual volunteers to add to the existing companies. They also sanctioned the raising of companies in various towns, supposedly for coastal defense, but with no special purposes mentioned. To increase the size of the militia, the bill also sanctioned the raising of new organizational units. "Select Militia," or volunteer troops of Fencible cavalry, composed of the gentlemen and yeomanry of various districts, would serve as cavalry auxilliaries to the militia infantry under the rules and regulations of the Home Guard. These were to be raised by the traditional recruiting for rank: the volunteers, fifty to eighty per troop, provided their own horses, saddles, and bridles, but arms, accoutrements, and uniforms were to be provided by government. These troops were often referred to as volunteers or the Yeomanry, which causes a bit of difficulty for the researcher, for the fourth provision of the orders called for the formation of units of cavalry, sanctioned by lord lieutenants in the various counties, composed of the gentlemen and yeomanry, to serve only in the counties, creating in effect county militias. Moreover, the dual purpose spoken of above was spelled out for these latter troops: they were not just to repel invasions but were to suppress riots and tumults, to act as both counterinvasion forces and police.[2]

This confusion of terminology and the clumsy method of introducing and financing these new forces forced Pitt to enter bills which would make private subscriptions in support of the government legal. The debates over these bills clarified the terminology somewhat, using volunteers only in reference to the town and county militias, but the serious purposes to which they would be put took months to be clarified. The volunteers had a difficult time aborning, and the blame for this can again be laid at the feet of the ministry and its unwillingness or inability to define the precise nature of the war they were fighting. The volunteers were intended to serve as anti-revolutionary as well as anti-invasion forces, and had the spokesmen of the government, Pitt or Grenville, explained or attempted to explain that they were fighting an ideological war at home as well as abroad, the devious tactics they used in introducing the volunteers would not have been necessary or would not have appeared devious.

Pitt apparently knew at least as early as March 4 that he was going to ask Englishmen not only to volunteer for home service but also to pay a large share of the costs. Newspapers as early as March 3 printed rumors of the augmentation of the militia, or that the grand juries for the Easter assizes would probably recommend to all Englishmen that they learn the use of arms. Indeed, the loyal association at Exeter published its intention to do just that in order to "convince our enemies, both abroad and at home, that as lovers of our King and Constitution, as Freemen and Britons, born and bred in a land of liberty, we will defend ourselves against invaders."[3] Englishmen were prepared, anticipating and even proceeding to do what Pitt wanted them to do. Royal proclamations had been used before in activating the loyalists with exceedingly good results, and one issued at this time calling for volunteer units to be formed would undoubtedly have been equally successful. Instead Pitt decided to test the reception to his plans by sending Lord Radnor to Reading, Berkshire, to present them to a meeting of the grand jury.

Radnor conscientiously carried out his duties, sending Pitt a copy of the resolutions carried at the meeting. These included the opening of a subscription and the formation of a Committee of the County of Berkshire to draw up plans for augmenting the forces of the Crown. Radnor included a partial subscription list, which totaled £1,484, pledged in half an hour. Two days later, according to instructions, he sent Pitt his analysis of the reception of the plan. There was, he said, "a strong, and general conviction that it was rather hard, that the Exertions which the urgency of Circumstances renders necessary should be at the Expense of Friends only." He had gathered a general notion that the plans would have been better received "if Government had enforced by Compulsion, and at the general expense such Measures," and while there was a "zeal" to assist the government, there was a resentment that this zeal was being taxed.[4] The plan had worked but Radnor pointed out that the portion of the plan asking for voluntary subscriptions might alienate some supporters.

When Pitt gave notice on March 6 of introducing a bill to augment the militia, he apparently was undecided whether to suggest that general subscriptions be used to support his plan. For while he explained the various parts of what was to be the bill, and the defensive purposes it was to serve, he said nothing about voluntary subscriptions. It was too late. Nicholas Vansittart, a member of the opposition, found out about the Berkshire meeting and called the attention of Parliament to the subscription raised there.[5] Because this did not as yet reflect official actions, Vansittart's observations did not lead to further debate, although it alerted some Parliamentarians. It was not until March 14 that Pitt sent a circular to the lord lieutenants containing his plan and his suggestion that general subscriptions be opened. When the Militia Bill was presented to the Commons on March 17, therefore, an immediate storm broke over whether or not "Voluntary aids for Public Purposes without the Consent of Parliament" were legal or constitutional.[6] This proved to be a vulnerable point of Pitt's plan. For if he was calling upon the loyalists, those most dedicated to preservation of the constitution, to come to the aid of that constitution by unconstitutional means, their support of the measure, and indeed of his government, could be threatened. Some loyalists had

already enrolled themselves in volunteer units, and undoubtedly plans to raise subscriptions had been made.
Aside from Captain Fremenheere's Penzance Volunteers, which had been formed on April 11, 1793, the first
of the new units, a volunteer infantry company, was
organized in Westminster at St. George's, Hanover Square.
Lieutenant Whitburn and Ensign Bellamy were commis-
sioned on March 5, 1794, and remained the commanding
officers of this small unit until it was reorganized into a
battalion of seven companies under the leadership of
Lieutenant Colonel Edward Foster on January 7, 1795.[7]
This new organization could very well have been raised
without a general subscription, avoiding the constitutional
complications discussed in Parliament. In March, while the
Parliamentary debate went on, commissions for three regiments of Fencible cavalry were issued to Charles Villiers,
M.P. for Dartmouth, Thomas Legh in Lancashire, and
Gerard Edwards in Rutland. But these regiments, supported by the militia rates as well as by the individuals involved, are less indicative of the confusion and indecision
of the loyalists than were the decisions reached by meetings called to decide whether or not to open subscriptions.
In March, for instance, four meetings—Warwick, Cornwall,
Somerset, and Dorchester—decided to collect pledges, and
three—Surrey, Essex, and Hertford—put the matter off.[8]
Others did not present the government's plans for raising
volunteers at all. The fate of the volunteers to a large
degree depended on the outcome of the decision reached
by Parliament over their constitutionality.
The Foxites managed to keep the issue unsettled from
March 17 through April 7. Contesting at first the right of
the government to ask Englishmen to contribute money
for public purposes without the consent of Parliament, the
Foxites forced Pitt to lay before the house all papers relative to such requests. The offending passage in the March
14 papers, presented March 26, stated that "it seems also
desirable [that] a general subscription should be opened

. . . for the purpose of assisting . . . the execution of all or any of the . . . measures . . . as circumstances shall appear to require." A royal message was also presented, asking Commons to help prepare the kingdom to resist an impending invasion. Pitt proved his mastery of parliamentary tactics by having Dundas move a response to the king's message promising support in this "just and necessary war." The tactic worked, for Fox and his friends at this time argued more about the justice and necessity of the war than about voluntary subscriptions. The original motion passed, and Pitt was given an additional two days to rally his forces. The Foxites tried again on March 28, introducing a motion that subscriptions, aids, loans, or any financings not approved by Parliament were unconstitutional. After much debate, the motion lost 34-204.[9]

The climax of the political debate on the legality of the use of volunteers and voluntary subscriptions occurred during the second and third readings of the Volunteer Corps Bill on April 1 and 7 respectively. Here the issue joined in public debate was whether or not the constitution was flexible enough to allow public participation in areas formerly the exclusive preserve of the houses of Parliament. Politicians came close to defining the new kind of war they were fighting and, in a sense, uncovered the opportunities and dangers that were presented to the development of the constitution in the face of new pressures.

The Foxite position rested chiefly on the provisions of the Bill of Rights which declare that Parliament has the exclusive right to raise money for public purposes. Indeed, Philip Francis had this provision read as part of his argument.[10] Knowing that this provision had been violated in the past, other speakers insisted that principle, not precedent, should determine the decision on this bill. In this approach, the followers of Fox were champions of the old constitution. In light of the issues involved, they supported the conservative cause.

It was not difficult for Pitt to answer this argument by

citing numerous instances in the eighteenth century when voluntary actions of the kind proposed in the bill had been treated as "salutory [*sic*] practices." His argument, simply stated, was that the conventions of constitutional practices had as much weight as did the letter of certain bills. Had he wished, this would have been sufficient, for many of the Foxite Whigs, including Fox himself, had sanctioned such departures from the Bill of Rights in 1782, and were spending much time attempting to demonstrate that their positions in 1782 and 1794 were consistent.[11] Pitt took this moment, however, to use the national forum to justify not only the pending bill but the entire volunteer movement.

Curwen earlier had criticized the bill as an attempt "to keep up a system of delusion among the people." Responding to this charge, Pitt argued that voluntary activities under Parliamentary sanction "mixed the zeal and warmth of individual will with the power of legal authority," giving them a power surpassing legalities. Moreover, at a time when "the avowed enemies . . . abroad, and the latent enemies who lurk at home in her bosom" were attempting to destroy the constitution, a voluntary outpouring of loyalty would demonstrate that the war was not between the governments of the two nations, but between the nations themselves.[12]

Here finally was Pitt's evaluation of the relationship between the Revolution and the war. Each depended upon the other. If the Revolution based its strength and justification upon the support given it by the French people, the demonstration that the English government derived its strength from the same source should put the lie to the claim that the French should invade England to liberate the English. Here also is a hint that Pitt realized the latent energizing force of the nationalism displayed by the loyalists—that their efforts to support their country far outran anything law and government could do to secure the national safety. Just as Grenville had privately admitted that the salvation of the country in November 1792 depended upon every man doing what he could, Pitt here was publicly and confidently asserting that, given the opportunity, every man "with few, very few exceptions" would do exactly that. The Revolution, the war, the outburst of patriotism, all were manifestations of enthusiasms which, if properly directed, could tap a national strength never used before. Here was Pitt's definition of the new kind of war: it was, in brief, a war between the national identities of the respective combatants, the first of the modern wars prompted and sustained by nationalism.

While Parliamentarians argued and finally settled the legality and constitutionality of the support the government asked from the English people, reports of the impending invasion from France and of possible preparations in England to assist it came into the Home Office. The Earl of Moira summed up his investigations about French preparations on March 22 after he interviewed a Captain Paterson. "His account does not go beyond a confirmation of what we have learned from others: that preparation is making at Havre, both in transports and Troops for some expedition." He guessed that these would be completed about the second week in April and proposed the Isle of Wight as their probable destination. On the same day Dundas received a letter, supposedly from the Earl of Fauconberg, that landing parties from French privateers had landed at Balmborough, about forty miles from Newcastle, had carried off all the cattle they could, and were remaining ashore. "Fauconberg" said that he had 400 men but would not march until the alarm had subsided. Two days later Dundas received a letter supposedly written by the mayor of Newcastle to the same effect. Dundas responded immediately, writing the mayor that ships were on the way and that the privateers would be dealt with. On March 25, however, Dundas learned that the letters were forged and that the whole story was a hoax. While rewards were offered for information about the forgers, the vulnerability of the Home Office to deceptions of this sort in the event of an invasion was vividly revealed.[13] The radicals, if they wished to assist a French invasion, could flood the mails with false reports of landings, confusing the direction of the defense. It was not a pleasant prospect, yet it confirmed the need for additional forces throughout the island to deal with real or imagined French landings as soon as possible. This hoax, however, pointed to the probable role the artisans would play should England be invaded. Should French sympathizers wish to do so, the military establishment in its various unit commands as well as the central directing agency, the Home Office, could be thrown into confusion just at the moment they needed to act with the greatest coordination.

In March, while government was digesting these possibilities and Parliamentarians were still struggling to settle the status of the volunteers, newspapers kept invasion fears alive. The actions of groups of individuals who decided on their own to prepare themselves in the use of arms were printed regularly, and rumors about the intentions of the French to invade, the size of their invasion fleet, and the areas they would likely invade appeared in the papers weekly. After the king's message about the impending invasion was sent to Parliament on March 25 the matter was considered all but settled. England was to be invaded and the only questions left were what to do about it and when it might happen.[14]

On April 4 the *Chelmsford Chronicle* accurately predicted that because of "the legality of private subscriptions . . . being now authorized by the largest majorities ever known in Parliament, we shall very shortly see all principal gentlemen and corporations of towns come forward with their donations in support of their King, their country and their laws, which are threatened to be invaded and overturned." The hiatus in this latest loyalty drive being over, the county meetings, put off until the question was answered, now met, and the subscriptions entered were the largest of their kind since the outbreak of war. The scattered records I have been able to discover of the amounts of money donated to raise volunteers reveal that between April 7 and May 7 at least £93,000 was pledged from seventeen counties, six cities, and two groups of individuals. Twelve counties alone collected £61,573.[15] If this was a representative showing and if all counties fared as well, over £150,000 was pledged at county meetings alone. For the most part this sum represented the opening pledges, that is, the amounts pledged at the original meetings. At most of the county meetings committees were appointed to open books for subscriptions at various locations throughout the county so that everyone would have a chance to subscribe. Thousands more did just that, and the amount donated to this cause grew in the months to follow.

There were four types of meetings used to obtain the funds necessary to answer the government's call. The largest was the county meeting, called by the lord lieutenant and attended by the principal landholders, merchants, and professional men in the county. The second was the city or town meeting, convened by the mayor or boroughreeve upon application from private citizens or upon the authority of the official himself. The third was the spontaneous gathing of private individuals pledging amounts of from £200 to £3,000. The fourth and last was, regrettably, the most difficult to discover. This was the meeting of an established loyal society which voted voluntarily to convert itself into a volunteer company. In many of these instances the associators did not appeal to the public for funding but merely subscribed the necessary amounts out of their own pockets. This occurred at Exeter in March and later at Sheffield, Manchester, and New Malton. These are noticeable only because of special circumstances: the novelty of Exeter, for instance, and the plea of financial difficulties at New Malton, the loyalists apologetically confessing, because of the growth of their unit, their inability to bear the costs alone.[16] While it would be impossible to discover the numbers of loyal associations which adopted this form of volunteering, it would be safe to state that it was greater than the numbers mentioned above.

The number of towns, cities, and counties opening subscriptions is equally undiscoverable. Judging by the units actually raised later and by reports of county, city, and town meetings in the newspapers, subscriptions were opened to form at least 136 military units of varying sizes. These consisted of 8 regiments of Fencible cavalry, 4 county infantry units, 28 county organizations of gentlemen and yeomanry, and 96 units, of varying sizes, of cavalry and infantry from cities and towns all over England.[17] How many additional men or companies were added to the existing militia through the committees formed to spend the pledged amounts of these subscriptions is impossible to calculate. But at a stroke and at very little cost the anti-revolutionary and defense forces of England were increased by thousands of men.

The chief subscribers were the aristocracy and gentry. In meetings called by the lord lieutenants, aristocratic subscriptions ranged from £1,000 by Earl Fitzwilliam in the West Riding to £100 by the Earl of Suffolk at the Wiltshire meeting. Knights and gentlemen pledged from £300 to £50. Sums ranging from one shilling to £1,000, however, were promised by people in all other ranks of society. County subscriptions generally raised the larger sums of money; the West Riding reached £16,000 in August from 412 subscribers. But the largest group of subscribers was at the Wiltshire meeting, where 2,531 people subscribed over £15,000. There were multiple subscribers who attended several meetings and contributed to each. Henry Addington, for instance, pledged £100 at the Wiltshire meeting and another £100 at the Devon. William Wilberforce gave £100 each to the three Yorkshire Ridings meetings. Others carefully noted that, while they had subscribed elsewhere, they were willing to subscribe again. While this sample of subscriptions is totally inadequate to estimate accurately the number of subscribers, at the

least 25,000 people donated money to this effort.[18]
The use made of the money collected varied from
county to county. The Essex subscribers, for instance, resolved to raise twenty additional men for each company of
the two battalions of Essex militia. In all Essex before
1796, Waltham Abbey raised an additional company of
volunteer infantry and Montague Burgoyne raised four
troops of cavalry. The East Riding committee used their
funds to restore Bridlington Fort as well as to raise a
company to man it before planning to raise infantry companies throughout the towns in the Riding. The Devon-
shire committee spent its money on coastal defense before
raising cavalry corps, although town meetings raised additional units. Inland counties usually tended to raise only
cavalry corps to serve only in the county, while coastal
counties generally divided their efforts between raising
infantry and artillery companies to guard the coasts and
bodies of cavalry to preserve internal peace as well as to
harass foragers of an invading army. The Sussex volunteers
attempted everything. Not only were cavalry units formed
in each rape and artillery units in six coastal cities, and
additional men raised for the militia, but a Fencible corps
of cavalry and a troop of horse artillery were also
planned.[19] Given the latitude of possibilities offered in
government's original call to act, it is not surprising that
such a variety of responses was received.

Not all agreed, however, that volunteers were necessary.
At least seven county meetings were contested on various
grounds. Fox and Sir Joseph Mawbey, who had opposed
the Surrey Address in June 1792 and the association in
December 1792, opposed the opening of the Surrey subscription. The Earl of Thanet and Lord Guildford opposed
the Kent subscription; Viscount Maynard and Lord Petre,
the Essex; a Mr. Blunt, the Sussex; and Christopher Wyvill,
the North Allerton. It is obvious from this partial list that
those who opposed the intentions of the meetings had
some standing in their communities. In the North Riding,
for instance, the assembled gentlemen, after voting their

loyalty to the king, negatived the motion to open a general subscription on the ground that all supplies for public services had to be voted by Parliament. In addition, there seems to have been a bit of confusion about the decision reached by the London Common Council. The *Chelmsford Chronicle* reported that the motion to open a subscription failed, the *York Courant* that it passed, and the *Sussex Weekly Advertiser* that it was evenly divided.[20]

The chief difficulty faced by the loyalists, especially after August, was finding men to volunteer to serve, and the most extreme example I have discovered of this difficulty was in Worcester. At the county meeting held there on April 29, the assembled gentlemen, yeomen, and principal inhabitants decided to open a subscription for internal defense. No decision as to the use of the money was reached until May 27, when it was decided to raise two volunteer companies to add to the militia. On the same day the city of Worcester opened a subscription for volunteers. While the total of amounts pledged grew through June, the members of the committee seemed to lose interest. The chairman could never hold a meeting because he could not obtain a quorum. In July the militia companies were finally raised but the subscriptions continued to roll in. By August these amounted to £5,392, and in consequence the committee decided to raise two troops of cavalry, fifty-six men per troop, with John Somers Cocks volunteering to lead them. The committee placed an ad in the *Berrow's Worcester Journal* calling for volunteers. After three weeks Somers Cocks placed his own ad in the *Journal,* in which he pleaded with readers to come to the colors, reminding them that "I have done my part—I call upon you to do yours." Two weeks later the mayor of Worcester, probably meeting the same difficulties as the county in raising men, suggested that a meeting be called to decide whether or not the city subscriptions should be given to the county. On October 2 a new advertisement was printed by the county committee urging all gentlemen and yeomen to urge their tenants to volunteer. Somers

Cocks's ad and the original county ad, of course, still were running.

In the meantime the city meeting was held and decided to join its funds with those of the county as long as a sufficient number of men would be made available for the internal defense of the city. This was probably a face-saving gambit, as it appeared there would be no men at all. The city subscriptions only totalled £688, while the county total was by then nearly £6,000. Through October the three advertisements continued to run with variations; on alternating weeks one of them would be left out. On October 30 the *Journal* reported that Somers Cocks finally had raised one troop and had them riding about the countryside.[21] For six months, as the subscriptions grew to nearly £7,000 and as numerous advertisements ran in the newspapers, the County of Worcester raised only fifty-six volunteers plus the two companies of volunteer militiamen.

This lukewarm, almost tepid, response to the call for volunteers is partially explainable by the relative isolation of Worcester from any immediate danger. Also because there were no radical clubs in the area there was little apprehension of subversion. The major explanation lies in the late call for volunteers made by the Worcester committee. By August the sinister equation—radical English artisans plus radical and successful French equals danger—had changed. Robespierre had fallen and the radicalism of the Revolution appeared to have ended. As we shall see, this was a major event in the ideological war and would have many implications for the loyal movement. The experiences of the Worcester volunteers, although extreme, illustrate some of the difficulties faced by the loyalists in 1794.

Throughout this hesitancy, confusion, and disorganization, however, it is still possible to trace the loyalists of 1792 once again volunteering their services to the nation when called upon. To be sure, exact correlations between the memberships of the two movements are difficult to pin down because of inadequate records. Of the two hundred-odd loyal associations in the Reeves papers and the few others I have found in local newspapers, less than half list the names of their committees, which might be compared with the lists of officers of the volunteer units. Moreover, a different organizational scheme was followed; where the loyalists in 1792 formed their associations according to the usual governmental divisions of the country—parishes, towns, hundreds, divisions, etc.—the volunteers formed theirs only in towns, cities, and counties. A further impediment to discovering common membership in both movements is the different sorts of services each performed. Debating, discussing, printing loyal tracts, and signing declarations of loyalty were activities possible for a greater number of people than were marching, riding, and operating heavy artillery on the coasts. At that, many loyal associations continued to meet and perform their services in their original character, and while they undoubtedly encouraged, helped finance, and supported the military units, their involvement in them cannot be traced.

In spite of these difficulties, a surprisingly large percentage of the military units had direct connections with the loyal associations. Of the 136 units listed by the War Office, 72 were in areas where I have no information of loyal clubs, and they may or may not have had common memberships. Ten units were in association areas, yet the associations' correspondence with Reeves or their advertisements in the local newspapers did not list their members' names. Of the remaining 54 military units, 41, or about 75 percent, had former members of the loyal associations as officers. It is relatively safe to assume that this percentage held true for the other units, so that at least 103 of the 136 military volunteer units were officered in part or in full by former association members. While there were undoubtedly many reasons why individuals joined the volunteers—simple patriotism, a desire to win social approval, perhaps even a desire to avoid service in the militia or to remain close to home and hearth—the inclusion of so many ex-associators gives the movement an ideological tone which justifies the definition of the volunteers as loyalists who, as the Birmingham volunteers put it, had "quit the Field of Argument for that of Arms."[22]

While the volunteers were busily, or tardily, organizing themselves, one can discern by the rate of formation of corps a hint of the growing anxiety in loyalists' minds about the growth of dangers to England domestically. There was a considerable time lag between the convening of the meetings to raise volunteers and the time when the units were fully manned. Because the government was attempting to raise additional men for the regular services at the same time, the manpower resources of England were severely strained. An indication of the growth of the volunteer corps as a whole, however, can be gleaned from the dates of the officers' commissions. These were generally applied for after it was reasonably certain that men and money were available for the proposed units, sometimes as much as a month after the subscription meeting. At that, these dates do not indicate when the volunteer unit was ready for service even if the men were instantly enrolled. With training periods of one or two days a week, considerable time passed before the volunteer units could be labeled "effective." The dates of the officers' commissions, therefore, should give us some insight into the urgency felt by members of a district one month or so earlier and the relative security bought by their practice some months later.

Using this measure, the months of deepest concern about internal and external dangers can be roughly gauged. By May 31 commissions had been issued for thirteen yeomanry cavalry units and thirty-eight infantry units. Thereafter the figures were ten yeomanry and twenty-two infantry units in June, nine and sixteen in July, five and twelve in August, five and seven in September, and only two and sixteen in the next four months. From January 1 to March 18, 1795, government issued commissions for only four yeomanry and eight infantry units.[23] This would mark the months of April through July as the months when loyalists felt the greatest need for military exertions against their domestic enemies, or the months of deepest concern about invasion. The activities of the loyalists in preparing themselves for the worst are indicative of the anxiety and concern felt in other sectors of society about the dangers facing England. Looking back later, Sir John Coleman Rasleigh noted that of all the war years, 1794 was the most crucial. Many individuals, like the loyalists, acted upon the same conclusion. The Portland and Windham Whigs, after almost two years of acting "in concert but not in conjunction" with government, now united with Pitt and his followers in a coalition ministry. The Duke of Portland was given the Home Office, William Windham the secretaryship at war, and Lord Fitzwilliam was elevated to the lord presidency. The principal politicians of England forgot old animosities and created the strongest government possible.[24] The formation of loyal volunteers outside government and the uniting of the major groupings in Parliament are of a kind. Each group indicated by actions its confusion, apprehensions, and fears about the growing complexity of foreign affairs and their relationship to domestic developments.

The domestic and international scenes were clouded and confusing. Allied defeats and victories, the growing radicalism in Paris, with its echo in England, the increased tempo of rioting, in some cases caused by the very anti-riot forces the government had called upon Englishmen to form, and finally the old bugbear of invasion coalesced into a contradictory and bewildering picture of threats to national security. Englishmen of all ranks attempted to interpret the situations, and, when they acted upon their conclusions, further increased the confounding nature of the evidence. The period between April and August 1794 was truly the time when circumstances seemed out of control.

The victories and defeats of the allies, for instance, seemed to happen simultaneously. The campaign began in

April and the newspapers were soon filled with victory reports from the Duke of York. Yet the victories were in reality only successes in repulsing an attacking enemy. The invasion of France or the containment of the revolution within French borders now were rarely spoken of. Indeed, the invading allied army now was converted to a defense force for protecting the Austrian Netherlands. By May admissions of British and allied defeats became commonplace. In June the French navy and privateers were so steadily taking English vessels that Lloyds reported rate increases of 20 percent and losses of over £400,000. The next week the *Sussex Weekly Advertiser* charged that the admiralty in the last six months had condemned only ten French vessels while the underwriters at Lloyds had lost another half million in sterling. For a moment it appeared that the English were losing control of the sea. Then the news of Howe's victory on June 1 arrived, and for the next few weeks Englishmen seemed obsessed with celebrating it. After the euphoria lifted, however, the war news was of continued allied defeats. Finally on July 21 the *York Courant* admitted defeat but blamed it on the allies' lack of determination. "Had all our Allies fought with the same zeal and spirit in the cause as the Duke of York and his British troops, . . . this retreat would have been prevented."[25] Once again, the revitalization of the revolution had resulted in a similar revitalization of French arms. This time, however, that revitalization appeared to be caused by new forces.

The radicalization of the Revolution in August and September 1792 had been evaluated as the result of the pressure of Brunswick's invasion and the panic and dismay of French leaders. This new wave of radical and extreme measures in France seemed to feed on successes. On April 21 the execution of Danton and his associates was duly reported in England with little comment. This event was seen as the result of a power struggle, something distasteful but understandable. On June 16, during the celebrations of Howe's victories, the directive of the French leaders to the armies that no British or Hanoverian prisoners should be taken was printed with no possible explanation other than barbaric reprisal. The arrests of thousands of people and the body counts of those executed filled the news sheets from June through July, with varying estimates of the numbers of people meeting death daily in French cities. The Revolution had created the perfect monster, one which needed no justification to continue its orgy of executions. On August 11, after the allied defeat was certain, the *York Courant* printed the plans of the French: to conclude peace with Spain, to continue the war with the greatest vigor possible against the Emperor, "and to try every means of corruption against England."[26] The "peaceful" war of 1793 was over and the English now found themselves at war with the new barbarians of Europe.

What was even more alarming to English leaders was the responsive echo in England to these extraordinary happenings in France. The growth and increased activities of the English radicals matched those of the French. Thelwall proposed the calling of a Convention on English soil, a proposal which awakened inactive societies all over England. An open-air radical meeting at Chalk Farm was attended by thousands, while a similar meeting was held at Sheffield, where an estimated 12,000 attended.[27] Not waiting for an organization to be formed which could coordinate radical activities in aid of a French invasion and serve as a provisional government should the invasion succeed, the government on May 12 began rounding up the leaders of the radical movement. The Habeas Corpus Act as it related to treason and sedition was suspended for six months. This quick action was successful in frightening some clubs out of existence, but, as could be expected, in other cases it only stimulated radical activities and indeed converted reform groups into groups dedicated to overthrowing the government.[28]

As tensions mounted in May, and as the Secret Committee in the House of Commons examined papers seized from the London Corresponding Society, newspapers once again were full of rumors and plots. The *York Courant* reported that the letters of a Mr. Rowan had revealed a plot in which 35,000 French soldiers would be landed in the north of England, where "75,000 defenders and others" would join them. The *Sussex Weekly Advertiser* hinted that the London Corresponding Society had 18,000 persons in London who were pledged to their support. The *Chelmsford Chronicle,* however, remained calm. On May 16, after printing news of the apprehension of William Stone, the brother of an Englishman in Paris, the editor thanked the government for putting the law into operation against "all the traitors, who fostered in the bosom of Great Britain, are industrious in destroying the vitals of her constitution." The law should determine guilt or innocence away from the popular outcry. Indeed, the editor reported his intention "not to prejudge any" and hoped that those arrested were indeed "firm friends" to England as they claimed, but the place to discover this was in the courts.[29] Newspapermen had no doubts that there were traitors in England. By printing rumors or notices that these internal enemies should be dealt with rationally, they undoubtedly convinced many readers that there were more traitors than there actually were and helped to sensitize the English public to activities they might not have noticed or might not have regarded as important before.

The Chalk Farm meeting speakers had hinted that the disaffected should arm themselves, and Englishmen discovered that many people indeed possessed arms. Lord Salisbury informed Nepean that people in "Hartford" who possessed weapons were evasive in answering questions as to their possible use. John Griffith in Manchester reported to Dundas that a case load of arms was deposited at "Mr. Walker's" home at Pithington near Manchester. "H.B." discovered casks of bullets at Yarmouth, and John White warned the Home Office about the manufacture of daggers at Sheffield. This latter was so generally known that "many of the most respectable inhabitants here are now learning their Military Exercises."[30] These people, incidentally, finally formed themselves into the Loyal Sheffield Volunteers. Much of this information was obviously incorrect or based upon misunderstandings. When the government later attempted to prove Hardy, Thelwall, and Tooke, of the London Corresponding Society and the Society for Constitutional Information, guilty of gathering arms, none of the information was used.[31] The situation does, however, point out the growing sensitivity of the English generally to any possibility of subversive activities. By July 11 even the cautious editor of the *Chelmsford Chronicle* noted that "since the late success of the French in Flanders, the spirit of republicanism has again jumped forth in this Kingdom."[32] This increasing propensity to leap to conclusions can be traced in the growing inclination of Englishmen to take physical action upon a moment's notice. From April through August, riots broke out all over England for reasons which seem, from this distance, less and less important.

At Manchester on April 21, one week after the Chalk Farm meeting in London, reformers attempting to hold their own meeting were attacked by loyalists and dispersed. Apparently two "recruits" had attempted to stop the meeting themselves but had been attacked by the "reformers" and "cut and abused." The local magistrate called for troops, but the loyalists had captured the leaders of the reformers before the troops arrived.[33] This almost resembled a full-scale battle. Presumably the loyalists mentioned here were not armed. While the first blood had been shed in the loyalist-radical struggle, no deaths were reported. The ideological war was turning into something quite different from what it had been.

It was in June, however, when things seemed to get out of hand. A Mr. Wells from Exeter notified Dundas on June 4 that violence at a riotous meeting of reformers was prevented only by the presence of troops. He said that the Exeter volunteers were not trained, but once they were they "would help keep these Fellows in order as well as the mad Democrats who are endeavouring every thing in their Power in an underhanded manner (not doing it openly) to create a Mob and confusion [in] any way." Two days later Nathaniel Bland, the magistrate at Bentford, notified the Home Office that rioting there was so dangerous that he was "obliged to make my Escape to Town." Rioting then broke out in London.[34] At Nottingham on July 10, it was the loyalists who rioted. There they seized "several people" (reformers) and threw them in the River Leen, where they dunked and beat them. At that the whole town got out of control. The reformers counterattacked and were counterattacked in turn. The reformers took refuge in a mill and, having artillery pieces available, fired on the loyalists, wounding a soldier. Undeterred, the loyalists attacked the mill and almost had it on fire when troops arrived to break up the battle.[35] The domestic situation was clearly getting out of hand.

The most senseless of all the rioting took place at Rochester. This disturbance began on July 29 in a theater "in consequence of some persons not taking off their hats when the tune of 'God Save the King' was played." Several officers of the Irish Artillery were present and, in the jostling and confusion, drew their swords and wounded a man. Two of the officers were taken into custody and one was put in prison. The next evening the whole company of artillery, with their field guns, assembled before the prison and demanded his release. The people of Rochester collected to assist the magistrate, but the artillerymen fired their weapons, dispersing the crowd. The officer was released but "refused to quit the gaol."[36] Fortunately no one was injured, but this propensity to violence, this sensitivity to imagined or trivial insults to the national pride, had an inherent potential to turn the previously humane English ideological war into a French-style bloodbath. For, as the example of the Irish Artillery officers demonstrates, many Englishmen now were armed and willing to use their weapons to settle arguments.

As early as June 5 reports arrived in the Home Office

indicating that the civilian population and military personnel were not on the best of terms. Lord Viscount Bateman, when attempting to parade the Hertfordshire militia through Lewes on May 21, found that some hostility was felt toward his regiment, which was "treated by the Mob in the most insolent manner." Whether this was because of the actions of his soldiers or because of general sentiments about the war Bateman did not indicate.[37] By July, when feelings ran high, the Rutland Fencibles, stationed in Lincoln, provoked a riot. For weeks the Fencibles had been patrolling the streets at night with drawn sabres and had conducted searches for weapons in various townsmen's homes. The incident which touched off the rioting was the exasperated exclamation of Henry Mitchell, a blacksmith, who in an argument cried, "Damnation Seize the King." The Fencibles then seized Mitchell, townsmen attempted to prevent them, and the resulting melee spilled into the streets. Colonel Gerard N. Edwards, the commander of the Fencibles, imposed martial law, but the civil magistrates overrode his decision and restored order.[38] The force stationed in Lincoln to preserve order, by overzealously pursuing that end, had achieved exactly the opposite result.

There were undoubtedly many more clashes of this sort than those reported to the Home Office, including those in which drunken soldiers carved townsmen with their swords or chased them off the streets with bayonets.[39] But they all pointed to the same conclusion—that affairs were approaching some sort of climax in which the results would be bloody. Too many people in England were convinced that internal enemies would aid the diabolical French to land and conquer England, and too many radicals had reached the same conclusions for action to be avoided. Williams explains the arrest of Hardy, Tooke, et al. as a result of a psychosis that affected both the government and the insurrectionists in May.[40] That psychosis was evident outside London through the months of June, July, and early August.

By mid-August a barely perceptible change in public apprehensions was revealed when Londoners rioted for three days (August 19-21) in the vicinities of recruiting houses. Newspapers reported a "spilling over" process, in which the rioters, if thwarted by the military in one location, merely moved to the next and continued their activities. Magistrates reported riots in Shoreditch, Cock Lane, Spitalfields, Rosemary Lane, Wapping, and Charing Cross. W. Colquhoun, a magistrate in Shoreditch, called upon the volunteers being organized in Hackney and the Tower Hamlets, but learned that they were not yet ready to help. Other military units, both regular and volunteer, assisted magistrates and the lord mayor in dispersing some rioters.[41] If the hair-trigger tempers that had caused so much trouble in July needed an excuse to relieve their tensions, these riots, directly affecting the war effort and concentrated in the metropolis, offered an ideal opportunity. Surprisingly, little violence was reported.

Government, of course, made an effort to discover the nature of the riots, their leaders, and whether they were coordinated by any agencies. Colquhoun was convinced that the leaders of the "Seditious Societies" had provoked the riots as a move in a larger plot. C.T. Kirby, the magistrate in Charing Cross, sent the government a handbill which certainly indicated some preparation for the riots:[42]

> Charing Cross, 19 August, '94
>
> Brother Citizens,
>
> Take no heed of Vermin Lifeguards nor any [of] the Slaves of Swine—Let us be avenged of the Murderers! Strike! Give no Quarter, Go on! Lose no Time. In the Lord is all our Trust
>
> Sympathy, Fraternity
> Citizen C

At any time since November or December of 1792, such reports would have been enough to cause the deepest alarm and, in the excited atmosphere of the previous months, to make the loyalists produce counter-riots. Instead, the opposite happened. The lord mayor, calling for extra troops to maintain the peace in his city, worked tirelessly to avoid bloodshed. Instead of rounding up a list of suspects suggested to him by Portland, the new home secretary, he began an investigation into the evils of the crimp shops and took steps to end the practice of crimping altogether. The *Sussex Weekly Advertiser* railed against this abusive method of recruiting and printed columns of testimony about the hardships it produced for individual families. William Devaynes, Reeves's successor at the APLP, advised the Home Office that the mobs "should be dispersed without Military Interference," for should someone be hurt, the subversives would make this into an added grievance against the forces for order. As alternatives, he suggested that handbills be distributed to the rioters and that magistrates be ordered to reason with the mobs before rioting broke out. Acting upon his own suggestions, he called the APLP together and led them in "parading" in the riot areas, actually preventing one riot by this method.[43] This was not the hysterical response one would have expected given the visible evidences of tension displayed round the country in July.

E.P. Thompson has noted the change of attitude in the English public in the autumn of 1794. He attributes this to the wearing off of the shock caused by the arrests of Hardy, Tooke, and the other radicals in May.[44] Those whose attitudes changed, however, were the loyalists and patriots, individuals who were not visibly shocked by the arrests in the first place. It is more likely that the implications of two events finally affected these people, and their hostility toward the domestic radicals was modified as a consequence. Howe's victory on June 1, it was gradually realized, at least delayed the possibility of an invasion. Robespierre's fall, on the other hand, changed the nature of the ideological war altogether.

Howe's victory was not known in England until June 9. In the first reports newspapers described universal celebrations in all parts of the country. For a few weeks the newspaper columns were taken up with the exploits of various individuals during the struggle and the lists of those killed and wounded. The newspapers also printed the French reception of the news, noting their version—that while Howe had scored a tactical victory, he had suffered a strategic defeat, for the grain ships Admiral Joyeuse was escorting arrived safely in France. A tactical victory, however, was good enough to revive English morale, which had taken a severe beating from the success of the French in capturing English prizes. The *York Courant* confidently predicted that this defeat would take years for the French to overcome. The *Chelmsford Chronicle* equated the enthusiasm for subscribing for internal defense with the vigor of the celebrations.[45] In the first instance, the satisfaction of the victory enhanced the other loyal exertions taking place in England.

It was in the latter part of June that the deeper implications of this sea encounter began to be realized. The *York Courant* speculated that it might have cut off any intentions the French may have had of invading England. The editor did not comment on the effect this might have upon the motivation to form volunteer units. Acts of gratitude to the victors, however, still occupied the most space in the newspaper. Subscriptions were opened at various cities and towns for the widows and orphans of the sailors killed in the engagement.[46] These grew to such an extent that the phenomenon captured the attention of the editors. On July 11 the *Chelmsford Chronicle*, after noting how much money had been pledged to various causes since the start of the war, noted: "The numerous and liberal donations made by individuals in this country during the present war will be an eternal monument of British liberality. We do not recollect, in the history of any former war, to have had such immense sums subscribed for different public purposes, as during the year and half of the present one. It is the most certain and substantial proof of the willingness of all ranks of people to support the government cf the country in the measures they have pursued."[47] The euphoria of the first naval victory of the war colored all other patriotic activities of Englishmen and lasted for over a month.

The newspapermen, however, could not ignore the news of military disasters on the continent in July, and in struggling to interpret their ultimate consequences for England, finally realized the effects of events in the various theaters of war. On July 24 the *Chelmsford Chronicle* concluded that the English public, in not reacting strongly to continental affairs, showed "good sense." The editor realized that ultimately a defeat on the Continent might work to England's disadvantage, but that superiority at sea would ensure England's victory in the war.[48] And this was the heart of the matter. Whether Howe scored a tactical or a strategic victory, the probability of invasion had been considerably lessened, possibly to the status of 1793. Military defeats on the Continent could not alter that conclusion. Suicide landings, the old bugaboo of 1793, were still possible, but English naval superiority meant that conquest was unlikely. Part of the driving necessity for volunteering to raise or serve in paramilitary units was dissipated.

Patriots and loyalists alike could draw comfort from the ultimate effects of Howe's victory, but the fall of Robespierre affected the very nature of the French Revolution, and in a direct sense, the *raison d'être* of the loyalists, for, whatever the English described that individual to be, the mystique, the power, and the threat of the Revolution had been intimately tied to him. For almost a year, as the French had solved the problems of indiscipline and anarchy which the English assumed were concomitants of the principles of the Revolution, and as they had managed to surmount impossible obstacles, Robespierre had appeared to be the individual responsible. By throwing off the restraints, inhibitions, and conventions which characterized the civilization of Europe, Robespierre had tapped a reservoir of energy, vitality, and resourcefulness that made the Revolution the threat that it was. Whatever deep, mysterious forces in human nature had been unleashed by the Revolution, whatever power existed in freedom and equality, Robespierre above all other French leaders had been attuned to them and had been their personification and embodiment. His fall meant more than the defeat of a faction in French politics, it signified a turning point in the process of the Revolution itself. As the radicalism of the Revolution fluctuated, so would the activities and enthusiasm of those supporting it in England. Finally, because the loyalists, the third link in this chain of causal sequences, were prompted by the second, their reason for being would fluctuate also.

The impact of Robespierre's fall upon the direction the Revolution would take was not quickly understood. The *Chelmsford Chronicle, York Courant,* and *Sussex Weekly Advertiser* reported that event between August 18 and August 22. The *Chronicle* hoped that it might lead the French to seek peace, but admitted its inability to predict the consequences. The *York Courant* was even more noncommittal, admitting that even the news it received of the French response was contradictory, one of its correspondents reporting that fifteen to eighteen thousand people had been massacred, a second that nothing was changed, and a third that there was universal rejoicing. The *Advertiser* was pessimistic about the consequences of Robespierre's fall. Noting that the guillotine was still operating at the same rate as before, the editor assumed that the French leader's demise meant nothing.[49]

From August through December English observers attempted to derive the new policies of France from the actions of the executive committees set up after Robespierre's death. As early as August 26 Grenville noted the weakening of the executive's effectiveness by the substitution of "twelve Committees, who are to be chosen with a sort of rotation, those who go out not being re-eligible" in place of a "Committee of six or eight efficient persons." He concluded that this would be "a substitution of the weakest possible form of Executive Government in lieu of the strongest." Newspapermen agreed, noting how the "destructive vigour" of the military commanders had evaporated with Robespierre's removal. The *Chelmsford Chronicle* summed it up best. Acknowledging that Robespierre had been a "monster" with Cromwellian ambitions, the editor concluded, "but that French affairs went on well during his despotism is equally certain, and it is an acknowledged truth that ever since they have been at a stand."[50] It appeared that some of the driving dynamism of the Revolution had been lost, and as a result France was not as formidable a foe as she had been.

The new French policy of moderation was the most significant result pertinent to the thesis of this book. As newspapermen and government officials attempted to discover the new policies of the republic, their one area of certainty was that the extremism of the Revolution was over. To be sure, France was still the enemy, but the degree of danger posed by the Revolution seemed considerably lessened. The *Chelmsford Chronicle,* for instance, commented that "the disavowal in the jacobine club, of that part of their doctrine which tends to the extending the blessings of their freedom to other nations, affords one trait of returning reason."[51] If the *Chronicle* had been correct, this would have been the end of the universal revolution, so much a cause of the belligerency of the two nations in the first place. It would have meant the conversion of the ideological war itself into an old-fashioned war—one which could result in defeat without annihilation. These were but conjectures, unproved and perhaps, even if valid, only temporary. The French could easily reverse their new policies with a change of ministers. In the meantime, the ideological danger was at least temporarily over and the rising hysteria of May, June, and July now had no foundation. Indeed, if France was no longer the supporter of revolution in other countries, there was no longer any reason for distinctions between loyalists and patriots. The war had to be fought, but the dangers of French-connected internal subversion were over. The discovery of these consequences would take time, but there was one important matter left over from the months of danger that had to be resolved. Those people indicted for treason in May had to be tried.

The adversaries in the treason trials of 1794 were in a curious position. Government had already achieved its primary object, preventing the leaders of the radicals from convening a British convention when the fears of invasion were at their height. Now, when the international situation appeared to be returning to relative understandability, the ministry faced the dilemma of justifying its indictments after the psychological moment had passed. Moreover, these politicians had already demonstrated in Paine's case that they were aware of the dangers of creating martyrs, so that their feelings about the desirability of convictions must surely have been mixed. In all likelihood London juries would have convicted the accused had the trials been held earlier, if their records in 1792-93 were any guide, but the chances of succeeding after Robespierre's fall were very dim in any case. Still, the thing had to be done. A similar dilemma faced the accused.

Hardy, Tooke, Thelwall, and the other defendants could have won by losing. Their whole justification for desiring change was that the present constitution was corrupt, inequitable, and a tyranny. Their conviction would have proven their assertions. Here was their supreme moment, their time on the national stage, where they could demonstrate dramatically to all Englishmen that change was necessary and that principles were more important than personal safety. Like the Protestant martyrs facing Mary Tudor, or William Prynne and John Hampden under Charles I, they could have lit a torch under the radical movement that would have made it independent of foreign influences. All that was necessary was an admission, or an invention if necessary, that they were preparing to overthrow the state by any means possible. Unfortunately for the radical movement, they chose to shelter themselves under the constitutional liberties they claimed they did not have. By doing so, they won the battle but lost the war. The trials were closely followed by the provincial and London papers. After Hardy's verdict of not guilty was reported, congratulations were given the system, not the defendant. As the *York Courant* put it: "What a fine contrast do the late Criminal Proceedings at the Old Bailey furnish to those of the Revolutionary Tribunal of France! The most solemn Criminal Court in the World has been occupied for eight days upon one Trial,—a space in which the Revolutionary Judges would have condemned, perhaps, as many hundreds." The *Sussex Weekly Advertiser* congratulated the system also. "The honest jury of Thomas Hardy has shewn to mankind that it would not be easy to make Englishmen forget the principles in which they were bred, nor surrender the security to which they were born." In *Rex* vs. *Hardy,* vs. *Tooke,* and vs. *Thelwall,* the constitution was the victor. The Londoners assembled outside Old Bailey may have realized this. Not only did they detach the horses from and pull the coaches of Hardy and his defender, Thomas Erskine, but they gave similar treatment to the lord mayor of London, who had assembled 200 special constables and the Temple Light Horse Volunteers to keep the peace.[52]

The anticlimactic nature of the treason trials and the Thermadorian Reaction in France marked the end of the radical threat in England, and indeed the end of the radical movement itself. Hardy and Tooke withdrew from the movement, the London Corresponding Society split into factions with different goals, and membership declined. Without the promise of France to aid them in their ambitions there was little hope for success or reason to continue. The diehards of the movement would continue their efforts for some years,[53] but as an organized movement they no longer threatened the constitution. For, regardless of whether or not their French connection persisted, the goals of the French had apparently changed. The artisans might be a danger to the state in the event of an invasion, as would an army of French agents, but the possibility of their convincing a large portion of the English population to overthrow the constitution was now past.

With the ending of the radical and revolutionary threat, part of the *raison d'être* of the loyal volunteers ended also. Securing the internal defense of the country as well as providing an auxilliary force in the event of invasion remained the goals of the volunteers, but the threat to the internal defense was not ideological. In 1795, when food riots broke out all over the country, the volunteers proved themselves to be excellent constabulary, containing and ending most riots quickly. They did not confront their ideological enemies, however, for these had all but disappeared. With relative ease Pitt passed the Two Acts at the end of the year which capped the demise of the radical movement and ended the reason to be a loyalist. The volunteer force continued for the remainder of the wars with France, and indeed, after a revival in 1846, for the rest of the nineteenth century. The role of the loyalists in their activities, however, ended. Now all were patriots, as there was no longer any reason to be loyalists.

Pitt knew quite well that the loyalist-radical conflict had ended. At the end of 1795, during the debates on the Two Acts, the Foxite Whigs again resorted to their earlier tactics of trying to delay legislation by charging that a pamphlet written by John Reeves, who was attempting to begin another loyal association movement, was a seditious libel on the constitution. Pitt could easily have quashed their motion. Instead he supported it, much to the discomfiture of the Foxites. Reeves was tried for seditious libel and of course acquitted.[54] Pitt's message was quite clear. There was no need for, and indeed a danger in, another loyal association movement because there were no longer any internal enemies to be fought by that method. Armed with the Two Acts, specifically designed to prevent the activities of radical clubs and clarify the laws on treason, the government could now protect the constitution, should it be necessary, through the normal processes of law. The laws, incidentally, were never used.

This last appearance of the loyalists was the strongest of all. Never easily defined or easily used against the groups which had called them into being, they formed the nucleus of a broader movement that was to persist throughout the French wars and continue until the twentieth century. It is probable that their gradual merging into the larger patriotic and nationalistic movement that was to sustain Britain for the long years of war passed unnoticed by their most outspoken leaders. Defense of one's country is easily confused with defense of one's constitution, especially in a nation wherein such sentiments are expressed in reference to one's king. Called into being with a dual purpose when the dangers to the society were felt most deeply, the volunteers could easily have not noticed the loss of one of those purposes once the dangers were passed.

Even the effect of the volunteers in lessening those dangers is difficult to state with any certainty. Their existence certainly had to be a factor in any plans radicals may have formed about the possibility of a successful insurrection or revolution, yet, in spite of speeches and brave words in handbills, no one is sure that the radical artisans ever seriously contemplated such a drastic step. One might argue that no plans were made because the loyalists were armed and ready for them, yet the loyalists were not ready and armed until the Revolution took a decided turn toward moderation and the radical artisans became decidedly less radical.

The existence of the loyal volunteers, therefore, can be pointed to only as an example of how far the loyalists were willing to go to defend their king, constitution, and country.

CONCLUSION

Circumstances and events created the loyalists, and circumstances and events ended their movement. In their brief, three-year existence they influenced much that happened in Britain. Their resolute defense of king, constitution, and country at the beginning of the war committed them to an endurance in the struggle which would reduce in importance petty annoyances, war-weariness, or setbacks in the military and diplomatic struggles of the next twenty-odd years that might have detracted from the ultimate goal of victory. English tenacity, and hence ultimate English success, owed much to the fervor and enthusiasm they imparted to the struggle. While it is impossible to state what kind of war would have been fought without the patriotism the loyalists infused into it, their justification of their cause made it possible for Englishmen to oppose the slogans and easy generalizations of their domestic and foreign enemies with a feeling that justice and common sense were on their side.

The career of the loyalists affords us as well an opportunity to reach several conclusions about the England of the last decade of the eighteenth century. For the crisis produced in England by the French Revolution forced Englishmen to reach decisions, and those decisions, and the manner of expressing them, tell us much about the state of political society. Normally the opportunity for political action remains as potential unrealized. It is during times of stress, of emergency, that the possible range of political actions is revealed. This period was such a time, and the actions of the participants in this national debate reveal much about the hidden nature of England's unwritten constitution, and expose the breadth of English liberties at the same time.

From another point of view, however, the motivations of the loyalists and radicals point to a different ingredient in the political life of England that would remain a factor in political decisions of the future, and they illustrate a state of mind which could only lead to an enlargement of the arena of participation in politics. This motivation was patriotism, love of country, a desire to be a part of the life of the state. The victory of the loyalists was largely due to their ultimate success in representing their view as the patriotic one, for at the very beginning of the struggle patriotism was not antithetical to the efforts of the artisans.

Patriots just as easily could have supported the efforts of those wishing to reform or improve the political and social institutions of the state. Excluding Paine and a few of the leaders of the radical movement who were obviously anti-English, Fox and his followers, along with those who supported Hardy, Tooke, and Redhead Yorke could have drawn strength from this patriotic fervor to make their country more virtuous and hence more deserving of being loved. Indeed, an early speech by Richard Price, a leading Dissenter, urged reform from this motive. For if patriotism gave loyalists endurance in attempting to achieve their goals, it also gave radicals the same endurance, even though reform or improvement was only dimly possible. These people, working for the good of their country, were, like the loyalists, conscious of their national identity and willing to volunteer their efforts to the realization of noble goals.

The lines which separated the two or perhaps three groups were defined in the clashes between them before and after the beginning of war. The first, and the less important, was the extent to which the radicals out of doors wished to modify the constitution. Their goals could only be derived or guessed at from the articles of their propaganda, chiefly those stated or hinted at in the writings of Paine. The Parliamentary group noted in the address of the Friends of the People only modifications of certain practices in the constitution. No manifesto or definite program was ever presented by either group. From this uncertainty of aims it is not difficult to see that the line separating the contending groups was a belief in the desirability of altering or maintaining the constitution. To be sure, this was a major question and one that transcended the ordinary operations of politics in England, but it was not an unusual one. Efforts to do just that had been partially successful during the American War and dismal failures after its cessation, with no real cleavages in the body politic resulting. Under normal circumstances, it is not unreasonable to believe that the advocates of change might have been partially satisfied. Given the existing patriotism, valid arguments about the commonality of interests of all Englishmen might have led to a slight measure of Parliamentary reform, continuing that slow evolutionary process by which the constitution of England has been transformed to this day.

From the beginning, however, the French Revolution affected English political decisions. The astonishing upheavals in the most civilized nation in Europe, inaugurated under the auspices of principles deemed inherent in the English constitution, yet manifesting themselves in France in ways repugnant to English sensibilities, captured the attention of all Englishmen who took note of political or constitutional affairs. Two large interpretations of the events of the Revolution emerged: France was either committing constitutional, political, and social suicide, or leaping into a glorious future. Reformers and radicals adopted the latter view, loyalists the former.

Whatever the origins of English radicalism, the inspiration to act, to press on, and to attempt the impossible certainly came from France. Here was living proof that the ideas which had animated the Commonwealthsmen throughout the eighteenth century had power. Equally the Revolution determined the timing and enthusiasm of the formation of artisan clubs—to work toward the realization of those ideas in concrete institutional reforms. The declaration of universal revolution by France on November 19, 1792, capped it all, for now the means by which the New Jerusalem could be built were at hand in the form of victorious French armies. Whether or not the English radicals ever contemplated accepting the French offer, the mere fact that it was made increased their enthusiasm and hope that their goals had a practical means of realization. Willy-nilly, radicalism in England was joined to radicalism in France. This French connection, however, proved fatal to the hopes of reformers and radicals alike. Not only were they supporting an ever-changing phenomenon, totally out of their control, and apparently out of anyone's control in France, but also by their choice they supported internationalism versus nationalism. They vacated the patriotic position and allowed an alliance of the great majority against them. This was the most important line separating the reformers from the patriots.

The chief spokesmen for this patriotic nationalism initially were the loyalists. They had not only to define the threat but also to build a counterargument which expressed their nationalistic feelings. This was a painstaking process, for their arguments had to be couched in a language which appealed not only to the underlying sentiment they felt, but also to the sentiment which they hoped was felt by their countrymen. Beginning with addresses of support for their king, the loyalists proceeded to venerate their constitution. Finally, under the impetus of war, their attention was focused on their country. This evolution of the symbolic references to their nation was only partially determined by the threats which called them forth. Addresses to the king, for instance, were at least a yearly practice on the occasion of the king's birthday, and were common on the dates of many other events in the king's life: the birth of a son or daughter, recovery from an illness, etc. The first indication of patriotic nationalism, therefore, was in the traditional method of paying respect to the sovereign.

The association movement of 1792-93 also followed the usual English practices of the past. Associations, societies, or clubs were semipermanent or permanent organizations of individuals working toward common goals. What distinguished the loyal associations in the growth of nationalistic expression was their goal—to defend the constitution against all enemies. Since the king was but a part of the constitution, the enlargement of the loyalists' goals is easily apparent. Moreover, their description of their enemies as allies of the French had an ideological, if not actual, ring of truth about it. In this manner, the associators preempted the patriotic sentiment for their own. The context of the argument changed. It was no longer a struggle between reformers and anti-reformers but one between patriotic Englishmen and traitors. The declaration of war by France cemented the dichotomy. Reformers could only by the most sophisticated reasoning oppose the loyalists and still be thought of as patriotic.

The subscription drives of 1793 and the volunteer movement of 1794 were manifestations of the further development of the conceptual framework in which individuals could satisfy their patriotic aspirations. Under the threat of invasion and the increased activities of radicals, the scope of their operations was enlarged to include the protection, not just of the king, not just of the constitution, but of the entire country. To achieve this they were willing to tax themselves and to serve in paramilitary capacities. After the domestic threats diminished they continued their support of their nation in increasing numbers. However we judge the effectiveness of their actions, their motivations are clear. They were patriotic nationalists, pure and simple.

It is of some significance to note the arena in which the contest was waged. It was a public debate, carried on in accepted fashion in organizations outside the formal constitution. Associations, clubs, and societies were the accepted means by which large sections of the body politic could express their opinions about state affairs. To be sure, Fox and his followers in Parliament kept the issue of reform alive within the walls of the constitution itself, but their efforts were puny compared to activities out of doors. Indeed, because of government's appeal to or manipulation of efforts in this area of organized public opinion, we can see, briefly, the creation of something resembling a transitory, informal constitution.

When government issued the royal proclamation of May 1792, it was responding to practices in the informal constitution hallowed by time. Movements for reform had traditionally originated in societies and associations outside the regular functioning constitution since the days of John Wilkes. Government's response was an appeal to the same area for support. It was as if those in power were requesting support for an ordinary measure proposed in Parliament. And they were successful. The number of addresses of loyalty demonstrated support enough to convince leading members of government that they had ended the movement for reform by a new section of society apparently politicized by the example of Frence. Office holders within the formal constitution had instigated a response from the informal to challenges from the same quarter. They accomplished more and less than they intended.

Contrary to the opinions of members of government, the radical clubs likely drew their inspiration, not from the response they obtained from the English public or from the approval or disapproval of the constituted authorities, but from the progress of the Revolution in France. The subduing of their activities in the summer of 1792 could be explained more by conditions in France than by those in England. On the other hand, those who chose to support the government, the loyalists, were sensitive both to the radical agitation in England and to the possible dangers to their society posed by the successes of the Revolution.

Government had offered them a means of expressing their concern more than it had informed them of what to be concerned about.

The next occasion for action by those within and without the formal constitution was prompted by the same stimuli as the first: actions within the informal constitution by the radicals, although with an added ingredient. This time there appeared the possibility of collusion between the radicals and the French. Once again government provided the means for expressing loyalist sentiments, but now the loyalists acted from a more or less permanently organized position. Their rout of the radicals did not end their participation in constitutional or semiconstitutional activities. If anything, their victory led them to take part in the war in any way they deemed beneficial. The informal part of the constitution had become almost a working part of the formal.

While it has been possible to follow government's plans to broaden the participation of the loyalists in constitutional duties by the formation of volunteer corps, it is also possible to observe that government was following the lead presented by the loyalists. It was not in raising men but in raising money that the volunteer corps bill attracted the most attention, for here loyalists were collecting money for public purposes, a function normally reserved to Parliament. It was not enough that government was arming tens of thousands of Englishmen to enforce good behavior upon other Englishmen; it also granted the loyalists power to accept contributions from everyone in order to pay part of the expenses. Because the loyalists had taxed themselves to provide for enlistments, widows and orphans, and so forth, in 1793 on their own initiative, government now incorporated this practice into the creation of a force to guard against domestic riots and tumults as well as to defend against invasion. In one sense, the informal practices of Englishmen were given sanction by the formal constitution to remain involved in its responsibilities for an indefinite period into the future. Fox and his followers were quite right in noticing this transformation of the formal constitution by the enlargement of powers of the informal.

The net result of the loyalists' responses to the challenges of the radicals, and of the enlargement of public participation in the defense of the nation, was to give the constituted authorities either the appearance or the reality of great strength. In the immediate crisis this was the goal sought by the patriots above all others. For, whether or not the radicals planned to cooperate with the French in weakening or invading Britain, whether or not they planned to incite domestic insurrections, whether or not they hoped to encourage the further progress of the Revolution, the reality of a militant consensus in Britain opposed to their ends would strengthen the possibility of stability at a chaotic time in European affairs.

This strength also made it unnecessary for the state to defend itself from internal subversion by excessive measures of suppression. There is no doubt that the English system of laws and liberties alone would have prevented even a mild approach to the French method of curbing dissent. Even steps in that direction were made unnecessary because the constituted authorities knew they held overwhelming support from the vast majority of the English public. Largely because of the loyalists, the English were spared even a mild legacy of violence which could have set dangerous precedents for the future. By supporting the constitution when they did, the loyalists allowed England to escape the extreme actions of the revolutionaries across the Channel.

The last inference we can draw from this study is the remarkable ability of the English to arrive at a consensus during times of stress and emergency. We shall probably never know whether the radicals ever seriously contemplated attacking the state in an attempt to foment a revolution, or to obtain assistance from the French. My personal guess is that they wished to use these possibilities only as a means of obtaining some part of their reforming plans. Contemporaries were probably as undecided on this issue as moderns are, yet even vague threats were enough to cause them to unite in defending their society and state. This indicates a community of interests transcending inequities of wealth, status, and position, the usual causes of human activities sought by historians. Patriotism was the order of the day, and in this respect the loyalists represented the true nature of Englishmen during those chaotic years.

NOTES

Abbreviations used:

Add. MSS: Additional Manuscripts. British Museum, London.

HO: Great Britain. Home Office Papers. Public Record Office, London.

HPD: Great Britain. *Hansard's Parliamentary Debates.* [All references are to the first series.]

PRO: Public Record Office, London.

CHAPTER I

1. *HPD* 29 (1817): 1476-77. HO 42/21: "List of Addresses to His Majesty, between the 1 June and the [sic] September, 1792 on occasion of His Majesty's late Proclamation," Sept. 10, 1792, f. 20; "Counties, Cities and Towns from which addresses have *not* been received—as of 10 September, 1792," f. 10.

2. E.C. Black, *The Association: British Extraparliamentary Political Organization, 1769-1793* (Cambridge, Mass., 1963).

3. R.R. Fennessee, *Burke, Paine and the Rights of Man* (La Haye, 1963) is the best account of the pamphlet controversy aroused by Burke's *Reflections.*

4. P.A. Brown, *The French Revolution in English History* (New York, 1965). This work, originally published in 1918, has not been superseded in its examination of the initial favorable response by English intellectuals and politicians to the Revolution.

5. Albert Goodwin, *Friends of Liberty: The English Democratic Movement in the Age of the French Revolution* (Cambridge, Mass., 1979), pp. 32-64.

6. Richard Grenville, Duke of Buckingham and Chandos, *Memoirs of the Courts and Cabinets of George the Third* (London, 1853), 2: 165 (hereafter cited as *Courts and Cabinets*). *HPD*, Fox, 27: 348.

7. Fennessee, *Burke, Paine, and the Rights of Man*, p. 181. Caroline Robbins, *The Eighteenth Century Commonwealthsman* (Cambridge, Mass., 1959). Add. MSS 40,100: George III to Dundas, July 16, 1791, f. 3. British Missionary Society, London, Hole Manuscripts: Porteus to H. More, July 1, 1791. Sheffield Public Library, Wentworth-Woodhouse Muniments F. 115(a): Loughborough to Fitzwilliam, Aug. 1, 1791 (n.f.).

8. Ian Christie, *Wilkes, Wyvill and Reform* (London, 1962).

9. Great Britain, Historical Manuscripts Commission, *Fourteenth Report*, Appendix V, "The MSS of J.B. Fortesque, Esq., Preserved at Dropmore," Mornington to Grenville, July 3, 1791, p. 118 (hereafter cited as Dropmore MSS).

10. HO 42/22: Vaughn to Nepean, Nov. 30, 1792, ff. 612, 613, 624. Vaughn reminded the government of the policy adopted toward Paine earlier when the government was debating whether another author (Cooper) should be apprehended. *HPD*, Dundas, 29: 1504.

11. E.P. Thompson, *The Making of the English Working Class* (New York, 1966).

12. Philip S. Foner, ed., *The Complete Writings of Thomas Paine* (New York, 1945), *Rights of Man*, pt. I: 283, 286, 287.

13. Ibid., pp. 341, 344.

14. Francis O'Gorman, *The Whig Party and the French Revolution* (London, 1967). J.H. Rose, *Life of William Pitt* (New York, 1924), p. 68.

15. Herbert Butterfield, "Charles James Fox and the Whig Opposition in 1792," *Cambridge Historical Journal*, no. 3 (1949): 296, 302.

16. *HPD* 29: 1303.

17. Ibid., p. 1306.

18. Ibid., p. 1481. D.G. Barnes, *George III and William Pitt, 1783–1806* (Stanford, 1939), p. 256.

19. *HPD* 29: 1312.

20. Ibid., p. 1315.

21. HO 42/20: Rutson to Nepean, May 31, 1792, f. 155.

22. *York Courant*, Jan. 3, 1792, p. 3.

23. Ibid., Jan. 10, 1792, p. 2; Jan. 24, 1792, p. 2; Feb. 28, 1792, p. 2.

24. *Sussex Weekly Advertiser* (Lewes), Feb. 20, 1792, p. 2; Jan. 30, 1792, p. 1; Apr. 30, 1792, p. 3; May 7, 1792, p. 3.

25. *York Courant,* May 15, 1792, p. 1. *Sussex Weekly Advertiser,* May 14, 1792, p. 3.

26. *Chelmsford Chronicle,* Jan. 25, 1792, p. 3. *York Courant,* May 1, 1792, p. 1; May 8, 1792, p. 1.

27. *York Courant,* May 15, 1792, p. 2. *Berrow's Worcester Journal,* May 17, 1792, p. 2. *Sussex Weekly Advertiser,* Feb. 13, 1792, p. 1; Apr. 16, 1792, p. 2; May 21, 1792, p. 2.

28. *York Courant,* June 11, 1792, p. 3; June 18, 1792, p. 2.

29. Ibid., June 25, 1792, p. 1. HO 42/21: Burdon to Nepean, Aug. 1, 1792, f. 89.

30. *York Courant,* June 18, 1792, p. 2. *Chelmsford Chronicle,* June 22, 1792, p. 2. *Sussex Weekly Advertiser,* June 4, 1792, p. 3.

31. *York Courant,* June 4, 1792, p. 1. *Chelmsford Chronicle,* June 22, 1792, p. 3. *Sussex Weekly Advertiser,* July 2, 1792, p. 3.

32. HO 42/22: DeLancey to Nepean acknowledging orders from Nepean dated June 24, 1792 (n.d.), f. 156. Add. MSS 40,100: George III to Dundas informing him of his pleasure at the good news, July 15, 1792, f. 45.

33. Grenville, *Courts and Cabinets*: Grenville to Buckingham, June 13 and Nov. 14, 1792, pp. 209, 227. Dropmore MSS: Grenville to Gower, July 19, 1792, p. 294.

34. Devon Record Office, Addington MSS 152M/C1792/OZ11: George Sloper to Addington, June 12, 1792 (n.f.).

CHAPTER II

1. Goodwin, *Friends of Liberty,* pp. 234–39. Gwyn A. Williams, *Artisans and Sans-Culottes* (New York, 1969), p. 58. Thompson, *Making of the English Working Class,* pp. 120, 17.

2. Northumberland Record Office, Woodman Family Letters M16-B35: F. Mackenney to Charleton Brand, Nov. 6, 1792 (n.f.).

3. Goodwin, *Friends of Liberty,* p. 239.

4. *Morning Chronicle* (London), Aug. 22, 1792, p. 2; Aug. 25, 1792, p. 2; Aug. 29, 1792, p. 2. *The Times* (London), Aug. 30, 1792, p. 2.

5. Dropmore MSS: Pitt to Grenville, Sept. 7, 1792, p. 319. Lord John Russell, ed., *Memorials and Correspondence of Charles James Fox* (London, 1853): Fox to Holland, Aug. 20, 1792, and Sept. 1792, pp. 366, 370.

6. Goodwin, *Friends of Liberty*, pp. 239-40. Goodwin notes the effects of French actions on radical ideas after July 1792, but not before.

7. J.M. Thompson, *The French Revolution* (New York, 1966), p. 347.

8. *The Annual Register, or a View of the History, Politics and Literature for the Year 1792* (London, 1799), p. 166.

9. HO 42/27: "Report on Sedition," Apr. 1794, ff. 863-77. See also Clive Emsley, "The Home Office and Its Sources of Information and Investigation, 1793-1801," *English Historical Review* 94 (July 1979): 544-48. HO 42/22: "Anon." to HO, Nov. 8, 1792, f. 305; (no sender) to HO, Dec. 30, 1792, f. 668. HO 42/23: (no sender) to HO, Dec. 1792, ff. 34-37; "A.Z." to Dundas, Dec. 3, 1792, ff. 89-92; "M." to HO, Dec. 8, 1792, ff. 263-64; "J.R." to HO, Dec. 10, 1792, f. 305; (no sender) to HO, Dec. 10, 1792, f. 293.

10. Library of Scotland, Melville MSS 7199: "News from Paris," Dec. 1, 1792-Jan. 19, 1793; "Ever Anonymous" to Dundas, Dec. 6, 1792, f. 115; "E.W." to Dundas, Dec. 1, 1792, f. 113; (no sender) to Dundas, Dec. 11, 1792, f. 119. The handwriting and contents of these letters leave no doubt as to their common origin. "E.W." was probably Lady Elizabeth Wallace, although I have not been able to find definitive evidence for this claim.

11. HO 42/22: Nepean to Wheate, Oct. 12, 1792, f. 115; Nepean to Brooke, Nov. 6, 1792, ff. 287-88.

12. HO 42/21: Dundas to Curry, Sept. 13, 1792, f. 533.

13. HO 42/22: Pitt to Lord Mayor of London, Oct. 26, 1792, f. 197; Bishop of Durham to Grenville, Nov. 11, 1792, ff. 354-56. HO 42/21: Nepean to Rose, Sept. 26, 1792, f. 83; Dundas to Lieutenant Governor Trigg, Sept. 15, 1792, f. 48.

14. HO 42/22: Walter to Nepean, Oct. 29, 1792, f. 206; De Lancey to Nepean, Nov. 25, 1792, f. 276.

15. George Lefebvre, *The French Revolution* (New York, 1962), p. 241. See also Robert R. Dozier, "Democratic Revolution in England—a Possibility?" *Albion: Proceedings of the Conference on British Studies* 4, no. 4 (Winter 1972): 185.

16. HO 42/21: Dundas to Curry, Sept. 13, 1792, f. 41; Dundas to the Rev. W. Manor, Sept. 16, 1792, f. 48. Dropmore MSS: Burges to Grenville, Sept. 14, 1792, p. 315.

17. HO 42/21: Dundas to Lord Hood, Sept. 21, 1792, f. 62. HO 42/22: Crowder to Long, Nov. 12, 1792, f. 360. This reply from the customs collector at Harwich dates the earliest request at September

11. HO 42/23: Westbeck to Hutson, Nov. 30, 1792, f. 7. Westbeck, the customs official at Ramsgate, mentions requests on September 13 and 21. Apparently the customs officials at various ports were alerted piecemeal.

18. *The Times*, Sept. 14, 1792, p. 2.

19. Add. MSS 40,100: Dundas to George III, Sept. 22, 1792, f. 63. HO 42/21: George III to Wilmot (n.d.), f. 66; draft of an advertisement "in favor of the French clergy," f. 113. P.J. Marshall and John A. Woods, eds., *The Correspondence of Edmund Burke* 7 (Chicago, 1968): Dundas to Burke, Sept. 21, 1792, p. 223. HO 42/21: Dundas to Nepean, Sept. 25, 1792, f. 75.

20. HO 42/21: Nepean to Rose [Ross?], Sept. 26, 1792, f. 83.

21. HO 42/22: Gibbon to Freeling, Oct. 1792, ff. 145, 172, 178.

22. HO 42/21: Nepean to Hobart, Sept. 1, 1792 (n.f.). Charles P. Miles, ed., *The Correspondence of William Augustus Miles on the French Revolution* (London, 1890): Miles to Long, Nov. 12, 1792, 1: 344-46. Miles reported that both Maret and Noel were sent to establish diplomatic connections as a prelude to the official recognition of Chauvelin as the accredited representative of the French Republic. His views, however, are highly colored by his attempt to magnify his own importance in these semiofficial negotiations.

23. HO 42/21: Miles to Aust, Sept. 8-9, 1792 (n.f.).

24. HO 42/21: Curry to Dundas, Sept. 28, 1792, f. 100. HO 42/22: Nepean to Lord Hood, Oct. 1, 1792, ff. 42-43; Nepean to Curry, Oct. 1, 1792, f. 30.

25. HO 42/21: Brooke to Nepean, Sept. 21, 1792, f. 64, and Sept. 28, 1792, f. 107. This latter document is curiously misdated Sept. 1789.

26. Carl Cone, *Burke and the Nature of Politics* (Lexington, Ky., 1964), 2: 404 n. Cone believes it was the same weapon. Marshall and Woods, in *Correspondence of Edmund Burke* (7: 328), state that Burke received a "pattern dagger" from J. Bland Burges. It was probably the same dagger as that remitted by Brooke.

27. HO 42/22: James Maxwell to Dundas, Oct. 2, 1792, f. 50; Newport to Nepean, Nov. 5, 1792, f. 281.

28. HO 42/23: Collins to Nepean, Dec. 4, 1792, ff. 214-15. Collins did not submit any proof that this was being done. Lefebvre (*French Revolution*, p. 280) estimates that 3,772 Frenchmen arrived in England in 1792. This is exactly the *Annual Register*'s figure for the number who arrived between August 30 and October 1 (*Annual Register*, "The Chronicle," p. 39). Contemporary estimates of the

number for the whole year ran as high as 8,000. See *HPD*, Lord Landsdown, 30: 147.

29. HO 42/22: Nepean to Brooke, Nov. 6, 1792, ff. 287-88.

30. HO 42/22: Nepean to Brooke, and Nepean to Wheate, Oct. 12, 1792, ff. 113, 115; Nepean to Onslow, Oct. 26, 1792, f. 185; Brooke to Nepean, Nov. 8, 1792, f. 316; Galton to Nepean, Nov. 14, 1792, f. 378; Nepean to Brooke, Nov. 14, 1792, f. 372; Mason to Nepean, Nov. 14, 1792, ff. 376-77.

31. The dating of this list is taken from the latest dated document in the series, HO 42/23: Hume to Nepean, Dec. 7, 1792, f. 179. Unless this list was intended to be used in prosecutions after the radical movement was crushed, I assume it to have been compiled in the week of December 7-14, when alarms were highest and before the loyal movement had reached its peak. After the success of the loyalists, there was little reason, other than that mentioned above, to gather such materials.

32. HO 42/23: "List of areas, reports and numbers of arms collected for people not connected with government" (n.d.), f. 181. The items listed are: No. 1, "Gun and Pistol makers at Birmingham," 1792, f. 183; No. 2, McGregory to McQueen (n.d.), f. 184; No. 3, Newport to Pitt, Sept. 25, 1792, f. 187; No. 4, Chalmers to Nepean, Sept. 25, 1792, f. 189; No. 5 (anon.) to Edmiston, Sept. 23, 1792, f. 191; "FFZ"(?) to HO, Dec. 3(?), 1792, f. 194; No. 6, (anon.) to HO (n.d.), f. 194; No. 7, "A friend to his Country" to HO, Sept. 20, 1792, f. 197; No. 8, Hudson to Wilberforce, Oct. 30, 1792, f. 200; No. 9, Woolley to Rose, Sept. 28, 1792, ff. 201-2; No. 10, Brooke(?) to HO, Oct. 1792, ff. 203-4; No. 11, Onslow to HO, Oct. 29, 1792, ff. 205-6; No. 12, Grenville to Nepean, Oct. 30, 1792, f. 209; No. 13 (Nepean's list mentions a letter from Brooke dated Nov. 8; this document has not survived); No. 14, "Extract of a letter from Maestricht," Nov. 14, 1792, f. 210; No. 15, Mason to Nepean, Nov. 14, 1792, ff. 376-77. HO 42/22: No. 16, Onslow to Nepean, Nov. 15, 1792, ff. 286-87; No. 17 (Nepean's list mentions "D⁰. from Stoarbridge that Daggers are making at Birmingham," Dec. 1, 1792; the document has not survived); No. 18, Hurd to Rose, Dec. 3, 1792, ff. 212-13; No. 19, Collins to Rose, Dec. 4, 1792, ff. 214-15; No. 20, Hume to Nepean, Dec. 7, 1792, f. 179.

33. HO 42/23: Nov. 14, 1792, f. 210.

34. It is difficult to arrive at an exact figure for the weapons ordered by nongovernmental agents. Most of the difficulty stems from the confusion created by a large order for 300,000 stands of

arms placed with Galton and Son and John Whatley. If these two arms manufacturers entered the contract jointly, the number of weapons noted by Nepean's tabulation would stand at 465,000. If each manufacturer had an order for 300,000, as some agents seemed to imply in their reports, 765,000 would be the correct figure. Deducting the weapons reported in the letter from Maestricht, which may have been part of the huge order from Galton or Whatley, the figure would stand at 635,000 or 335,000.

35. HO 42/23: Collins to Williams, Dec. 12, 1792, ff. 343-44; Nepean to Alderston, Dec. 14, 1792, f. 378.

36. *The Times,* Oct. 8, 1792, p. 2. Because of the extended negotiations after the battle of Valmy and the inconclusive results of the battle itself, the victor was not determined until Brunswick began his retreat.

37. HO 42/22: (n.d.) ff. 216-18. The cities were Stockport, Yarmouth, Derby, Ipswich, Leicester, Birmingham, Manchester, Chester, Shrewsbury, Liverpool, Sheffield, London, Norwich, and Cambridge. It is difficult to date this list. Williams does not examine every society in Nepean's list, yet he states, without citing evidence, that the Birmingham society was not founded until November 1792 (Williams, *Artisans,* p. 64). John Brooke in Birmingham, involved in tracking down the destinations of arms made in that city for people not in the government, reported to Nepean on November 1, 2, and 4 about activities there. Nepean answered all three letters on November 6 and mentioned a "Debating Society" which he wanted investigated. It is possible that the society was formed in the early part of November in time for Brooke to have discovered it before reporting to Nepean.

38. Library of Scotland, Melville MSS 7199: "E.W." to Dundas, Dec. 20, 1792, f. 118. HO 42/22: Vaughan to Nepean, Nov. 30, 1792, ff. 612-13. Dropmore MSS: Grenville to Auckland, Dec. 4, 1792, p. 351.

39. HO 42/22: Townshend to Grenville, Oct. 31, 1792, f. 219; Burdon to Dundas, Nov. 3, 1792, ff. 261-62; Townshend to Nepean, Nov. 11, 1792, f. 353; Stisted to HO, Nov. 15, 1792, f. 303. Apparently the riot at South Shields began first. Townshend, when reporting the riots at Yarmouth, intimated that the rioters there had heard about the earlier riots in the Newcastle area.

40. HO 42/22: Townshend to Dundas, Nov. 5, 1792, ff. 278-78A; Townshend to Nepean, Nov. 11, 1792, f. 353. Powditch to Pitt, Nov. 3, 1792, ff. 265-67. One means of maintaining discipline

within their ranks was to drive reluctant seamen or officers, stripped naked, through the town.

41. HO 42/22: Townshend to Dundas, Nov. 5, 1792, ff. 278-78A. At Yarmouth, the rioters stormed the jail to free their imprisoned leaders and were partially successful.

42. HO 42/22: Townshend to Grenville, Oct. 31, 1792, f. 219; Burdon to Dundas, Nov. 3, 1792, ff. 261-62; Powditch to Pitt, Nov. 3, 1792, ff. 247-53. Powditch estimated that "about 400 sail" were tied up by the riot.

43. HO 42/22: Grenville to Townshend, Nov. 2, 1792, f. 243; Nepean to Burdon, Nov. 5, 1792, f. 274; Nepean to Bulmer, Nov. 5, 1792, f. 276; Nepean to Mayor of Newcastle upon Tyne, Nov. 5, 1792, ff. 283-84; Nepean to Bishop of Durham, Nov. 7, 1792, ff. 302-3.

44. HO 42/22: Reedman to Nepean, Nov. 8, 1792, ff. 312-13. Burdon concurred, although he criticized the delay in restoring order. HO 42/22: Burdon to Nepean, Nov. 8, 1792, ff. 314-15.

45. HO 42/22: Nepean to Reedman, Nov. 10, 1792, f. 345; Nepean to DeLancey, Nov. 13, 1792, ff. 366-68; Burdon to Nepean, Nov. 16, 1792, f. 387. While disagreements between the sailors and ships' owners continued, the port was no longer out of control. The best account of this strike is found in Norman McCord and David E. Brewster, "Some Labour Troubles of the 1790's in North East England," *International Review of Social History* 13, pt. 3 (1968): 366-83.

46. HO 42/22: Lacon(?) to Townshend, Oct. 30, 1792, ff. 220-21. Lacon(?), the Mayor of Yarmouth, also sent Townshend a letter he had received in which the writer threatened that his "head shall come from his sholders [sic] and his house to the ground." HO 42/22: Anon. to Lacon(?), Oct. 21, 1792, f. 222. In his covering letter on this date, however, Townshend attributed wage disputes as the primary causes for the riots at Yarmouth and Lynn. The same causes were given by those reporting the riots at South Shields and Ipswich. HO 42/22: Burdon to Nepean, Nov. 3, 1792, ff. 261-62; Stisted to HO, Nov. 15, 1792, f. 383.

47. HO 42/22: Bulmer to Nepean, Nov. 1, 1792, ff. 263-64.

48. HO 42/22: Powditch to Pitt, Nov. 3, 1792, ff. 247-53, 265-67; Reynolds to Grenville, Nov. 9, 1792, f. 330; Townshend to Nepean, Nov. 11, 1792, ff. 343-54.

49. Grenville, *Courts and Cabinets*, Grenville to Buckingham, Nov. 14, 1792, pp. 227, 228.

50. HO 42/22: Massey to Freeling, Nov. 22, 1792, ff. 474-75. Miles, *Correspondence*: Miles to Long, Nov. 12, 1792, p. 345. See also Clive Emsley, "The London 'Insurrection' of December, 1792: Fact, Fiction, or Fantasy?" *Journal of British Studies* 17, no. 2 (1978): 66-86. HO 42/22: Sproule to HO, Nov. 24, 1792, f. 502.

51. Goodwin, *Friends of Liberty*, pp. 252-58.

52. Grenville, *Courts and Cabinets*, Grenville to Buckingham, Nov. 7 and Nov. 14, 1792, pp. 224, 227-28. Dropmore MSS: Buckingham to Grenville, Nov. 8, 1792, p. 327.

53. Dropmore MSS: Buckingham to Grenville, Nov. 15, 1792, p. 333, and Nov. 8, 1792, p. 327.

54. Dropmore MSS: Auckland to Grenville, Nov. 16, 1792, p. 335. Burke, *Reflections*, p. 124.

55. Dropmore MSS: Buckingham to Grenville, Nov. 18, 1792, p. 336.

56. *HPD*, Fox, 30: 28. Dropmore MSS: Buckingham to Grenville, Nov. 18, 1792, p. 336. HO 42/23: Blackett to Freeling, Nov. 22, 1792, f. 2. HO 42/22: Massey to Freeling, Nov. 22, 1792, f. 474; Chrees to Freeling, Nov. 23, 1792, f. 479; Austwick to Freeling, Nov. 23, 1792, ff. 481-82; Poole to Nepean, Nov. 23, 1792, f. 496.

57. Goodwin, *Friends of Liberty*, p. 259. Goodwin repeatedly refers to those who disagreed with the goals and methods of the radicals as "Alarmists."

CHAPTER III

1. Black, *Association*, ch. 7.

2. Austin Mitchell, "The Association Movement of 1792-3," *Historical Journal* 4 (1961): 61. *Sussex Weekly Advertiser*, Dec. 17, 1792, p. 3; Dec. 24, 1792, p. 3. *York Courant*, Dec. 17, 1792, p. 2; Dec. 24, 1792, p. 2. Dropmore MSS: Grenville to Auckland, Dec. 18, 1792, p. 359; Whitworth to Grenville, Jan. 5, 1793, p. 364. Whitworth reported a conversation he had had with Empress Catherine.

3. *Sun* (London), Nov. 23, 1792, p. 2; Nov. 24, 1792, p. 2. *The Times*, Nov. 24, 1792, p. 2. *Morning Chronicle* (London), Nov. 24, 1792, p. 2. *York Courant*, Jan. 3, 1792, p. 3. Add. MSS 37,835: Portland to Windham, Nov. 30, 1792, f. 7.

4. Historians disagree on the involvement of the government. Black and Goodwin argue that the APLP was founded by the government, while Mitchell notes the lack of evidence either way.

5. PRO 38/8/170: Reeves to Pitt, Sept. 7, 1794, ff. 259-60. John Reeves, *The Association Papers* (London, 1793), p. iv.

6. Grenville, *Courts and Cabinets*, Grenville to Buckingham, Nov. 25, 1792, p. 229. Carl B. Cone, *The English Jacobins* (New York, 1968), p. 147.

7. *HPD*, 32: 661-62

8. Add. MSS 16,919: J. Dick to Reeves, Nov. 29, 1792, f. 132. Dick declined on the grounds that it would have been improper for an "official man" to be on the executive committee. It is not possible to state when the vacancy created by Dick's refusal was filled.

9. Add. MSS 16,919: John Heriot to Reeves, Nov. 29, 1792, p. 111.

10. Add. MSS 16,930: Manchester, Dec. 18, 1792, f. 19. Add. MSS 16,931: Penzance, Dec. 14, 1792, f. 117; Wednesbury, Dec. 3, 1792, f. 159; Rotherham, Dec. 17, 1792, f. 133.

11. Add. MSS 16,929: Folkstone, Jan. 4, 1793, f. 84; Birmingham, Dec. 7, 1792, f. 13; Bromsgrove, Dec. 26, 1792, ff. 24, 25. Add. MSS 16,930: Shepton Mallet, Dec. 29, 1792, ff. 54, 55. Add. MSS 16,931: Hawes, Jan. 2, 1793, f. 67; Stapleford, Dec. 20, 1792, f. 145; Banbury, Dec. 24, 1792, f. 6. *Sussex Weekly Advertiser*: Poultny, Dec. 12, 1792, p. 4; Lewes, Dec. 22, 1792, p. 3. *York Courant*: Whitby, Dec. 12, 1792, p. 2. *Berrow's Worcester Journal*: Worcester, Jan. 27, 1793, p. 3; Bromsgrove, Jan. 3, 1793, p. 4; Tewksbury, Jan. 3, 1793, p. 4. *Chelmsford Chronicle*: Saffron Waldon, Dec. 28, 1792, p. 3; Dunmow Hundred, Jan. 4, 1793, p. 4; Haverhill, Jan. 18, 1793, p. 3.

12. Add. MSS 16,929: Porters, Dec. 6, 1792, f. 81; Butchers, Jan. 9, 1793, f. 29. Add. MSS 16,930: Stationers, Dec. 12, 1792, f. 46. Add. MSS 16,931: Underwriters, Dec. 12, 1792, f. 99; Bakers, Dec. 7, 1792, f. 152. *York Courant*: Masters and Pilots, Dec. 31, 1792, p. 3.

13. Add. MSS 16,931: Kings Bench Prison, Dec. 22, 1792, ff. 83-84. *York Courant*: Debtors at York Castle, Jan. 7, 1793, p. 1.

14. *The Times*, Nov. 24, 1792, p. 2. Add. MSS 16,929, 16,930, and 16,931 are collections of this correspondence.

15. *Sun*, Dec. 13, 1792, p. 2.

16. Add. MSS 16,929: Birmingham, Dec. 7, 1792, ff. 12-13. *Berrow's Worcester Journal*, Dec. 27, 1792, p. 4. Add. MSS, 16,930: Dec. 11, 1792, f. 20. Add. MSS 16,931: Dec. 14, 1792, f. 132; Dec. 17, 21, 24, 27, 1792, f. 68.

17. Add. MSS 16,931: Peterborough, Dec. 19, 1792, f. 118; Wey-

mouth, Dec. 8, 1792, f. 158. Add. MSS 16,929: Falmouth, Dec. 17, 1792, f. 78; Add. MSS 16,931: St. Albans, Dec. 26, 1792, f. 1; Canterbury, Dec. 13, 1792, ff. 31, 32; St. Mary-le-bone, Dec. 8, 1792, f. 101. Bath, Dec. 8, 1792, ff. 8, 9.

18. Add. MSS 16,929: United Parishes of St. Andrew, Holborn, above the Bar, and St. George the Martyr, Dec. 7, 1792, ff. 101, 102; Carshalton, Dec. 11, 1792, ff. 34, 35; The Liberty of Saffron Hill, Glatton Gardens, Ely Rents, Dec. 11, 1792, ff. 94, 96; London Liberty of St. Andrew Holborn, Dec. 13, 1792, ff. 97-99. Add. MSS 16,930: Parish of St. John the Evangelist, Dec. 7, 1792, f. 83. Add. MSS 16,931: Wakefield, Dec. 10, 1792, f. 155; New Sarum, Dec. 12, 1792, f. 134; Lindfield, Dec. 24, 1792, f. 95; Pevensy Rape, Upper Division, Dec. 28, 1792, f. 120.

19. *Sussex Weekly Advertiser,* June 25, 1792, p. 3. Add. MSS 16,930: Dec. 22, 1792, f. 1. *York Courant,* June 11, 1792, p. 2; Dec. 17, 1792, p. 2; June 18, 1792, pp. 3, 4. Add. MSS 16,931: Dec. 12, 1792, f. 130; Dec. 10, 1792, f. 155.

20. *Chelmsford Chronicle,* Nov. 30, 1792, p. 3. Add. MSS 16,931: Nov. 30, 1792, f. 142; Wednesbury, Dec. 3, 1792, f. 159; Highgate, Dec. 4, 1792, f. 73; Parish of St. Savior, Dec. 4, ff. 143, 144. *Observer* (London): St. Martin in the Fields, Dec. 9, 1792, p. 3, reporting a meeting held Dec. 4, 1792. The difficulty of assigning causal sequences stems from the lack of announcements of proposed meetings and the lack of news about the distribution of the militia proclamation of December 1, which was, of course, read aloud across the nation.

21. Grenville, *Courts and Cabinets,* Grenville to Buckingham, Dec. 1 and Dec. 5, 1792, pp. 231, 232. See also HO 40/18. HO 50/18: "State of the Rank and File of the Following Corps of H. M. Militia as of last returns—29 January '93" (n.f.); "List of Militia Corps which have not transmitted Returns" (n.f.).

22. *Chelmsford Chronicle,* Dec. 7, 1792, p. 1. *Sun,* Dec. 8, 1792, p. 2. *York Courant,* Dec. 10, 1792, p. 2.

23. Reeves, *Association Papers,* p. iv.

24. Dropmore MSS: Burges to Grenville, Sept. 3, 1792, pp. 308, 309; Nov. 4, 1792, p. 325. Goodwin, *Friends of Liberty,* pp. 261-62.

25. Marshall and Woods, *Correspondence of Edmund Burke*: E. Burke to R. Burke, Nov. 29, 1792, p. 317.

26. Grenville, *Courts and Cabinets,* Grenville to Buckingham, Nov. 29 and Dec. 1, 1792, pp. 230, 231. HO 42/22: Anon. to

Nepean, Nov. 30, 1792, f. 319. Emsley, "London 'Insurrection,'" p. 74. Emsley identifies this person as Dubois de Longchamp.

27. Devon Record Office, Addington MSS 152M/C1793, OZ 12: John Hiley Addington to Henry Addington, Dec. 5, 1792 (n.f.).

28. *HPD* 29: 1556-57.

29. O'Gorman, *Whig Party.*

30. Sheffield Public Library, Wentworth-Woodhouse Muniments, F. 31(a): Portland to Fitzwilliam, Nov. 30, 1792 (n.f.).

31. *HPD* 30: 29-30.

32. Ibid., pp. 28, 40, 43, 59.

33. Ibid., p. 36.

34. Ibid., pp. 72-73.

35. Ibid., p. 130.

36. Ibid., pp. 130-31, 137.

CHAPTER IV

1. *Observer*, Dec. 9, 1792, p. 3.

2. Thompson, *English Working Class*, p. 23. Thompson labels the APLP "a great semi-official agency for the intimidation of reformers."

3. Add. MSS 16,929: Hundreds of Bosmere Clayton and Stow, Jan. 28, 1793, ff. 14, 15; Crediton, Dec. 26, 1792, f. 52. Add. MSS 16,930: Saffron Walden, Dec. 7, 1792, f. 51. Add. MSS 16,921: Lambeth, Dec. 10, 1792, f. 89; Ongar Division, Dec. 14, 1792, f. 111; Blything Hundred, Dec. 12, 1792, f. 21; Southhampton, Nov. 30, 1792, f. 142.

4. Add. MSS 16,931: Jan. 3, 1793, f. 53. Add. MSS 16,929: Dec. 15, 1792, ff. 27, 28; Dec. 7, 1792, ff. 12, 13; Dec. 27, 1792, ff. 54, 55.

5. Add. MSS 16,931: Dec. 24, 1792, f. 21. Add. MSS 16,929, Dec. 29, 1792, ff. 115, 116.

6. Add. MSS 16,931: Dec. 8, 1792, f. 80.

7. Add. MSS 16,931: Dec. 8, 1792, ff. 8, 9.

8. Add. MSS 16,931: Horbury, Dec. 17, 1792, f. 76; Pontefract, Dec. 27, 1792, f. 121; Woolwich, Dec. 27, 1792, f. 168.

9. Add. MSS 16,929: Feb. 11, 1793, ff. 72, 73.

10. Donald E. Ginter, "The Loyalist Association Movement of 1792-93 and British Public Opinion," *Historical Journal* 9, no. 2 (1966): 179-90. Ginter suggests that because of the large number of reformers involved in the movement, a "sizeable proportion" of the

loyal movement was captured by reformers. It seems likely that the opposite happened.

11. Goodwin, *Friends of Liberty*, p. 265. Goodwin argues that magistrates encouraged "Church and King" mob action against reformers. If so, the magistrates were working against the goals of the loyal clubs, whose primary function was to prevent disorders of this sort.

12. *York Courant*, Dec. 17, 1792, p. 2. *Observer*, Dec. 9, 1792, p. 3.

13. Add. MSS 16,929: Hundreds of Bosmere Clayton and Stow, Jan. 28, 1793, ff. 14, 15; St. Nicholas, Deptford, Dec. 13, 1792, f. 56. Add. MSS 16,930: Wangford Hundred, Dec. 17, 1792, ff. 72, 73; Parishes of Burgh Castle and Belton, Dec. 26, 1792, ff. 75, 76. Add. MSS 16,931: Penzance Constitutional Club, Dec. 14, 1792, f. 117.

14. Add. MSS 16,931: Dec. 31, 1792, ff. 57-60.

15. *Chelmsford Chronicle*, Oct. 26, 1792, p. 3.

16. Add. MSS 16,929: Bath, Dec. 20, 1792, f. 1; Hinckley, Jan. 8, 1793, f. 110. Add. MSS 16,930: Market Marlborough, Dec. 26, 1792, ff. 25, 26. Add. MSS 16,931: Somerset, Jan. 24, 1793, f. 62. *Sussex Weekly Advertiser*, Jan. 21, 1793, p. 2.

17. Add. MSS 16,929: Chelsey, Dec. 14, 1792, f. 41: Deptford, Dec. 13, 1792, f. 56. Add. MSS 16,930: Wellington, Dec. 26, 1792, ff. 77, 78; New Windsor, Dec. 5, 1792, f. 95. Add. MSS 16,931: Emsworth, Dec. 19, 1792, f. 58.

18. *Chelmsford Chronicle*, Feb. 24, 1792, p. 4; June 1, 1792, p. 3. *Berrow's Worcester Journal*, Nov. 29, 1792, p. 3; Dec. 6, 1792, p. 4.

19. Add. MSS 16,930: Jan. 1, 1792, f. 15.

20. Add. MSS 16,930: Jan. 29, 30, Feb. 3, 4, 1792, ff. 14, 16-18.

21. Add. MSS 16,929: Deal, Dec. 17, 1792, ff. 54, 55; Devises, Nov. 28, 1792, f. 63. Add. MSS 16,930: Lewes, Dec. 6, 1792, f. 9; Wellington, Dec. 26, 1792, ff. 77, 78. Add. MSS 16,931: St. Savior, Dec. 4, 1792, ff. 143, 144; Peckham, Dec. 13, 1792, f. 113.

22. Add. MSS 16,930: Kidderminster, Dec. 22, 1792, f. 1; Lewes, Jan. 25, 1792, f. 10; New Windsor, Dec. 17, 1792, f. 95.

23. *Chelmsford Chronicle*, Dec. 14, 1792, p. 3. *York Courant*, Dec. 31, 1792, p. 3. *Berrow's Worcester Journal*, Jan. 17, 1793, p. 3.

24. *Sussex Weekly Advertiser*, Dec. 24, 1792, p. 3. *York Courant*, Jan. 14, 1792, p. 3.

25. *Chelmsford Chronicle,* Jan. 25, 1793, p. 3. *Sussex Weekly Advertiser,* Dec. 31, 1792, p. 3.
26. Add. MSS 16,929: Holborn, Jan. 15, 1792, f. 103; Saffron Hill, Jan. 18, 1792, f. 105. Add. MSS 16,930: Richmond, Dec. 7, 1792, ff. 46-48; Titchfield, Dec. 22, 1792, f. 64.
27. Add. MSS 16,919: Thomas to APLP, Nov. 29, 1792, f. 140; Rivers to APLP, Nov. 26, 1792, f. 33; Allen to APLP, Nov. 27, 1792, f. 67; Robinson to APLP, Nov. 27, 1792, f. 73. Add. MSS 16,920: Tracey to APLP, Nov. 30, 1792, f. 25.
28. Reeves, *Association Papers,* pt. 1, "Publications printed by special order of the Society": no. 5, *The Fatal Effects of Republican Principles, exemplified in the History of England from the Death of Charles I to the Restoration of Charles II*; no. 6, Archdeacon Paley, *Reasons for Contentment.*
29. W. Roberts, ed., *Memoirs and Correspondence of Mrs. Hannah More* (London, 1834); More to Mrs. Boscawan, 1793, 1: 128. Add. MSS 16,924: Fulham APLP to APLP, Jan. 5, 1793, f. 33.
30. Add. MSS 16,924: "A.B." to APLP, Jan. 3, 1793, f. 9. Porteus actively collected materials and sent them to Pitt for the same reasons. Woodside, Compton Guilford, Surrey, Hoare MSS 172: Porteus to Pitt, Dec. 12, 1792 (n.f.).
31. Reeves, *Association Papers,* p. ii.
32. Great Britain, Historical Manuscripts Commission, *Fourteenth Report,* Appendix IV, Kenyon: Jones to Lord Kenyon, Dec. 2, 1792, p. 536.
33. *The Times,* Dec. 11, 1792, p. 1. A special meeting of the Committee of the APLP was held on December 6, but no mention was made of Jones in the APLP advertisement.
34. Dropmore MSS: Buckingham to Grenville, Nov. 27, 1792, p. 344. Add. MSS 16,919: Yorke to APLP, Nov. 26, 1792, f. 27; Smear to APLP, Nov. 27, 1792, f. 54; Robinson to APLP, Nov. 27, 1792, f. 73; Heriot to APLP, Nov. 29, 1792, f. 111.
35. PRO 30/8/229: Dec. 28, 1792, f. 302 (a payment of £58/18/6); Mar. 10, 1793, f. 134 (a payment of £172/16/3).
36. Hannah More, *Village Politics* (London, 1793), pp. 9-13.
37. Reeves, *Association Papers,* pt. 2. There were four tracts in this series: *One Penny-worth of Truth from Thomas Bull, to his brother John* (n.d.); *One Penny-worth of Answer from John Bull to his Brother Thomas,* Dec. 3, 1792; *John Bull's Second Answer to his*

Brother Thomas (n.d.); *A Letter from John Bull to his Countrymen,* Dec. 6, 1792.

38. *A Letter from John Bull,* p. 11.

39. Reeves, *Association Papers,* pt. 1, "Publications printed by special order of the Society": no. 1, *Mr. Justice Ashhurst's Charge to the Grand Jury of Middlesex*; no. 2, *A Charge to the Grand Jury of Middlesex,* by William Mainwaring, Esq.; no. 3, *A Protest against T. Paine's Rights of Man,* by John Bowles; no. 4, *Speech of the Lord President of the Session, addressed to the Lord Provost of Edinburgh*; no. 5, *The Fatal Effects of Republican Principles, exemplified in the History of England from the Death of Charles I to the Restoration of Charles II*; no. 6, *Lord Loughborough's Speech on the Alien Bill* and Archdeacon Paley, *Reasons for Contentment*; no. 7, *The Second Charge of Mr. Justice Ashhurst to the Grand Jury in the Court of King's Bench*; no. 8, *Mr. Justice Buller's Charge to the Grand Jury of the County of York, at the Lent Assizes, 1793*; no. 9, *The Earl of Radnor's Charge to the Grand Jury of the County of Berks*; no. 10, *Cautions against Reformers,* by Lord Bolingbroke.

40. Reeves, *Association Papers,* pt. 1: anon., *A Word in Season to the Traders and Manufacturers of Great Britain*; anon., *Ten Minutes Caution from a Plain Man to His fellow Citizens*; anon., *A Country Curate's Advice to Manufacturers—Recommended to the serious Consideration of every Workman in the various Manufacturing Towns of England and Scotland*; anon., *Reflections on the Present Crisis*; J. Bowles, *A Protest against T. Paine's Rights of Man*; idem, *Answer to the Declaration of the "Friends of the Liberty of the Press"*; S. Jenyms, *Thoughts on a Parliamentary Reform*; W. Mitford, *Additional Proof of the Excellence of the English Constitution.* On Bowles, see PRO 30/8/229, Nov. 10, 1792, f. 16 (payment of £100 "to 1st Dec.").

41. Reeves, *Association Papers,* passim. See especially *One Pennyworth of Answer from John Bull,* pp. 3-4; *A Word in Season,* pp. 8-9; *Lord Loughborough's Speech,* p. 12; *Mr. Justice Ashhurst's Charge to the Grand Jury of Middlesex,* p. 4.

42. *One Penny-worth of Truth,* p. 2.

43. Great Britain, Historical Manuscripts Commission, *Thirteenth Report,* Appendix VIII, Charlemont, II: Malone to Charlemont, Dec. 14, 1792, p. 207. HO 42/23: Sayors to Alderson, Dec. 15, 1792, f. 128.

44. Add. MSS 37,873: Mullarton to Windham, Feb. 20, 1792, f. 204.

45. *Sussex Weekly Advertiser*, Jan 7, 1793, p. 2.

46. Williams, *Artisans*, p. 71.

47. *Sussex Weekly Advertiser*, Dec. 24, 1792, p. 3. HO 42/24: Dundas to Lord Mayor, Jan. 24, 1792, f. 244. PRO 30/8/159: Miles to Pitt, Feb. 14, 1793, f. 239. HO 42/25: N. Conant to HO, Mar. 4, 1793, f. 45.

48. Elie Halevy, *England in 1815* (London, 1949), p. 425. Thompson, *Making of the English Working Class*, p. 116.

CHAPTER V

1. *York Courant*, Feb. 4, 1793, p. 1. *Sussex Weekly Advertiser*, Mar. 4, 1793, p. 2.

2. *Sussex Weekly Advertiser*, Jan. 28, 1793, p. 3; Feb. 11, 1793, p. 3. *York Courant*, Feb. 11, 1793, p. 2. *Observer*, Feb. 24, 1793, p. 2.

3. HO 42/24: Feb. 16, 1793, f. 526. *Observer*, Feb. 24, 1793, p. 3; Mar. 17, 1793, p. 3.

4. HO 42/24: "Friends and Fellow Seamen," Feb. 2, 1793, f. 356.

5. *Observer*, Feb. 24, 1793, p. 2.

6. Ibid.; Mar. 10, 1793, p. 2; Mar. 17, 1793, p. 4. *Sussex Weekly Advertiser*, Feb. 25, 1793, p. 3; Mar. 11, 1793, p. 3. *York Courant*, Mar. 18, 1793, p. 2.

7. *York Courant*, Apr. 15, 1793, p. 2.

8. *Sussex Weekly Advertiser*, Mar. 25, 1793, p. 1; Apr. 22, 1793, p. 1; July 8, 1793, p. 2. *York Courant*, Apr. 15, 1793, p. 2; May 20, 1793, p. 2; May 29, 1793, p. 2.

9. *York Courant*, Mar. 4, 1793, p. 2; May 20, 1793, p. 2; May 27, 1793, p. 2; June 3, 1793, p. 2.

10. Ibid., Oct. 14, 1793, p. 2. HO 42/27: Brookfield to HO, Nov. 13, 1792, f. 131; Baugh to HO, Nov. 14, 1793, f. 145.

11. *York Courant*, Nov. 18, 1793, p. 2; Dec. 2, 1793, p. 2; Dec. 9, 1793, p. 2; Dec. 16, 1793, pp. 2-3. HO 42/28: Lodge to Nepean, Jan. 28, 1794, ff. 88-89

12. *Sussex Weekly Advertiser*, Mar 4, 1793, p. 1. *York Courant*, Sept. 9, 1793, p. 1.

13. Thompson, *Making of the English Working Class*, p. 116.

14. PRO 30/8/45: "The Dover Association," Dec. 16, 1793, f. 91.

15. *Observer,* Dec. 30, 1792, p. 3; Feb. 10, 1793, p. 3; Mar. 17, 1793, p. 3. Devon Record Office, Addington MSS OZ 21: W. Wright to Lord Amherst, Mar. 6, 1793 (n.f.). PRO 30/8/245: Deal Association to Pitt, Feb. 11, f. 94. HO 42/25: "Extract of a plan which has been proposed and since approved . . .," May 11, 1793, f. 438.

16. HO 42/27: Bentham to Nepean, Nov. 10, 1793, ff. 87-90. HO 42/24: "Pro bono publico" to HO, Jan. 28, 1793, f. 95. HO 42/28: "Pro Bono Publico" to HO, Jan. 9, 1794, f. 57. HO 42/24: W. Devaynes to Nepean, Feb. 13, 1793, f. 464; "Mr. Goring" to Sir George Younge, Feb. 15, 1793, f. 505 B.

17. *HPD* 30: 280, 347, 356-57.

18. *HPD* 30: 212, 611, 566, 1476, 592. *HPD* 31: 379. *HPD* 33: 860.

19. *HPD* 30: 1059-60.

20. Joceline Bagot, *George Canning and His Friends* (New York, 1909), p. 191.

21. Richard Glover, *Britain at Bay* (New York, 1973), pp. 40-43. These problems were not solved even during the Napoleonic wars.

22. Cone, *English Jacobins,* p. 188.

23. *Observer,* July 14, 1793, p. 4. *Sussex Weekly Advertiser,* Mar. 10, 1794, p. 4.

24. *Sussex Weekly Advertiser,* Apr. 7, 1794, p. 4.

25. Cone, *English Jacobins,* pp. 187-89.

26. Thompson, *Making of the English Working Class,* pp. 114-21.

27. *Observer,* July 7, 1793, p. 2; July 14, 1793, p. 3. Devon Record Office, Addington MSS OZ 21: Earl of Mornington to Addington, Aug. 26, 1793 (n.f.).

28. *York Courant,* Sept. 9, 1793, p. 1. *Sussex Weekly Advertiser,* Oct. 21, 1793, p. 1.

29. *York Courant,* Oct. 28, 1793, p. 1. *Sussex Weekly Advertiser,* Oct. 14, 1793, p. 2.

30. Cone, *English Jacobins,* p. 190. Thompson, *Making of the English Working Class,* pp. 121-23, 125.

31. Williams, *Artisans,* pp. 77, 78.

32. HO 42/26: Hugh Cleghorn to Nepean, July 23, 1793, ff. 172-73; James Greene to HO, Aug. 29, 1793, f. 430; C. Stuart to HO, Oct. 27, 1793, ff. 806-8.

33. HO 42/27: "Report on Sedition," April (?) 1794, ff. 863-77.

34. HO 42/26: "A Society of Loyal Britons," Oct. 10, 1973, f. 701. HO 42/27: Grove Taylor to Dundas, Dec. 3, 1793, ff. 510-15.
35. HO 42/26: Richmond to Dundas, Oct. 13, 1793, ff. 723-25.
36. *York Courant,* Oct. 28, 1793, p. 1.
37. HO 42/27: "X.Y.Z." to HO, Nov. 4, 1793, f. 21.
38. *York Courant,* Feb. 3, 1794, p. 2; Feb. 17, 1794, p. 2; Feb. 24, 1794, p. 1.
39. *Chelmsford Chronicle,* Feb. 7, 1794, p. 4; Feb. 21, 1794, p. 2; Feb. 28, 1794, p. 2.
40. *Sussex Weekly Advertiser,* Feb. 24, 1794, p. 3.
41. HO 42/28: R.H. Gibbon to Aust, Jan. 27, 1794, f. 133.
42. PRO 30/8/245: "After 1793, R.P.C.—Defense" (n.d.), ff. 3-6.
43. Devon Record Office, Addington MSS 152M/C1794, CM1: W. Ogelvie, "On Military Associations" (n.f.).
44. HO 42/29: "Observations on the means of repelling Invasion," Mar. 1794, ff. 281-88.
45. Glover, *Britain at Bay,* pp. 129-31.
46. J.R. Western, *The English Militia in the Eighteenth Century* (London, 1965), pp. 164, 205. Glover, *Britain at Bay,* pp. 128, 129.
47. HO 42/24: "Amicus" to HO, Jan. 24, 1793, f. 238; De-Lancey to Nepean, Feb. 7, 1793, f. 384. PRO 30/8/225: Feb. 14, 1793, ff. 98-101.
48. HO 42/25: John Borwis to HO, Feb. 28, 1793, f. 5; Lord Carysfort to HO, Mar. 1, 1793, f. 13; "Extract of a Plan . . .," May 11, 1793, f. 438.
49. HO 42/28: Buckingham to Grenville, Feb. 2, 1794, ff. 193-99; Amherst to Dundas, Feb. 13, 1794, f. 269.
50. HO 42/28: Devaynes to HO, Feb. 17, 1794, f. 311; J.M. Bingham to Dundas, Feb. 24, 1794, f. 365.
51. HO 42/29: J. Fremenheere to Dundas, Mar. 1, 1794, f. 23.

CHAPTER VI

1. *HPD* 31: 89.
2. *Chelmsford Chronicle,* "General Orders for the Security of the Country," Mar. 21, 1794, p. 2.
3. *York Courant,* Mar. 3, 1794, p. 2. *Sussex Weekly Advertiser,* Mar. 3, 1794, pp. 2, 3.
4. PRO 30/8/245: Radnor to Pitt, Mar. 4, 1794, f. 107. PRO 30/8/170: Radnor to Pitt, Mar. 6, 1794, f. 12.

5. *Sussex Weekly Advertiser,* Mar. 10, 1794, p. 2. *HPD* does not report Pitt's speech of March 6. *Chelmsford Chronicle,* Mar. 14, 1794, p. 1.

6. *HPD* 31: 83-84.

7. British Museum, State Papers, B.S. 45/148: "List of the Officers of the Several Regiments and Corps of Fencible Cavalry and Infantry; of the Officers of the Militia; and of the Corps and Troops of Gentlemen and Yeomanry; and of the Corps and Companies of Volunteer Infantry," 2: 137.

8. PRO 30/8/245: 110, 114, 118. *Chelmsford Chronicle,* Mar. 28, 1794, p. 2. *Sussex Weekly Advertiser,* Mar. 31, 1794, p. 3.

9. *HPD* 31: 84-89, 91, 92-97, 107, 122.

10. Ibid., p. 212.

11. Ibid., p. 215.

12. *Chelmsford Chronicle,* Apr. 11, 1794, p. 2. Pitt's speech was not recorded in *HPD.*

13. HO 42/29: Moira to Nepean, Mar. 22, 1794, f. 163; Fauconberg to Dundas, Mar. 22, 1794, f. 171; William Yeilder to Dundas, Mar. 24, 1794, f. 179; Dundas to Yeilder, Mar. 24, 1794, f. 186; Thomas Dundas to Dundas, Mar. 25, 1794, f. 203; Clayton to Dundas, Mar. 28, 1794, ff. 243-44.

14. *Sussex Weekly Advertiser,* Mar. 31, 1794, pp. 1-2.

15. *Chelmsford Chronicle,* Apr. 4, 1794, p. 2. *York Courant,* Apr. 19, 1794, p. 2. The counties were Chester, Hampshire, Kent, Leicester, Lincoln, Norfolk, North Hampshire, Oxford, Rutland, Somerset, Suffolk, and Surrey.

16. *Sussex Weekly Advertiser,* Mar. 3, 1794, p. 2. HO 42/30: John Brooke to Nepean, May 6, 1794, ff. 21, 23. *York Courant,* Dec. 15, 1794, p. 3.

17. British Museum, State Papers, B.S. 45/148: vols. 1-2, passim.

18. *York Courant,* May 26, 1794, p. 3; August 11, 1794, p. 3. Wiltshire Record Office, Savernake Manuscripts 9: Sept. 1794 (n.f.); June 1794 (n.f.). Devon Record Office L5, 1262M (n.f.).

19. *Chelmsford Chronicle,* May 2, 1794, p. 2; Apr. 11, 1794, p. 3. *York Courant,* Apr. 28, 1794, p. 2. Devon Record Office L5, 1262M (n.f.). East Sussex Record Office LCV-1, EW2 (n.f.).

20. *Chelmsford Chronicle,* Apr. 25, 1794, p. 2. *York Courant,* Apr. 21, 1794, p. 1. *Sussex Weekly Advertiser,* Apr. 28, 1794, p. 1.

21. *Berrow's Worcester Journal,* May 1, 1794-Oct. 30, 1794, passim.

22. HO 42/30: "Resolutions of the Loyal True Blues" (n.d.), f. 23.

23. British Museum, State Papers B.S. 45/148: vols. 1-2, passim.

24. Cornwall Record Office, "Rasleigh Memoirs": 1846(?), p. 33. PRO 30/8/168: Portland to Pitt, May 13, 1792, f. 103. O'Gorman, *Whig Party*.

25. *York Courant*, Apr. 21, 1794, pp. 1-2; May 26, 1794, p. 1; June 16, 1794, p. 2; June 30, 1794, p. 1; July 7, 1794, p. 2; July 21, 1794, p. 1. *Chelmsford Chronicle*, May 23, 1794, p. 3; June 20, 1794, p. 2. *Sussex Weekly Advertiser*, June 2, 1794, p. 1; June 9, 1794, p. 1; June 16, 1794, p. 2.

26. *York Courant*, June 16, 1794, p. 2; Aug. 11, 1794, p. 2.

27. Thompson, *Making of the English Working Class*, pp. 130, 131. *Sussex Weekly Advertiser*, Apr. 21, 1794, p. 3.

28. HO 42/30: May 12-21, 1794, ff. 74, 78, 80, 146, 148, 150, 152, 154, 158. *Chelmsford Chronicle*, May 23, 1794, p. 1. Thompson, *Making of the English Working Class*, pp. 132-33.

29. *York Courant*, May 19, 1794, p. 3. *Sussex Weekly Advertiser*, May 19, 1794, p. 2. *Chelmsford Chronicle*, May 16, 1794, p. 4.

30. HO 42/31: Salisbury to Nepean, June 14, 1794 (n.f.); John Griffith to Dundas, June 14, 1794 (n.f.); "H.B." to Pitt, June 20, 1794 (n.f.); John White to Nepean, June 23, 1794 (n.f.).

31. Thomas B. Howell, Esq., *A Complete Collection of State Trials* (London, 1818) 24: 199-1387; 25: 1-745.

32. *Chelmsford Chronicle*, July 11, 1794, p. 2.

33. Ibid., Apr. 25, 1794, p. 3. *York Courant*, Apr. 28, 1794, p. 2.

34. HO 42/31: "Mr. Wells" to Dundas, June 4, 1794 (n.f.); Nathaniel Bland to HO, June 6, 1794 (n.f.); W. Mainwaring to Nepean, June 12, 1794 (n.f.); "Mr. King" to Dundas, June 12, 1794 (n.f.).

35. *Berrow's Worcester Journal*, July 10, 1794, p. 3. *Sussex Weekly Advertiser*, July 14, 1794, p. 4.

36. *Chelmsford Chronicle*, Aug. 1, 1794, p. 4.

37. HO 42/31: Viscount Bateman to Dundas, June 5, 1794 (n.f.).

38. HO 42/32: "Informations filed by William Noon, John Rutkin and Sampson Cot, Light Fencibles," July 18, 1794 (n.f.).

39. HO 42/32: T. Worde to HO, Aug. 18, 1794 (n.f.).

40. Williams, *Artisans*, p. 79.

41. HO 42/32: C.T. Kirby to Portland, Aug. 19, 1794 (n.f.); W.

Colquhoun to Nepean, Aug. 21, 1794 (n.f.). *York Courant,* Aug. 25, 1794, p. 2.

42. HO 42/32: "Papers Relating to Riots, etc." (28 depositions), Aug. 21, 1794 (n.f.); Colquhoun to Portland, Aug. 21, 1794 (n.f.); Colquhoun to "Magistrates," Aug. 22, 1794 (n.f.); C.T. Kirby to Portland, Aug. 19, 1794 (n.f.).

43. HO 42/32: Lord Mayor to Portland, Aug. 21, 1794 (n.f.); Devaynes to HO, Aug. 20, 1794 (n.f.). *Sussex Weekly Advertiser,* Aug. 25, 1794, p. 2. *York Courant,* Aug. 25, 1794, p. 2.

44. Thompson, *Making of the English Working Class,* p. 134.

45. *York Courant,* June 16, 1794, p. 2. *Chelmsford Chronicle,* June 20, 1794, p. 3.

46. *York Courant,* June 23, 1794, p. 2.

47. *Chelmsford Chronicle,* July 11, 1794, p. 4.

48. Ibid., July 24, 1794, p. 2.

49. Ibid., Aug. 22, 1794, p. 3. *York Courant,* Aug. 18, 1794, p. 2. *Sussex Weekly Advertiser,* Aug. 18, 1794, p. 3.

50. Grenville, *Courts and Cabinets:* Grenville to Buckingham, Aug. 26, 1794, pp. 271-72. *Sussex Weekly Advertiser,* Aug. 25, 1794, p. 3. *Chelmsford Chronicle,* Aug. 29, 1794, p. 2.

51. *Chelmsford Chronicle,* Aug. 29, 1794, p. 2.

52. *York Courant,* Nov. 3, 1794, p. 2; December 1, 1794, p. 2. *Sussex Weekly Advertiser,* Nov. 10, 1794, p. 1. HO 42/32: Lord Mayor to Portland, Nov. 22, 1794 (n.f.).

53. Thompson, *Making of the English Working Class,* pp. 137-40.

54. *HPD* 32: 643-44, 681.

BIBLIOGRAPHIC NOTE

Of the many works dealing with the period investigated in this monograph, several are useful in understanding the context in which these events transpired. Because of their numbers, the selection of works listed below is not meant to be inclusive, but only illustrative of the rich storehouse of historical writings we possess dealing with the period covered by this book. Steven Watson's *The Reign of George III, 1760-1815* (Oxford, 1960) is the best short introduction to various facets of English life. *History of England in the XVIII Century*, vols. 6 and 7 (New York, 1891), by W.E.H. Lecky, though dated in many respects, still contains much information valuable to a student of the period. Other works, less broadly conceived yet instrumental in adding to a picture of the context, include G.M. Trevelyan's *British History in the Nineteenth Century, 1782-1901* (London, 1922); Asa Brigg's *The Age of Improvement* (London, 1959); H.W. Carless Davis's *The Age of Grey and Peel* (Oxford, 1929); and in an even more restricted manner, Clive Emsley's *British Society and the French Wars, 1793-1815* (Totowa, N.J., 1979). A work much dated but still sparkling with insights is Elie Halevy's *England in 1815* (reprinted, London, 1949).

Several works which deal generally with the revolutionary nature of the period are R.R. Palmer's *The Age of the Democratic Revolution*, 2 vols. (Princeton, 1959, 1964); Crane Brinton's *A Decade of Revolution* (New York, 1934); and Franklin Ford's article, "The Revolutionary Napoleonic Era: How Much of a Watershed?" *American Historical Review* 69 (Oct. 1963): 18-29. Two articles somewhat at variance with the conclusions of Palmer and Ford are R.R. Dozier's "Democratic Revolution in England—A Possibility?" *Albion: Proceedings of the Conference on British Studies* 4, no. 4 (Winter 1972): 183-92; and Clive Emsley's "The London 'Insurrection' of December, 1792: Fact, Fiction, or Fantasy?" *Journal of British Studies* 17, no. 2 (1978): 66-86. These provide a general view of the period, but the subject touched upon in this work, the

British response to the French Revolution, has long been of interest
to historians. Two developments coincident with the French Revolution have
provided historians a means of gauging its effects. The eclipse of the
reform movement headed by prominent Whig politicians, and the
spectacular rise and fall of the radical movement have been studied
extensively to that end. From the beginning of the twentieth
century, all have recognized some connection between the two. Most
have attributed the failure of both movements to the activities of
William Pitt, rather than to domestic currents of opinion. The works
mentioned below illustrate the trends of thought on the subject.

Three works written before World War II illustrate the views held
about Pitt's involvement in the cessation of the reform movement
and the repression of the radicals. Joceline Bagot's *George Canning
and His Friends* (New York, 1909), G.M. Trevelyan's *Lord Grey of
the Reform Bill* (London, 1929), and D.G. Barnes's *George III and
William Pitt* (Palo Alto, 1939), attribute the decline of reform and
radical movements to Pitt's mistaken and wrong-headed policies.
Herbert Butterfield, in "Charles James Fox and the Whig Opposition
in 1792," *Cambridge Historical Journal,* no. 3 (1949): 293-330,
raised some questions about this evaluation of Pitt's policies, given
the domestic situation at the time, but held to the overall view as to
the cause of the demise of radicalism and the tempering of the
power of the old Whig connections. The influence of Sir Louis
Namier in structural analysis led historians to a closer look at the
foundations of the problem. Richard Pares, in *King George III and
the Politicians* (Oxford, 1954), while examining another problem,
posed the question of the freedom of action of a prime minister of
the time; while Keith Feiling, in *The Second Tory Party* (London,
1959), noted particularly the liberal policies Pitt followed. Interest
centered on the organization and connections of the Whigs, and
works such as Donald Ginter's "The Financing of the Whig Party
Organization," *American Historical Review* 62 (Jan. 1966): 421-
40, and Francis O'Gorman's *The Whig Party and the French Revolution* (London, 1967), finally put the matter in the right perspective. The changing position of the Whigs was caused more by internal
disunity in their responses to external events than by any manipulation by Pitt. These last works were published coincidentally with
E.P. Thompson's *The Making of the English Working Class* (New
York, 1966), which cast a new interpretation of the period based
upon the activities of the radicals.

The radicals had received much attention by historians by the time of Thompson's publication. Most of the works already mentioned included some references to them. One of the most important twentieth-century books to incorporate these activities into a thematic whole was written by G.S. Veitch. In his *Genesis of Parliamentary Reform* (London, 1913, reprinted 1965), Veitch demonstrated the importance of the radicals in influencing the 1832 Reform Bill. P.A. Brown's *The French Revolution in English History* (London, 1918; reprinted New York, 1965) emphasized their appearance in the 1790s as one of the most significant influences of the Revolution upon English society. Their origins were tentatively hinted at by S. Maccoby in *The English Radical Tradition* (New York, 1957); while Austin Mitchell in his unpublished M.A. thesis, "Radicalism and Repression in the North of England, 1791-1793," Victoria University of Manchester, 1958, revealed the extent of their activities in that area. Caroline Robbins, in her work, *The Eighteenth Century Commonwealthsman* (Cambridge, Mass., 1959), traced their intellectual origins back to the seventeenth century. A rash of excellent studies followed, such as Ian Christie's *Wilkes, Wyvill and Reform* (London, 1962), and George Rude's *The Crowd in History* (New York, 1964), which was followed by the publication of Thompson's work mentioned above.

Thompson's work released a flood of books and articles about the radicals, not the least of which was Gwyn Williams's *Artisans and Sans-Culottes* (New York, 1969), to be capped, quite fittingly, by Veitch's student, Albert Goodwin, in his *Friends of Liberty: The English Democratic Movement in the Age of the French Revolution* (Cambridge, Mass., 1979). While Thompson's methodology and emphasis were challenged by many historians, only a few, notably Carl Cone in *The English Jacobins* (New York, 1968), attempted to moderate or challenge his conclusions. This present work is intended to help restore a balanced perspective of the period.

Other works useful in understanding the period include, for administrative matters, A. Aspinall's *The Cabinet Council, 1783-1835* (Oxford, 1952); Kenneth Ellis's *The Post Office in the Eighteenth Century* (London, 1958); R.R. Nelson's *The Home Office* (Durham, N.C., 1969); supplemented by Clive Emsley's "The Home Office and Its Source of Information and Investigation 1793-1801," *English Historical Review* 94, no. 572 (July 1979): 532-61; and the older yet still worthwhile work by Howard Robinson, *The British Post Office: a History* (Princeton, 1948). Sidney and Beatrice Webb's *English Local Government from the Revolution to the Municipal*

Corporation Act (London, 1906), 9 vols., is still one of the most useful works on that subject, although Philip Styles's "The Development of County Administration in the Late 18th and Early 19th Centuries," address delivered to the Dugdale Society, 7 October, 1933, *Dugdale Society Occasional Papers*, no. 4, corrects some details of their work. D.M. Clark's "The Office of Secretary to the Treasury in the 18th Century," *American Historical Review* 42 (Oct. 1936): 22-45, and W.R. Ward's "Some 18th Century Civil Servants: The English Revenue Commissioners," *English Historical Review* 70 (Jan. 1955): 24-54, go much beyond their titles in explaining the inner workings of the central government.

For an age bubbling with new ideas it is not surprising that there is no single study of them all. Leslie Stephen's *English Thought in the 18th Century* (reprinted, New York, 1962) presents bits and pieces illustrating the intellectual ferment of the period. Alfred Cobban, in his *Edmund Burke and the Revolt against the 18th Century* (London, 1929), complemented and superseded by Carl Cone's *Burke and the Nature of Politics* 2 vols. (Lexington, Ky., 1964), gives insights into the deep changes in attitudes taking place. Political views are explored in ·R.R. Fennessey's *Burke, Paine and the Rights of Man* (La Haye, 1963); and political propaganda is dealt with in Mary D. George's "Political Propaganda 1793-1815: Gillory and Canning," *History* n.s. 31 (1946): 9-28; and Robert Dozier's "Ministerial Efforts to Combat Revolutionary Propaganda," Ph.D. dissertation, University of California, Berkeley, 1969.

Other useful works on facets of English society include A. Aspinall's *Politics and the Press* (London, 1949), supplemented by Lucille Werkmeister's *A Newspaper History of England* (Lincoln, Neb., 1967), which is more a case study of the *Morning Chronicle* than a complete history of the press. Military-diplomatic issues and actions are revealed satisfactorily in Richard Glover's *Britain at Bay* (New York, 1973); J.T. Murley's "The Origin and Outbreak of the Anglo-French War of 1793," Ph.D. dissertation, University of London, 1954; and J.W. Fortesque's *A History of the British Army*, 10 vols. (London, 1899-1920). The loyal associations have been investigated by Eugene Black in *The Association: British Extraparliamentary Political Organization, 1769-1793* (Cambridge, Mass., 1963); Austin Mitchell, "The Association Movement of 1793-3," *Historical Journal* 4: 56-77; and Donald Ginter, "The Loyalist Association Movement of 1792 and British Public Opinion," *Historical Journal* 9, no. 2: 179-90. Only two old and one fairly new works deal with the volunteers: Robert Berry's *A History of the Formation and Development of the Volunteer Infantry, From the Earliest Times, Illustrated by the Local Records of Huddersfield and Its Vicinity, from 1784 to 1874* (London, 1903); Cecil Sebag-Montefiore's *A History of the Volunteer Forces from the Earliest Times to the Year 1860* (London, 1908); and J.R. Western's "The Volunteer Movement as an Anti-Revolutionary Force, 1792-1801," *English Historical Review* 71: 603-14.

Several works reveal some of the methods of popular protest. Supplementing Rude's work already mentioned are Christopher Hibbert's *King Mob* (New York, 1958); Norman McCord and David Brewster's "Some Labour Troubles of the 1790's in the North East England," *International Review of Social History* 13, pt. 3 (1968): 366-83; R.B. Rose's "The Priestly Riots of 1791," *Past and Present*, Nov. 1960, pp. 68-85; and E.P. Thompson's "The Moral Economy of the English Crowd in the Eighteenth Century," *Past and Present*, no. 50 (Feb. 1971): 76-136.

Unpublished manuscript materials can best be described by location. In London the most important papers investigated are in the Public Records Office and the British Museum. At the latter, Additional MSS 16,919-931, 37,834, 37,843-847, 37,873-874, 37,914-916, 40,100-102, and 42,772-780 contained the Reeves materials. In the State Papers, BS 45/148, vols. 2-7, proved very useful. At the Public Record Office, the Home Office Papers 33/1, 42/20-32, 50/18-19, and 97/1-2 were the most frequently consulted; Foreign Office MSS 94/3 and 428/20, plus the Treasury Solicitors MSS 11/954/3498, were useful. In the Chatham MSS, also in the Public Record Office, 30/8/102-104, 140, 158, 163, 168, 170, 173, 229, and 245 contain the material used in this work. The Melville Manuscripts most valuable to this author at the National Library of Scotland in Edinburgh were vols. 6, 19, 20, 1041, 1076, 6524, and 7199. At the Sheffield Public Library, the Wentworth-Woodhouse Muniments, FF. 31(a), 44(a), 44(b), 44(g), 65(d), and 115(a) were relevant. T.C. Hoare, from his collection at Woodside, Compton Guilford, Surrey, graciously supplied me with several documents. Documents located at local record offices in Cornwall (Rasleigh MSS); Devon (Addington MSS 152M/C1793/OZ11-OZ12, 152M/C1793/OZ21, and 152M/C1794/CMI, plus the Lieutenancy Papers, L5, 1262M); East Sussex (Lieutenancy Papers, LCV-1, EW2); Northumberland (The Woodman Family Letters, M16, 1334); and Wiltshire (Savernake MSS), were of value.

Contemporary published materials include ten newspapers: the *Argus of the Constitution* (London), 1792; *Berrow's Worcester Journal* (Worcester), 1792-95; the *Chelmsford Chronicle* (Chelmsford), 1792-95; the *Morning Chronicle* (London), 1792-95; the *Morning Herald* (London), 1792-93; the *Observer* (London), 1792-95; the *Sun* (London), 1792-95; the *Sussex Weekly Advertiser* (Lewes), 1792-95; *The Times* (London), 1792-95; and the *York Courant,* 1792-95. Other contemporary published materials used were: *The Annual Register, or a View of the History, Politics and Literature for the Year 1792* (London, 1816); Great Britain, Hansard, *The Parliamentary History of England from the Earliest Period to the Year 1803,* vols. 29-34 (London, 1817); and Thomas Howell's *A Complete Collection of State Trials,* vols. 24-25 *(London, 1818).*

The published collections of letters, diaries, etc., used in this work include: Mrs. Henry Boring's *The Diary of the Right Honorable William Windham, 1784-1810* (London, 1836); Philip Foner's edition of *The Complete Writings of Thomas Paine,* 2 vols. (New York, 1945); and especially Richard Grenville, Duke of Buckingham and Chandos, *Memoirs of the Courts and Cabinets of George the Third,* 2 vols. (London, 1843-55). This latter work, the letters of William Grenville, Pitt's foreign secretary, when used in conjunction with the letters of his brother, the Marquise of Buckingham, found in the Historical Manuscripts Commission publications, *Fourteenth Report,* Appendix V, Fortesque II, provides the researcher with letters and answers of two informed, intelligent men commenting upon the events of the day. Other useful works from the Commission are the *Thirteenth Report,* Appendix VIII, Charlement II; and the *Fourteenth Report,* Appendix IV, Kenyon. The letters of Edmund Burke and Charles James Fox can be found respectively in P.J. Marshall and John A. Woods, *The Correspondence of Edmund Burke,* vol. 7 (Chicago, 1968); and Lord John Russell, *Memorials and Correspondence of Charles James Fox,* 4 vols. (London, 1843). A truncated selection of William Pitt's letters, inadequately complemented by the Chatham MSS mentioned above, can be found in Bishop George Tomline's *Memoirs of the Life of the Right Honourable William Pitt* (London, 1822). *The Correspondence of W.A. Miles* by the Rev. Charles P. Miles (London, 1926), and R. Johnson's *The Letters of Hanna More* (London, 1925) offer some insights into lesser characters in the drama of the English response to the French Revolution.

INDEX

Abingdon, Earl of, 116
Addington, Henry, 131, 149
Addington, John Hiley, 70
Amherst, Lord, 136
APLP (Association for the Preservation of Liberty and Property against Republicans and Levellers): advertisements by, 57; founder controversy, 57-59; support of war fund, 108; pension fund, 110; as coordinator of subscription drives, 111. *See also* Devaynes, William; loyal association movement; Reeves, John
arms purchases: in 1792, 40-43; dangers of, 41; sources of, 41-42; gatherings in 1794, 158-59. *See also* Crisis of 1792
Auckland, Lord (ambassador to the Netherlands), 50

Barwis, John, 135
Bateman, Lord Viscount, 161
"Beaumarchais," 40
Bentham, Jeremy, 112
Berrow's Worcester Journal, 16, 18-19, 91
Bingham, J.M., 136
Birmingham riots, 5
Bland, Nathaniel, 160
Briellat, Thomas, 120
Brooke, John, 40-41, 43
Buckingham, Marquise of, 135-36
Burdon, R., 44-45

Burges, J. Bland, 56, 69
Burke, Edmund: *Reflections,* 2-3; on relief of clerical exiles, 38; on danger of French connection, 69; defines ideological war, 115-16

Canning, George, 117-18
Catherine I, Empress, 189 n.2
Chalk Farm meeting, 157-58
Chelmsford Chronicle; war news in 1792, 16; on Paine, 19; on loyal addresses, 20; response to May Proclamation, 22; on founding of APLP, 65; on mobilization of militia, 65; on plot rumors, 65, 158-59; resolutions of publicans, 85; on effigy burnings, 90; on invasion rumors, 129; on volunteer subscriptions, 147; on Howe's victory, 164-65; on military defeats on continent, 165; on Robespierre's fall, 166-67; on moderation of French in 1794, 167
civilian-military hostility, 161
Cocks, John Somers, 151-52
Colquhoun, James, 124, 162
constitutional societies (Manchester, Penzance, Rotherham, Wednesbury), 59
Crisis of 1792, 32-33. *See also* intelligence gathering
Curry, Thomas, 36, 39-40

DeLancey, Col. Oliver, 23; on volunteers, 135

Windham, William, 74
Wright, Thomas, 58
Wyvill, Christopher, 150

York, Duke of, 118-19, 134, 156
York Courant: on French Revolution, 16-17, 121, 157, 166; on war,
16-17, 68, 121, 128-29, 156-58, 164; on radicals, 18, 68, 90-91, 128-29, 158, 169; on loyalists, 22, 109-11; on subscription drives, 109-11; on treason trials, 169

Zouch, Henry, 64-65